Qualitative Inquiry

Qualitative Inquiry

Thematic, Narrative and Arts-Informed Perspectives

Lynn Butler-Kisber

SAGE

Los Angeles | London | New Delhi
Singapore | Washington DC

© Lynn Butler-Kisber 2010

First published 2010

SAGE Publications Ltd
1 Oliver's Yard
55 City Road
London EC1Y 1SP

SAGE Publications Inc.
2455 Teller Road
Thousand Oaks, California 91320

SAGE Publications India Pvt Ltd
B 1/I 1 Mohan Cooperative Industrial Area
Mathura Road
New Delhi 110 044

SAGE Publications Asia-Pacific Pte Ltd
33 Pekin Street #02-01
Far East Square
Singapore 048763

Library of Congress Control Number: 2009931803

British Library Cataloguing in Publication data

A catalogue record for this book is available from
the British Library

ISBN 978-1-4129-4819-7
ISBN 978-1-4129-4820-3 (pbk)

Typeset by C&M Digitals (P) Ltd, Chennai, India
Printed in the United States of America
Printed on paper from sustainable resources

Contents

Acknowledgements

I would like to thank the many wonderful graduate students at McGill University, and other special colleagues, who contributed directly to this book in the examples they provided, and less directly, but significantly in the exchanges and discussions we have had over many years. They helped to push my thinking and supported my efforts along the way. I would also like to thank the excellent professors I had at the Harvard Graduate School of Education who ignited my passion for qualitative inquiry and sowed the seeds for this initiative.

I also wish to thank my editor, Patrick Brindle, at Sage Publications, who, after a brief conversation in Montreal, had sufficient faith in me to invite me to write a book proposal about the work I was doing in qualitative inquiry. His helpful suggestions and support over the past three years have made the task both easier and most pleasant. In addition, I am very grateful for the thorough comments and helpful feedback provided by the reviewers of both the proposal and the manuscript.

Finally, I want to thank my family – my husband Stephen, my son Jasen and daughter-in-law Laura, grandchildren Mackenzie and Lyla, my daughter Lisa, and my father Cliff, all of whom contributed to this endeavour with their love, support, good humour, and patience. I am indebted to them all.

Every effort has been made to obtain all the necessary permissions from those who contributed examples to this book, and from all the copyright holders. If any have been inadvertently overlooked, the publishers will be pleased to make the necessary arrangements at the first opportunity.

Figures 2.1 and 2.2	Visual consent forms from class assignment by Kelly Howarth with kind permission.
Figure 3.2	Multitasking, State of heightened alert, and Interpreting the disease from L. Furlini, (2007). *Living with chronic dementia: A case for educational support.* Unpublished doctoral dissertation, McGill University, Montreal, QC. With kind permission from the author.
Figure 3.3	Deana's concept maps from S. Kerwin-Boudreau (2008). *The evolving practitioner: A qualitative inquiry into reflections on teacher perspectives in a professional development program in higher education.* Unpublished doctoral dissertation, McGill University, Montreal, QC. With kind permission from the author.

Table 4.1   Significant statements: Collaboration from class assignment by Kim Havard with kind permission.

Table 4.2   Formulated meanings of significant statements: Collaboration from class assignment by Kim Havard with kind permission.

Table 4.3   Clusters of common themes from class assignment by Kim Havard with kind permission.

Table 4.4   Exhaustive description of collaboration in an academic environment from class assignment by Kim Havard with kind permission.

Figure 5.2   Explanation of Ann's story from L. Butler-Kisber (2002). Artful portrayals in qualitative inquiry: The road to found poetry and beyond. *The Alberta Journal of Educational Research, XLVIII*(3), 229-239. Reprinted with kind permission of the publisher.

Page 85   'That Rare Feeling': poem from C. Glesne (1997). That rare feeling: Re-presenting research through poetic transcription. *Qualitative Inquiry, 3*(2), 202-221. Reprinted with kind permission of the author and publisher.

Figure 6.1   Excerpts from transcript with words and phrases highlighted from class assignment by Melanie Stonebanks with kind permission.

Page 88   'Ode to the Embellisher and the Slasher': poem from class assignment by Melanie Stonebanks with kind permission.

Pages 89-90   'By My Own Light': poem from class assignment by Gail Fairbank with kind permission.

Page 94   'Putting My Father Down': poem by Mary Stewart from L. Butler-Kisber & M. Stewart (2009). The use of poetry clusters in poetic inquiry. In M. Prendergast, C. Leggo & P. Sameshima (Eds.), *Poetic inquiry: Vibrant voices in the social science* (pp. 3-11). Rotterdam: Sense. Reprinted with kind permission of the authors and publisher.

Page 96   'Walking My Mother': poem by Lynn Butler-Kisber from L. Butler-Kisber & M. Stewart (2009). The use of poetry clusters in poetic inquiry. In M. Prendergast, C. Leggo & P. Sameshima (Eds.), *Poetic inquiry: Vibrant voices in the social science* (pp. 3-11). Rotterdam: Sense. Reprinted with kind permission of the authors and publisher.

Page 96   'Fani': poem by Lynn Butler-Kisber from L. Butler-Kisber & M. Stewart (2009). The use of poetry clusters in poetic inquiry. In M. Prendergast, C. Leggo & P. Sameshima (Eds.), *Poetic inquiry: Vibrant voices in the social science* (pp. 3-11). Rotterdam: Sense. Reprinted with kind permission of the authors and publisher.

Figure 7.1   *Pathways*: collage from class assignment by Ramona Parkash with kind permission.

Pages 106-107   Notes on collage from class assignment by Ramona Parkash with kind permission.

Figure 7.2   *Who am I?*: collage from class assignment by Michele Pinard with kind permission.

Pages 107-113   Notes on collages from class assignment by Michele Pinard with kind permission.

List of Figures and Tables

FIGURES

TABLES

1

Introduction

PURPOSE OF THE BOOK

This book is intended for graduate students at all stages in the qualitative inquiry process, and who are in search of ways to match the best possible perspectives and approaches to their research focus. It will be helpful for professors involved in graduate supervision, as well as for other researchers in the field. The content of the book emerged from my own research and supervision of graduate students and was shaped more specifically from my 15 years teaching qualitative inquiry courses to graduate students in the Faculty of Education at McGill University. For the past eight years, I have been teaching a course entitled Interpretive Inquiry that includes a rich cross-section of students from dietetics, education, epidemiology, geography, law, nursing, physical and occupational therapy, and social work. It is a course that I proposed and developed because of a need expressed repeatedly by graduate students for a broader exposure to a variety of inquiry approaches and perspectives, and a more in-depth look at how to implement these. They need to be able to choose, match and then defend their inquiry approaches with their research focuses and questions, their beliefs and assumptions, and their communicative abilities and passions (Patton, 2002).

> Doing, reading and writing qualitative research are part of the same complex craft. Each is an act of inquiry that aims at making meaning of the world. Although people often perceive them as discrete and disconnected, these three acts are interrelated and require many of the same skills, approaches, and attitudes. In each, we construct meanings, understandings, and interpretations about others' behaviors or interpretations of events. (Brizuela, Stewart, Carrillo, & Berger, 2000: xi)

This book focuses on various approaches to inquiry and at the same time grounds these in the appropriate perspective(s) so that a researcher can argue convincingly for the approach taken, and explain clearly and convincingly how this has been done. It attempts to move away from the dichotomy that separates methods from the overall inquiry process, and to show the overlap and complexities that exist when trying to situate a study within a particular perspective. It provides the theoretical underpinnings that guide the various forms of inquiry including the newer, burgeoning arts-informed approaches in qualitative work, and discusses some of the salient issues such as ethics, validity, representation and evaluation, and suggests strategies for addressing them. However, the main thrust of the book is to examine carefully a range of inquiry approaches, from the older, more traditional constant comparison and phenomenological ones to the many and varied artful approaches that are helping to push the boundaries of research. It provides an overview that 'shows rather than just tells' what is available for conducting the work. This book demonstrates how to choose these approaches appropriately and, most importantly, explains with examples how to rationalize and carry out the processes.

OVERVIEW

This introductory chapter traces the evolution of qualitative research. It uses as a backdrop Denzin and Lincoln's (2005) notions of the eight moments of qualitative research and provides more detail of what has happened in the last four decades, from the 1970s until the present. It highlights how in the 1970s, educational anthropologists and sociolinguists did much to promote this work in order to understand human activity in context, and make research more useful and accessible. It discusses the influence of narrative and feminist work in the 1980s that opened the doors to more storied, embodied and ethical/participatory approaches to research. This was followed closely by the shift to nontraditional and, more recently, arts-informed methodologies to counteract the hegemony inherent in traditional texts that came as a result of the postmodern movement and the search for more authentic forms of representation. Next it discusses various worldviews (Creswell, 2007) and the typical categories of research that are outlined in most qualitative research texts. It suggests that these typologies are more about labeling and fitting work into a particular tradition and/or field, or establishing *what* kind of research it is, rather than matching the focus, questions, and researcher orientation to the process or *how* of inquiry.

An initial way for thinking about *how* inquiry is carried out has been suggested by Maxwell and Miller (2008). They discuss how each inquiry process is based on one or the other of

> two types of relationships: those based on similarity, and those based on contiguity ... The similarity-based relations involve resemblances or common features ... generally used to define categories and to group and compare data[1] ... by category ... Contiguity-based relations ... are connections that are identified among data in an actual context. (p. 462)

Maxwell and Miller refer to the former as categorizing approaches, and the latter as connecting approaches. For example, both constant comparison and phenomenological inquiry discussed in Chapters 3 and 4 are predicated on categorizing approaches, while narrative and poetic inquiry use connecting approaches. This frame is a helpful beginning for classifying the various approaches to inquiry. But the *how* of inquiry as I am defining it extends beyond classifying the approaches based on categorizing and connecting dimensions. I argue that inquiry is the method. It is the way of being in and doing the work from its inception to its conclusion.

Finally, this chapter continues with an overview of the evolution of qualitative inquiry, and a section where I position myself as a researcher. It concludes with a brief summary of each of the chapters.

EVOLUTION OF QUALITATIVE INQUIRY

Sexton (1997) as outlined in Raskin (2002: 2) has divided the history of humankind into three eras: the premodern, the modern, and the postmodern. The premodern from the 6th century B.C. through the Middle Ages emphasized the mind/body dualism of reality where faith and religion played central roles. In the modern era, from the Renaissance to the end of the 19th century, and I would add beyond, empiricism, positivism, and scientific methodology were stressed, as well as the belief in objective truths. In fact, 'scientific knowledge was assumed to be a mirror image of objective reality' (Sexton, 1997: 7). Finally, the postmodern or present era represents the thinking that evolved through the second half of the 20th century until now. It emphasizes the creation rather than the discovery of social and personal realities, and 'highlights human participation in the construction of reality' (Raskin, 2002: 2).

Denzin and Lincoln (2005) have mapped out a series of what they call 'eight moments' in qualitative research that correspond to Sexton's description of the latter modern era and its transition to the postmodern way of thinking. The first of these was the *traditional phase* (1900–1942), where work was presented as objective but was actually colonizing depictions of reality that led to misunderstandings about other people and their cultures. The second was the *modernist phase* (1940–1970s), where qualitative researchers attempted to develop their work in ways that matched the rigor of quantitative research. Third was the *blurred genres phase* (1970–1986), during which time researchers experimented with narrative ways of doing and knowing and attended to relational aspects of research. The fourth phase was the *crisis of representation* (mid 1980s–1990) that emphasized how all phases of the research process are a series of constructions made and interpreted by the researcher and called for the researcher to situate herself reflexively in the work. Fifth was the *postmodern phase* (1990–1995), where researchers engaged in what was then considered experimental forms of writing and participatory inquiry. Sixth was the *postexperimental phase* (1995–2000), during which time new arts-informed ways were used to study and portray lived experience. Seventh was the *methodologically contested phase* (2000–2004), where methods were being questioned. Finally, they suggest that the current eighth moment is the *fractured future* (2005–), marking a time when qualitative inquiry will have to confront conservative measures attempting to reign in qualitative inquiry and align it more closely with positivistic orientations (pp. 14–20).

By using these phases as broad brushstrokes and a backdrop for how qualitative inquiry has evolved, it can be seen that it has a substantial history. This will be spelled out more specifically in subsequent chapters. For the moment, I return in more detail to the four most recent decades in qualitative inquiry. In the 1970s, a major shift took place when cognitive psychologists discovered in the translated works of Vygotsky, the social, constructivist, and contextual nature of language. Sociolinguists saw the need to study language from a pragmatic or functional perspective, while theorists began to question the existence of an objective reality. The nature of interaction, the importance of context and the need to understand interaction as a process rather than a product, forced researchers to turn to qualitative approaches to conduct their work. Borrowing from naturalistic studies of anthropology and sociology, and the subjective, lived-experience orientation of phenomenology, researchers produced micro-ethnographies, ethnomethodologies, and phenomenological studies that used natural and everyday contexts to get rich and deep understandings of the particular.

The work of narrative and feminist inquirers in the 1980s pushed the boundaries of this evolving work further. Their efforts highlighted the fact that narrative is a legitimate and natural way of doing and knowing. The relational nature of their work brought ethical issues around equity, voice and reflexivity to the forefront, while the challenges of postmodern critiques emanating from critical and race theory continued to challenge the thinking about the nature of reality and the need to examine the local as a political site where inequities exist that can be challenged and changed with action.

By the 1990s, and after a long, hard struggle, qualitative inquiry began to receive acceptance as a legitimate form of research. Within qualitative inquiry, however, researchers were questioning the linear and hegemonic practices inherent in traditional texts and began to experiment with artful forms and processes in their research. They wanted their work to be more embodied and capable of evoking intellectual, aesthetic and affective responses and to reach wider audiences and ignite social action and change. The increasing visual world we live in and the advances in technology have provided support and opportunities for pushing the boundaries even more. Since the turn of the 21st century, arts-informed work has continued to increase and flourish. While by no means universally accepted (Silverman, 2007), arts-informed inquiry has gained prominence around the globe and has sparked important, ongoing, and necessary conversations about how to develop and evaluate this type of work. The future for qualitative inquiry holds much promise; it will not disappear. But there are concerns about the backlash associated with the 'evidence-based' research movement that is taking place. It puts pressure on qualitative researchers to adopt a more 'quantitative' methodology to 'improve' the quality and robustness of the work (Yanow & Schwartz-Shea, 2006: xvii). Discussions about quality and how to evaluate qualitative inquiry, and ways to deal with the backlash, will be issues confronting qualitative inquirers for the remainder of this decade and beyond.

WORLDVIEWS AND CATEGORIES OF INQUIRY

Guba (1990: 17), cited in Creswell (2007), defines a paradigm or worldview as 'a basic set of beliefs that guide action'. Furthermore, Creswell (2007) states that there are four worldviews: post-positivism, social constructivism, advocacy/participatory, and pragmatism. He suggests that worldviews 'used by qualitative researchers vary with the set of beliefs they bring to research', and that researchers often mix worldviews if they are compatible with each other (p. 19). Post-positivism has a scientific and reductionist approach aiming for cause and effect findings from empirical data. Post-positivist researchers align themselves closely to clearly delineated research steps and the products/reports of quantitative researchers. Social constructivism is predicated on the idea that lived experience is socially constructed, understood in context, and influenced by the historical and cultural experiences known to individuals. Social constructivist researchers situate themselves in their work, use open-ended questions, emergent analysis and develop close relationships with participants in order to explain in great detail the particular experience or phenomenon under study. The advocacy/participatory worldview focuses on making changes for marginalized groups and creating spaces so these voices can be heard. In certain work, the participants take part in delineating the focus of the research and work actively with the researchers throughout the process. Researchers coming from a worldview of pragmatism are most interested in the 'actions, situations and consequences of inquiry … and will emphasize the importance of conducting research that best addresses the research problem' and by using the best available approaches (pp. 22–23). Creswell (2007: 23–29) also suggests that at a less philosophical level there are interpretive communities or, as Bentz and Shapiro (1998) call them, 'cultures of inquiry'. They draw on postmodern, feminist, critical and critical race, queer and disability theories to inform their work. Creswell posits that there are five basic approaches to inquiry: narrative, phenomenological, grounded theory, ethnographic, and case study and provides some descriptions and discussions of each too lengthy to summarize here. Other authors have similar classifications for qualitative inquiry (Denzin & Lincoln, 2005; Miles & Huberman, 1994; Munhall & Oiler, 1986; Strauss & Corbin, 1990; Yanow & Schwartz-Shea, 2006). These typologies tend to use overlapping terminology and mix the 'what and the how'. They are confusing because terms for approaches vary according to the culture of inquiry when often they are referring to the same thing.

This book takes a different approach for mapping out the terrain of qualitative inquiry. It focuses on acknowledging the stance or perspective of the researcher and the form of inquiry based on a typology discussed below. As noted above, the inquiry is considered the method, not separate from it. Moreover, it is predicated on the kinds of inquiry that are emergent in nature, ones where researchers do not begin their work with a specific theoretical lens as critical theorists might do. Rather, the researcher accounts for her researcher perspective and monitors this clearly and transparently throughout the work, and allows understandings to emerge. Then she may use a particular lens(es) to interpret the work further (Butler-Kisber, 2001), and to suggest possibilities for action and change.

Establishing a researcher perspective is not a clear-cut exercise because 'rather than having one fixed version of who we are, we all move between multiple identities' (Silverman, 2007: 1–2). That being said, it is useful to try to sort out the ontological perspectives (beliefs about the nature of being/reality) and epistemological perspectives (beliefs about how knowledge is acquired) that the researcher brings to her work. A helpful way of doing this is to think of an ontological continuum (see Figure 1.1) that

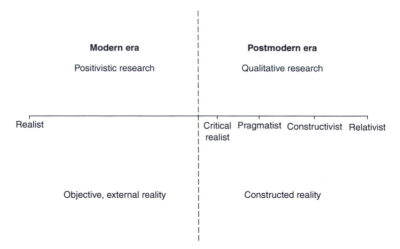

FIGURE 1.1   QUALITATIVE INQUIRY CONTINUUM

on the far left represents a realist perspective, one that is predicated on the idea that an external reality exists independent of beliefs or understanding, in other words, there is a clear difference between beliefs about the world and the way the world is. Inquiry done by researchers holding a realist or positivist perspective is predicated on the ideas that it is 'possible to conduct objective and value free inquiry, observations are the final arbiter in theoretical disputes' and 'the methods of the natural sciences … are appropriate for the study of social phenomena because human behaviour is governed by law-like regularities' (Snape & Spencer, 2003: 16).

On the far right, or other end of the continuum, is the relativist perspective, or the belief that reality is known only through socially constructed meanings. There is no single shared reality, just a variety of social constructions. From the mid-point of this continuum to the far left would represent, for the most part, the modern era of thinking described above. From the mid-point to the right would represent, again with a qualified 'for the most part', the postmodern or interpretivist/post-positivist era of thinking during which time qualitative inquiry evolved and began to flourish. Inquiry done from this perspective is predicated on the ideas that

> the researcher and the social world impact on each other, facts and values are not distinct and findings are inevitably influenced by the researcher's perspective and values … and … the methods of natural science are not appropriate because social world is not governed by law-like regularities but is mediated through meaning and human agency. (Snape & Spencer, 2003: 17)

It should be noted that from hereon I avoid the term 'interpretivist' inquiry because of the uneven and inconsistent way that it is used in the literature as an umbrella term for many different ways of discussing qualitative inquiry. Also, I avoid the term 'post-positivist' inquiry because this term is defined as a binary opposition of positivism, as what it is not, rather what it is − a completely different orientation to research.

The ontological perspectives that are situated from the mid-point to the right of this continuum represent the postmodern era of thinking. They have been classified in many different ways, using varying terms, and overlap considerably. For the purposes of a brief overview, I have decided to discuss three general stances. It should be noted that all three share the common beliefs about qualitative inquiry described above that drive much of the current, emergent-oriented qualitative work, but each of them also has some basic differences. These are the perspectives of critical realists, pragmatists, and constructivists.

Critical realists retain 'an ontological realism while accepting a form of epistemological constructivism and relativism' (Maxwell, 2008: 165) because they accept the 'possibility of alternative valid accounts of any phenomenon' and that 'all theories of the world are seen as grounded in a particular perspective and world view, and all knowledge is partial, incomplete, and fallible' (Maxwell, 2008: 164). They do not shy away from making judgments about the merit of various theories about the world. They are comfortable drawing causal conclusions about human behaviour that emerge from inquiry that is derived preferably from observational work (Silverman, 2007). Critics suggest that, 'while critical realism contests some of the default assumptions of empiricism and realism which treat social systems as closed systems, it is still predicated on an inherent order of things that is graspable by research' (Mir & Watson, 2001: 1169). Critics are wary of this 'epistemologically conservative stance' that 'provides a very stable consensus about a knowledge base for social science inquiry' (Clandinin & Rosiek, 2007: 44).

The key feature of the pragmatist perspective emanating from the work of John Dewey, William James and George Herbert Mead, among others, is that ontology and epistemology are conflated. There is no gap between knowledge and everyday action. Knowing is in the doing/experiencing, truth is the equivalent to whatever is known at a particular time, and social knowledge is cumulative and provides the basis for the evolution of thought and society (Munhall, 2007: 4). Thus knowledge is both temporal and continuous as one experience grows out of another and ordinary, everyday experience is valued but can never be fully represented. Representations are necessarily selective, and the challenge is to use knowledge in ethical ways to 'enhance human experience' (Clandinin & Rosiek, 2007: 40-42). Critics of the pragmatist perspective find an emphasis that always starts first from the individual and local experiences to be a slow and cumbersome way to ultimately enact social action and change.

The ontological stance of constructivists born out of the work of Gregory Bateson, Jean Piaget and Lev Vygotsky, among others, is that reality is socially constructed/created through social practices, interaction, and experiences. Therefore, all constructed meanings represent a particular point of view. There is no such thing as a single reality. The constructivist epistemological stance accepts that there are multiple ways of understanding/knowing the world that are always constituted and contextually dependent.

> The perspective of the observer and the object of observation are inseparable; the nature of meaning is relative; phenomena are context-based; and the process of knowledge and understanding is social, inductive, hermeneutical, and qualitative. (Sexton, 1997: 8)

Both the critical realist and pragmatist perspectives share much in common with constructivism. There has been less and less criticism of constructivist perspectives as qualitative inquiry gained legitimacy. The main argument against constructivist views are that taken to extreme, there is an inherent relativism and inability to act and/or improve resulting from the belief that all meaning is constructed.

What is probably most important to remember when talking about qualitative inquiry and researcher perspectives is that 'any given qualitative researcher … can be more than one thing at the same time, can be fitted into both the tender and tough-minded categories' (Denzin, 1998: 338). It is the way researcher perspectives are explained and made transparent that is most important.

ORGANIZATION OF THE BOOK

The organization of this book is based on a form of typology that I have devised in order to categorize the different kinds of qualitative inquiry. I have used a pragmatist lens to do so because I have focused on inquiry as a holistic process, not just an approach or a method. I have moved away from some of the historical typologies which use varying criteria that mix the notion of *what* kind of inquiry a study is with *how* the inquiry is done. I contend that this muddies the waters for researchers looking for direction and a way of 'being' in their work. I am suggesting that the term 'qualitative inquiry' is the operative or umbrella term for all kinds of inquiry that utilize interpretation. It is based on a single case and a particular situation, or involves a small number of participants, and is predicated on narrative ways of doing, thinking, and understanding. The term 'qualitative inquiry' works against the age-old qualitative/quantitative dichotomy, and the concern expressed by Yanow & Schwartz-Shea (2006) that currently 'qualitative research' is being used frequently to 'refer *not* to the traditions of meaning-focused or lived experience-focused research, but to small "n" studies that apply large "n" tools … following methodologically positivist approaches' (pp. xvi–xvii), as well as to the evidence-based research mentioned above.

I am proposing a new typology for classifying qualitative inquiry, that qualitative inquiry can be subdivided into three basic types of inquiry: *thematic, narrative,* and *arts-informed.* All three emphasize holistic inquiry processes, and a way of being in the research, not just a certain method or series of analytic steps. Each does these in different ways. Thematic inquiry uses categorization as an approach (Maxwell & Miller, 2008) for interpretation that produces a series of themes that emerge in the process of the research that account for experiences across groups or situations. Narrative inquiry uses a number of connecting approaches (Maxwell & Miller, 2008) to produce a contextualized and contiguous interpretation and storied account of the particular situation(s), while arts-informed[2] inquiry uses various forms of art to interpret and portray the focus of the particular study. All three types of inquiry can be informed by any one, or more than one, of the ontological and epistemological stances outlined above, and can be carried out with participants in more or less participatory ways, or can have a more inward and autobiographical or self-study focus. It should be emphasized that there is no perfect, one-to-one match suggested. It behooves the researcher to try to make her stance clear, and to use the knowledge about different perspectives to interrogate the inquiry process in transparent and reflexive ways.

POSITIONING MYSELF IN THE WORK

In my work, I have used or am using all three types of qualitative inquiry – thematic, narrative, and arts-informed, depending on the focus of the research and who the audience happens to be (Butler-Kisber, 1988, 2002, 2005a, 2005b, 2007, 2008; Butler-Kisber & Stewart, 2009). Also, I am influenced in the ways mentioned above by critical realist, pragmatist, and constructivist perspectives, depending on the inquiry in which I am involved. For example, I draw a particular salience from the work of critical realists and their penchant for finding the 'remarkable in the mundane' and the 'mundane in the remarkable' (Silverman, 2007: 16–18), their imperative to listen and observe things anew through attention to detail and self-conscious reflection. From the pragmatists I am heavily influenced by the notion that knowledge is experience. Therefore inquiry is a way of knowing that includes all aspects of what is fundamentally a relational and holistic process that takes place over time. It involves not just the approach to interpretation, or a series of methodological steps, but is the overall way of being in and doing the research. What I draw particularly from the constructivist perspective comes from the Vygotskian (1978) notion that the tool/language or the form mediates understandings in different and potentially interesting ways. This opens the doors to artful forms of inquiry where different mediums reveal different interpretations and possibilities. Furthermore, my work is guided by feminist and postmodern notions with a view to action and social change.

I was fortunate to have been taught and/or mentored by a number of outstanding scholars. In the early years in my doctoral work I was taught by sociolinguist Courtney Cazden and anthropologist Karen Watson-Gegeo who provided me with a wonderful foundation in thematic inquiry illustrated in the educational ethnography and classroom discourse analysis of the 1970s and 1980s. Later, I was introduced to multiple approaches to qualitative inquiry in courses with Joseph Maxwell and Michael Huberman. It was Michael who introduced me to the work of Laurel Richardson and provided me with my first taste of poetic inquiry. Subsequently, I was privileged to have been enticed, encouraged, and guided in narrative and arts-informed inquiry by Jean Clandinin, Elliot Eisner, and Tom Barone. My interest and stances in what I am classifying as thematic, narrative and arts-informed inquiry have been influenced extensively by the work of these innovative scholars.

Finally, my teaching and supervision have had, and continue to have, a significant impact on how I think about and conduct qualitative inquiry. Students over many years and from varying disciplines have helped me to question more fully and probe more deeply, and have acted as an inspiration and a sounding board for exploring and reflecting upon new avenues and possibilities.

SUMMARY OF CHAPTERS

The qualitative inquiry described in this book is not exhaustive. I have divided the book into chapters that give examples of thematic, narrative, and arts-informed inquiry based on what I have experienced in my own work, and in work I have done with colleagues and graduate students.

As a precursor to the various forms of inquiry, Chapter 2 provides an overview of the general issues that all qualitative researchers face. These are described and examples are provided to elaborate. Issues that are more germane to a particular type of inquiry are discussed in the subsequent chapters.

Thematic inquiry is discussed in Chapters 3 and 4, where I have introduced constant comparison and phenomenological inquiry as two examples of researcher stances and types of practices and processes. Included are examples from existing research and graduate student work. These elaborate and show in some detail how the research can unfold, and the challenges that researchers face when conducting this kind of inquiry. It should be noted that these two chapters do not exhaust the possibilities that exist for thematic inquiry; for example, they do not include critical incident inquiry (Musanti & Halquist, 2008) or examples of practitioner inquiry (Cochran-Smith & Lytle, 2009).

Chapter 5 focuses on narrative inquiry; its roots and perspectives are described. Because of the scope of narrative inquiry, various approaches and stances that include 'living the story with participants', 'starting with the story', and 'finding the story' are outlined, and examples are provided. The chapter concludes with a discussion about issues and quality in narrative inquiry.

Chapters 6 through 9 focus on arts-informed inquiry and include poetic inquiry, collage inquiry, photographic inquiry, and performative inquiry. Again, these chapters do not exhaust the examples and possibilities of arts-informed inquiry. Missing, among others, are painting, sculpture, dance, and music as inquiry, but I have chosen to focus on the art forms with which I am most familiar. Each chapter traces the background and underpinnings of the particular form of inquiry, provides some concrete examples, and culminates in a discussion about challenges and quality in the work.

Chapter 10 is brief and meant to be so. It does not attempt to summarize the earlier chapters, but rather discusses future thinking and possible directions for various forms of qualitative inquiry. Many of these have been foreshadowed in the preceding chapters.

NOTES

1. I prefer and will use the term 'field texts' coined by Clandinin and Connelly (2000) instead of data, to underscore, as they have suggested, the subjective and constitutive nature of materials used for research, and to avoid perpetuating the notion that 'data' exists in and of itself.

2. I am purposely using 'arts-informed' rather than 'arts-based' as a term for qualitative inquiry. 'Arts-based' inquiry was coined by Elliot Eisner at Stanford University in

the early 1990s. He opened the doors to this kind of research and largely through his efforts it has burgeoned in the last decade. Subsequently, the term 'arts-informed' was introduced by Gary Knowles and Ardra Cole at the Ontario Institute for Studies in Education at the University of Toronto. Their preference for the term arts-informed stemmed from the fact that as educational researchers they were using art to inform their research rather than basing it on art. Perhaps artists venturing into this kind of research should use the term 'arts-based', while those of us who came to art from research should remain with the term 'arts-informed'. The distinction could be a helpful one when addressing issues of quality and evaluation in this type of inquiry.

REFERENCES

Bentz, V. M., & Shapiro, J. J. (1998). *Mindful inquiry in social research.* Thousand Oaks, CA: Sage.

Brizuela, J. P., Stewart, R. G., Carrillo, R. G., & Berger, J. G. (2000). (Eds.), Introduction. *Acts of inquiry in qualitative research.* Harvard Educational Review, Reprint Series No. 34, xi–xxii.

Butler-Kisber, L. (1988). *Peer collaboration around educational tasks: A classroom ethnography.* Unpublished doctoral dissertation, Harvard University, Cambridge, MA.

Butler-Kisber, L. (2001). Whispering angels: Revisiting dissertation data with a new lens. *Journal of Critical Inquiry into Curriculum and Instruction, 2*(3), 34–37.

Butler-Kisber, L. (2002). Artful portrayals in qualitative inquiry: The road to found poetry and beyond. *The Alberta Journal of Educational Research, XLVIII*(3), 229–239.

Butler-Kisber, L. (2005a). The potential of artful analysis and portrayals in qualitative inquiry. In F. Bodone (Ed.), *What difference does research make and for whom?* (pp. 203–217). New York: Peter Lang.

Butler-Kisber, L. (2005b). Arts-based qualitative research and self-study: A poetic approach. In K. O'Reilly-Scanlon, C. Mitchell, & S. Weber (Eds.), *Just who do we think we are? Methodologies for self-study in teacher education* (pp. 95–110). NY: Routledge Falmer.

Butler-Kisber, L. (2007). Collage as analysis and representation. In J. G. Knowles, T. C. Luciani, A. L. Cole, & L. Neilsen (Eds.), *The art of visual inquiry* (pp. 265–280). Halifax, NS: Backalong.

Butler-Kisber, L. (2008). Collage as inquiry. In J. G. Knowles, & A. L. Cole (Eds.), *Handbook of the arts in qualitative research* (pp. 265–276). Thousand Oaks, CA: Sage.

Butler-Kisber, L., & Stewart, M. (2009). The use of poetry clusters in poetic inquiry. *Poetic inquiry: Vibrant voices in the social sciences.* Rotterdam: Sense.

Clandinin, D. J., & Connelly, F. M. (2000). *Narrative inquiry: Experience and story in qualitative research.* San Francisco: Jossey-Bass.

Clandinin, D. J., & Rosiek, J. (2007). Mapping a landscape of narrative inquiry: Borderlands spaces and tensions. In D. J. Clandinin (Ed.), *Handbook of narrative inquiry* (pp. 35–75). Thousand Oaks, CA: Sage.

Cochran-Smith, M., & Lytle, S. (2009). *Inquiry as stance: Practitioner research in the next generation.* New York: Teachers College Press.

Creswell, J. W. (2007). *Qualitative inquiry and research design: Choosing among five approaches* (2nd ed.). Thousand Oaks, CA: Sage.

Denzin, N. K. (1998). The art and politics of interpretation. In N. K. Denzin & Y. S. Lincoln (Eds.), *Handbook of qualitative research* (pp. 313–371). Thousand Oaks, CA: Sage.

Denzin, N. K., & Lincoln, Y. S. (2005). *The Sage handbook of qualitative research* (3rd ed.). Thousand Oaks, CA: Sage.

Guba, E. G. (1990). The alternative paradigm dialog. In E. G. Guba (Ed.), *The paradigm dialog* (pp. 17–30). Newbury Park, CA: Sage.

Maxwell, J. A. (2008). The value of a realist understanding of causality for qualitative research. In N. K. Denzin & M. G. Giardina (Eds.), *Qualitative inquiry and the politics of evidence* (pp. 163–181). Walnut Creek, CA: Left Coast.

Maxwell, J., & Miller, B. (2008). Categorizing and connecting strategies in qualitative data analysis. In P. Leavy & S. Hesse-Biber (Eds.), *Handbook of emergent methods* (pp. 461–477) New York: Guilford.

Miles, M. B., & Huberman, A. M. (1994). *Qualitative data analysis: A sourcebook of new methods* (2nd ed.). Thousand Oaks, CA: Sage.

Mir, R., & Watson, A. (2001). Critical realism and constructivism in strategy research: Towards a synthesis. *Strategic Management Journal, 22*(12), 1169-1173.

Munhall, P. L. (2007). *Nursing research: A qualitative perspective* (4th ed.). Sudbury, MA: Jones & Bartlett.

Munhall, P. L., & Oiler, C. J. (Eds.) (1986). *Nursing research: A qualitative perspective.* Norwalk, CT: Appleton-Century-Croft.

Musanti, S. I., & Halquist, D. (2008). Critical incidents and reflection: Turning points that challenge the researcher and create opportunities for knowing. Paper presented at the *Annual Meeting of the American Educational Research Association.* New York (March).

Patton, M. Q. (2002). Two decades of development in qualitative inquiry: A personal, experiential perspective. *Qualitative Social Work, 1*(3), 261–283.

Raskin, J. D. (2002). Constructivism in psychology: Personal construct psychology, radical constructivism, and social constructionism. In J. D. Raskin & S. K. Bridges (Eds.), *Studies in meaning: Exploring constructivist psychology* (pp. 1–25). New York: Pace University Press.

Sexton, T. L. (1997). Constructivist thinking within the history of ideas. The challenge of a new paradigm. In T. L. Sexton & B. L. Griffin (Eds.), *Contructivist thinking in counseling practice, research, and training* (pp. 3–18). New York: Teachers College Press.

Silverman, D. (2007). *A very short, fairly interesting, and reasonably cheap book about qualitative research.* London: Sage.

Snape, D., & Spencer, L. (2003). The foundations of qualitative research. In J. Ritchie & J. Lewis (Eds.), *Qualitative research practice: A guide for social science students and researchers* (pp. 1–23). London: Sage.

Strauss, A., & Corbin, J. (1990). *Basics of qualitative research: Grounded theory procedures and techniques.* Newbury Park, CA: Sage.

Vygotsky, L. (1978). *Mind in society: The development of higher psychological processes.* Cambridge, MA: Harvard University Press.

Yanow, D., & Schwartz-Shea, P. (2006). *Interpretation and method: Empirical research methods and the interpretive turn.* Armonk, NY: M. E. Sharpe.

2

Issues in Qualitative Inquiry

There are six main issues that qualitative researchers face when conducting their work: validity (commonly referred to as the trustworthiness of a qualitative study); generalizability (or what I like to refer to as particularizability in qualitative work); access and consent; reflexivity; voice; transparency. This chapter defines the terms validity, reliability and generalizability as they pertain to qualitative inquiry and argues that questions of reliability have no relevance in qualitative inquiry. It is necessary to do this in order to explain why, in qualitative work, many researchers — although not all (Maxwell, 1992) — particularly those who embrace a pragmatist and/or constructivist stance described in Chapter 1, prefer to use the term ('trustworthiness' or credibility and persuasiveness) (Reissman, 1993) instead of 'validity'. These same researchers also prefer the idea of 'particularizability' (Donmoyer, 1990) instead of 'generalizability'. Factors that enhance credibility are described, such as length of time in the 'field', multiple sources of field texts (data), and participant checks. Access and consent are explored as an ongoing negotiation rather than a single moment of consent, and illustrate the importance of relationships in all research endeavours. Examples are given about access difficulties and how these can be solved. It is suggested how to ensure that very young participants, or others who might have difficulty understanding, can be part of the consent process, even when it is not legally mandated. The importance of including the voices of the participants for more authentic portrayals and more ethical practices is discussed. Researcher reflexivity is explored and elaborated upon by showing how identity memos (Maxwell, 1996) and reflective memos can help to make sure that the researcher is continually aware of the assumptions that she brings to her work. The researcher must acknowledge and critically question these in the research process, while being cognizant of the fact that the socially situated nature of research brings the assumptions of others into play as well. The chapter culminates in a discussion about transparency, suggesting that for a study to be trustworthy/credible and ethical it must be transparent, and this may indeed have other benefits (Eisner & Peshkin, 1990). Transparency can be enhanced if the researcher deals adequately with these fundamental issues, and makes very clear the inquiry processes that have been followed. The remaining chapters on thematic, narrative, and arts-informed work will build on these issues and show how to make the various inquiry approaches very transparent.

VALIDITY

> A multitude of approaches to and conceptualizations of validity have emerged, differing significantly depending on the research methodologies and paradigms that guide each particular research project. From positivist to postpositivist perspectives ... validity is often broadly described as being dependent on the degree to which a study actually measures what it purports to measure – whether 'the truth' is accurately identified and described. (Miller, 2008: 909)

From the point of view of qualitative inquiry, this realist notion of defining and describing a 'truth' to demonstrate validity has very little meaning. Critical realists (Maxwell, 1992) have argued that it is impossible to demonstrate validity in this realist way. They believe that validity in qualitative work can be evaluated on 'the fact that there exist ways of assessing accounts which do not depend entirely on features of the account itself, but in some way relate to those things that the account claims to be about' (p. 281). Maxwell (1992) suggests that these ways are 'descriptive validity' or factual accuracy of the account, and 'interpretive validity' or the degree to which the account reflects the insider/participant perspectives. Finally, there is 'theoretical validity' or how well the interpretation functions as an account of a particular phenomenon (pp. 283–288). It has become preferable more recently in qualitative inquiry, particularly in narrative and arts-informed work, to move away from the term 'validity' because it still carries with it the realist/positivist understandings that misconstrue how it is defined for these types of inquiry (Eisner, 1991). So while different terms and emphases are used depending on the nature of a particular study, as will be shown in subsequent chapters, many qualitative inquirers prefer to evaluate inquiry based on its trustworthiness or credibility.

Trustworthiness is determined by its degree of persuasiveness, authenticity, and plausibility (Reissman, 1993). A rigorous or trustworthy study indicates its persuasiveness by including a coherent and transparent research process and illustrating an adherence to researcher reflexivity and reflection, or a clear statement of how the researcher accounts for assumptions and biases. Also it shows how the researcher is situated in the work and accounts for the social and contextual influences, and how she interrogates all of these on an ongoing basis. Trustworthiness is enhanced when there is clear evidence that a length of time has been spent in the field and there are multiple forms of field texts that can help to corroborate explanations. Also, it is useful to have some breadth or range in terms of participants, in other words to get different perspectives from others who know and/or understand the context. For example, Furlini (2005) was conducting in-depth interviews with a number of caregivers of family members with chronic dementia. She also interviewed some doctors, health care professionals and social workers to get a variety of perspectives. A continual verification of findings, an involvement of participants in the verification process, and the use of peer debriefing all contribute to trustworthiness. Authenticity and plausibility are increased when explanations are clearly grounded in the field texts, the voices of the participants are present in the work, and the researcher reveals and analyzes discrepant 'cases' or instances. In so doing, she offers alternative explanations, and is frank about tensions that arise in the work (Clandinin & Connolly, 2000). Last but certainly not least, there needs to be clear evidence that the work has been founded on, and guided by, ethical practices.

> In sum, trustworthiness provides qualitative researchers with a set of tools by which they can illustrate the worth of their project outside the confines of the often ill-fitting quantitative parameters. (Given & Saumure, 2008: 896)

GENERALIZABILITY

In positivistic/quantitative research, the term 'generalizability' is deemed possible if there is a sufficiently large sample size and an adherence to clearly defined and prescribed procedures. These measures are intended to rule out the possibility of the results occurring by chance, therefore making the findings of a study generalizable to other contexts. In qualitative inquiry, the philosophical underpinnings described in Chapter 1, the small number of participants, and the varied, emergent and contextualized processes and 'results' rule out any willingness or attempt to claim that one situation can be generalized to another (Donmoyer, 1990, 2008). In fact, the term 'particularizability' might be more appropriate, meaning how a certain study resonates (Conle, 1996) with people in other situations so that they are able to find both confirmation and/or new understandings of experiences and phenomena. In addition, Donmoyer (2008) has suggested that 'reading qualitative accounts of radically different cases … produce enriched cognitive schema and that these schema … allow for a kind of intellectual generalization even when settings are radically different' (p. 372). Thus, generalizability as it is defined in terms of positivistic research has no currency in qualitative inquiry. In fact, even some positivistic researchers have questioned whether generalizability is ever really possible in quantitative research (Cronbach, 1975).

In quantitative research, reliability is another measure of quality. Reliability is the degree to which multiple researchers would arrive at the same conclusions if they were engaged in the same study and adhered to identical procedures. Based on the discussion above, it can be seen why in qualitative inquiry, reliability is not considered possible or desirable, as it undermines the very assumptions on which qualitative inquiry is based. In qualitative work, transparency and researcher reflexivity might be considered the equivalent. Transparency permits a clear understanding of the inquiry process which persuades the reader/audience of the trustworthiness or rigor of the study, and allows other researchers to build on or adapt processes that are revealed in the work (Saumure & Given, 2008). In researcher reflexivity, as mentioned earlier and discussed below, the researcher accounts for and attends to the biases and assumption she brings to the study. It is incumbent upon the researcher to attend to how the research is socially situated and what influences this has on the study. Insights garnered from participants by having them or peers review what is emerging in the inquiry can provide important and different perspectives for thinking about what is transpiring.

ACCESS AND CONSENT

Research access and informed consent are ongoing, negotiated processes (Personal Communication, Margaret Sommerville, January, 1999), that continue throughout the life of a project and beyond (Feldman, Bell, & Berger, 2003). They are predicated on relational and ethical behaviour that means conducting an 'authentic investigation' (Maykut & Morehouse, 1994: 29) that does no harm (Eisner, 1991) and embraces the practices that Lugones (1994) suggests people employ as they 'world travel' or move in unfamiliar spaces. These include understanding the language and conventions of the participants and their contexts, engaging in dialogical exchanges (Madison, 2005: 105), interrogating power relations and hegemonic practices, and acting with empathy and reflexivity.

The legal protection of human participants emanated from the Nuremberg Code established in 1947 that posited a way of evaluating medical research involving humans (Feldman et al., 2003: 13–14). As this work evolved in different countries, research review became formalized, institutionalized, and mandatory and regulated by research ethics boards (REBs). Feldman et al. (2003: 15) suggest that the formally instituted safeguards help the participants understand more clearly what a researcher is doing. These enhance the research relationship and help prevent withdrawal. Also, they force researchers to think through the plans for the research carefully in advance. This helps to avoid subsequent, unforeseen difficulties. As well, an REB provides an avenue of recourse for the researcher should a complaint arise. While the language may vary, most REBs require a summary of the project, examples of letters to participants outlining the project, and copies of the consent forms indicating how the participants will be protected. The ethics submission and the consent forms must emphasize the right of participants to be fully informed, to know all the risks and benefits, the right to privacy and confidentiality, the right of cultural groups to accurate and respectful description of their customs and heritage, and the right to withdraw without pressure or penalty. Also, they must provide consideration for the vulnerability of children or any other particular group of participants. In addition, REBs require a description of how participants will be recruited, an outline of any potential harms and risks, and whether these are acceptable given the benefits of the research. Researchers are expected to anticipate and outline any potential ethical issues that might arise during the research, and to request a subsequent review should the research change for some reason. Usually researchers must go through review at their home institutions and, where applicable, the institutions in which the participants are a part.

These procedures are extremely important, albeit sometimes overly bureaucratic, because they have helped greatly to regulate research in the last 25 years by putting ethical issues squarely on the table. They are, however, the tip of the iceberg. What is critical is how these measures are actually implemented over the course of a study and beyond. Given how the lines between research and everyday activity have blurred with the increasing forms of inquiry, it is also imperative that new issues are identified and brought to the surface as they emerge. Mostly, it is the everyday conduct of the researcher, informed by issues and committed to ethical practices, that establishes the degree of integrity of the ongoing inquiry process.

In 1998 a graduate student, Kelly Howarth, was conducting a study of the home-schooled literacy learning of her 5-year-old for a course on qualitative inquiry. To do a project, all students were required to go through an expedited, departmental ethics review. Her challenge was to find a way to get informed consent from her young son who did not know how to read. She found a very creative approach. She outlined in very simple statements the steps she envisioned for the project. She presented him with the written steps and provided spaces in the text between each statement. She read each statement aloud to him while pointing to the words. After each statement she asked him to draw what the statement said (see Figure 2.1). When he finished there was a space for his signature, her signature and the date (see Figure 2.2). This has proven to be an excellent way of opening up discussions about just how 'informed' informed consent is in certain situations, and how alternative ways of conveying the research process can contribute to informed consent. With digital technologies that are now available, there may be some visual avenues to explore in the area of informed consent.

ACCESS

Access is the reciprocal process of informed consent. One cannot get consent without some initial access to people and/or contexts, but true access only comes with informed consent. There are no direct routes to access, but having a statement that outlines the project is helpful because it enables the researcher to leave a tangible product with a participant(s) that can be revisited after the contact is made. Naturally, in certain contexts where language or literacy presents a problem, a written document is not helpful.

Finding appropriate participants and/or sites can be pursued in different ways. One can seek an endorsement (Bogdan & Biklen, 1992) from an expert in the field to first locate some possible participants or a site. There are some problems associated with seeking several participants or sites and then choosing only one. Both the endorser and the participants can feel rejected when not selected. A researcher can

CONSENT FORM

MOMMY GOES TO SCHOOL AT McGILL UNIVERSITY. THAT IS THE PLACE UP ON THE HILL WHERE WE WENT TO THE LIBRARY AND ONE OF MOMMY'S FRIENDS GAVE ME A PIECE OF PAPER TO DRAW ON.

FOR MOMMY'S SCHOOL, SHE HAS TO DO WORK TO GIVE TO HER TEACHERS.

FIGURE 2.1   EXAMPLE OF A VISUAL CONSENT FORM

THE ONLY PEOPLE WHO WILL SEE MOMMY'S WRITING, THE PICTURES AND TAPES ARE HER TEACHERS AND THE OTHER STUDENTS IN HER CLASSES.

I KNOW THAT I CAN STOP BEING IN MOMMY'S STUDY AT ANY TIME.

I WANT TO HELP MOMMY. ALL THIS IS OKAY WITH ME.

SIGNED _CRICTAN DIAMD_

MOMMY _Kelly Howatt_

DATE _October 5, 1998_

FIGURE 2.2   SIGNATURE ON VISUAL CONSENT FORM

go formally through the organizational hierarchy to seek access, or more laterally through colleagues and/or friends. The former takes longer but ensures that all necessary approval is sought and granted; the latter may proceed much more quickly, but may slow down and possibly create unanticipated difficulty when other mandatory levels of access become involved, after the fact. The delicate balance is to be able to inspire interest and even excitement in the research without having to promise the impossible. The researcher has to be able to show that there are reciprocal benefits to be gained, and that she is legitimate and credible in her work. Perseverance is often necessary, and the shape of the research may change, but caution should be taken to avoid trading off too many aspects of the project to gain access only to find as a result that, ultimately, the research is impeded (Butler-Kisber, 2006).

REFLEXIVITY

Who we are as researchers, or our research identities, changes with time and experience, just as our everyday identities do. For novices, the idea of having a research identity without a wealth of research experience comes as a surprise, but we are all constantly researching as naturally interpretive beings, using the small 'r' idea of research, to consider and analyze things around us to make meaning of our worlds. And clearly we all bring beliefs, often unarticulated ones, to the research process. What needs to be accounted for and interrogated, as discussed in Chapter 1, is what perspectives are brought to the work and why we see things the way we do. In qualitative inquiry, no apologies are needed for identity, assumptions, and biases, just a rigorous accounting of them.

Dowling (2008) suggests that there are four kinds of researcher reflexivity. On the more realist end of the qualitative continuum, this is seen as the practice of bracketing out assumptions largely associated with phenomenological inquiry (see Chapter 4). The second she calls 'epistemological reflexivity', where 'researchers are required to ask questions of their methodological decision making and are encouraged to think about epistemological decisions regarding the research and findings' (p. 747) often associated with constant comparison inquiry (see Chapter 3). The third type probes more deeply beyond the actual research process to examine political and social influences on the inquiry, seen in many different kinds of inquiry that seek social justice and change. The fourth type embraces a reciprocal reflexivity on the part of both the researcher and participants typically associated with feminist and participatory inquiry (p. 748).

Identity memos (Maxwell, 1996), or short, concise statements addressing the questions of 'who I am, the beliefs I have that might impact on the work, and how I will account for my beliefs and assumptions during my study' are helpful ways of making tacit assumptions explicit. This is a way for researchers to interrogate and monitor their subjectivity as Peshkin (1991) has suggested:

> I see this monitoring as a necessary exercise, a workout, a tuning up of my subjectivity as a researcher, why I chose my study, what beliefs I bring to my study, and why, how these get it in shape. It is a rehearsal for keeping the lines of my subjectivity open – and straight. And it is a warning to myself so that I may

avoid the trap of perceiving just what my own untamed sentiments have
sought out and served up as data. (pp. 293–294)

A helpful exercise to show how beliefs are used unconsciously to make interpretations is to view a short, silent videotaped clip of some activity and have the viewers interpret what is transpiring. The clip I find particularly helpful is taken from a
study of an early childhood classroom (outlined more fully later), where the students
are working independently at their desks and the teacher is overseeing the work
while she uses the time to conference with individual students. The desks are clustered in groups of four, and the camera focuses in on Naomi and Kimie who are
working side by side. Naomi moves from her seat out of view and reappears moving at a rather slow pace. The camera then shows Naomi glancing over at Kimie's
work several times. Then she gets up from her seat and goes to the corner of the
room where she appears to dawdle for a few seconds. She finally picks up some
crayons and returns to her seat.

Repeatedly, the responses to the clip suggest almost unanimously that Naomi
appears distracted and off-task, and that she seems to be trying to look at Kimie's
work to help her do her own. There is surprise when the audience hears that
Naomi is an extremely capable student who gets her work done quickly and is
often pensive as she moves about the classroom. Kimie is the one asking for help,
and does this frequently during other work as peer help is encouraged in this classroom. When Naomi first left her seat she went to get a pencil, very permissible in
this particular classroom, and the second time she went to get some crayons so she
could do other work, having finished the assignment. Student responsibility for
accessing supplies, books and other materials is also a fundamental dimension of
this classroom. Further discussion with the viewers of this clip always reveals some
of the preconceived notions that they carry with them, either from their own
experiences as young learners, or as teachers, or both. These include how on-task
work in school is defined, and how looking over at someone's work suggests difficulty, and perhaps even cheating. It is a way of showing how easy it is to jump to
a conclusion/interpretation prematurely based on held assumptions.

Reflective memos or short statements written regularly and reflectively about
what is occurring, questioning understanding by attending to assumptions, is another
way for a researcher to keep track of how she is positioned and may be unduly influ-
encing what is transpiring, or to monitor other contextual or social dimensions that
may be having an impact on what is transpiring. It is a way for the researcher to
'dialogue with herself' about questions, issues, and intuitions as they arise and to
keep track of these. Because reflective memos are written over time, they chronicle
an interesting, temporal path and can be used in peer debriefings, or with supervisors,
to push to a more critical form of reflexivity.

VOICE

Historically in qualitative research, the voices of participants were glossed over
and/or 'aggregated'. Research reports were written in an 'objective' manner that

portrayed an authorial, all-knowing voice with no attention to 'voicing' the researcher identity and assumptions brought to and shaped in the work (Guba & Lincoln, 2005: 209). This changed substantially with the advent of more relational research that emerged in the 1980s. It put many ethical issues on the table, including that of participant and researcher voices. The appropriation of participant voices and stories/experiences was highly criticized and reflexivity became an important element in terms of meeting the needs of ethical and transparent practices. Now there is a widespread understanding that

> voice is more than a metaphor for individual perspective ... The qualitative researcher, therefore, must strive to understand the reality of voice as a process of the lived creation of meaning and not merely as a vague ethical gesture or an attempt to understand the opinion or perspective of one's sources. (Fabian, 2008: 943)

The issue of voice in inquiry is multifaceted and fraught with tensions. It requires vigilant and ethical attention to power and appropriation while attending to ownership, advocacy, and protection of participants on the inquiry continuum – through the ongoing work with participants, the explanations derived from this work, and the publication or 'product' that emerges (Kirsch, 1999: x). Many of the newer forms of arts-informed inquiry have moved away from more traditional texts to deal with issues of voice and to counter the hegemonic dimensions of linear texts. These new forms of representation have nuanced ethical issues of voice and given rise to important discussions, as will be shown in subsequent chapters.

TRANSPARENCY

It should be noted that the inquiry process begins long before the researcher formally accesses a site/participants and has implications for those involved long after the work has been completed. The ethical and relational dimensions of the work are critical, as these profoundly shape all aspects of the inquiry. Throughout this chapter, transparency has been mentioned as a way to enhance trustworthiness, as a way to be reflexive in the inquiry process, to share productively the inquiry process with colleagues, and as a way to act ethically and relationally with participants. On the surface it seems straightforward enough, but in practice it is less so. There is a qualitative difference between telling and showing, and much of the published research tends to tell rather than show. Transparency requires not only a careful and detailed documentation of the entire process of inquiry for subjective use, but also a 'public transparency' that adds trustworthiness and persuasiveness to the work, and helps other inquirers, particularly novice researchers, to expand their horizons (Hiles, 2008: 890).

CONCLUDING REMARKS

In the chapters that follow there is an emphasis on showing rather than just telling, not to prescribe or suggest that there are recipes for doing qualitative inquiry, but rather to open up discussions and possible actions. No matter what the form of inquiry, whether thematic, narrative or arts–informed, these basic issues are integral to the work and require attention throughout any inquiry process.

REFERENCES

Bogdan, R., & Biklen, S. (1992). *Qualitative research for education: An introduction to theory and methods* (2nd ed.). Boston: Allyn & Bacon.

Butler-Kisber, L. (2006). Revisiting and reflecting on qualitative research: Three stories. *National Forum of Teacher Education Journal, 16*(2), 43–72.

Clandinin, D. J., & Connolly, F. M. (2000). *Narrative inquiry: Experience and story in qualitative research.* Thousand Oaks, CA: Sage.

Conle, C. (1996). Resonance in pre-service teacher inquiry. *American Educational Research Journal, 33*, 297–325.

Cronbach, L. (1975). Beyond the two disciplines of scientific psychology. *American Psychologist, 30*, 116–127.

Donmoyer, R. (1990). Generalizability and the single case study. In E. W. Eisner & A. Peshkin (Eds.), *Qualitative inquiry in education* (pp. 175–200). New York: Teachers College Press.

Donmoyer, R. (2008). Generalizability. In L. M. Givens (Ed.), *The Sage encyclopedia of qualitative inquiry, Vol. 1* (pp. 371–372). Thousand Oaks, CA: Sage.

Dowling, M. (2008). Reflexivity. In L.M. Givens (Ed.), *The Sage encyclopedia of qualitative inquiry, Vol. 2* (pp. 747–748). Thousand Oaks, CA: Sage.

Eisner, E. W. (1991). *The enlightened eye: Qualitative inquiry and the enhancement of educational practice.* New York: Macmillan.

Eisner, E. W., & Peshkin, A. (Eds) (1990). *Qualitative inquiry in education: The continuing debate.* New York: Teachers College Press.

Fabian, S. C. (2008). Voice. In L. M. Givens (Ed.), *The Sage encyclopedia of qualitative inquiry, Vol. 2* (pp. 943–944). Thousand Oaks, CA: Sage.

Feldman, M. S., Bell, J., & Berger, M. T. (2003). *Gaining access: A practical and theoretical guide for qualitative researchers.* Walnut Creek, CA: AltaMira.

Furlini, L. (2005). *Living with chronic dementia from the caregiver perspective: A case for educational support.* Unpublished doctoral dissertation, McGill University, Montreal, QC.

Given, L. M., & Saumure, K. (2008). Trustworthiness. In L. M. Givens (Ed.), *The Sage encyclopedia of qualitative inquiry, Vol. 2* (pp. 895–896). Thousand Oaks, CA: Sage.

Guba, E. G., & Lincoln, Y. S. (2005). Paradigmatic controversies, contradictions, and emerging confluences. In N. K. Denzin & Y. S. Lincoln (Eds.), *The Sage handbook of qualitative research* (3rd ed.), (pp. 191–215). Thousand Oaks, CA: Sage.

Hiles, D. R. (2008). Transparency. In L. M. Givens (Ed.), *The Sage encyclopedia of qualitative inquiry, Vol. 2* (pp. 890–892). Thousand Oaks, CA: Sage.

Kirsch, G. (1999). *Ethical dilemmas in feminist research: The politics of location, interpretation, and publication.* Albany, NY: State University of New York Press.

Lugones, M. (1994). Playfulness, 'world'-travelling, and loving perception. In D. S. Madison (Ed.), *The woman that I am: The literature and culture of contemporary women of color* (pp. 628–638). New York: St. Martin's.

Madison, D. S. (2005). *Critical ethnography: Method, ethics, performance.* Thousand Oaks, CA: Sage.

Maykut, P., & Morehouse, R. (1994). *Beginning qualitative research: A philosophic and practical guide.* New York: RoutledgeFalmer.

Maxwell, J. A. (1992). Understanding and validity in qualitative research. *Harvard Educational Review, 62,* 279–300.

Maxwell, J. A. (1996). *Qualitative research design: An interactive approach.* Thousand Oaks, CA: Sage.

Miller, P. (2008). Validity. In L. M. Givens (Ed.), *The Sage encyclopedia of qualitative inquiry, Vol. 2* (pp. 909–910). Thousand Oaks, CA: Sage.

Peshkin, A. (1991). *The color of strangers, the color of friends: The play of ethnicity in school and community.* Chicago: University of Chicago Press.

Reissman, C. K. (1993). *Narrative inquiry.* Newbury Park, CA: Sage.

Saumure, K., & Given, L. M. (2008). Rigor. Trustworthiness. In L. M. Givens (Ed.), *The Sage encyclopedia of qualitative inquiry, Vol. 2* (pp. 795–796). Thousand Oaks, CA: Sage.

3

Constant Comparison Inquiry

This chapter discusses the early contributions of grounded theory (GT) to qualitative research (Glaser & Strauss, 1967), and how, currently, its proponents have suggested it can be considered a constructivist approach (Charmaz, 2005), if the researcher 'adopts grounded theory guidelines as tools, but does not subscribe to the objectivist, positivist assumptions in its earlier formulations' (p. 509). It focuses on a form of work that has emerged from GT, called 'constant comparison inquiry' (Maykut & Morehouse, 1994), and outlines how such a form of inquiry is implemented from the accessing and organizing of the data, through the initial unitizing of the material and assigning early, descriptive labels or codes. It shows, with an example, how to write rules of inclusion to define the categories so that they can be expanded and/or collapsed, and how to move to a process of renaming the categories in more conceptual/functional ways (Strauss & Corbin, 1990) in order to reveal deeper understandings and connections. It includes an interesting example of a study on the educational needs of caregivers of persons with dementia, showing how the researcher used constant comparison inquiry to tease out similarities across the interviews of five women caregivers who, on the surface, had very different experiences (Furlini, 2005). A third example is provided from the work of Strauss and Corbin (1990) to highlight the process of moving from descriptive to conceptual understandings. This analytic move is not an easy one and often requires looking at the field text material in new and innovative ways. A discussion of two forms of visual mapping – concept and cartographic mapping – are included to illustrate how such tools can help the researcher understand, interpret and even present the work more conceptually. Finally, the challenges researchers face when conducting constant comparison inquiry are discussed. This section argues that when used across 'cases' as in this example, constant comparison inquiry can produce common elements of phenomena that can be both helpful and persuasive in making recommendations resulting from the research. The trade-off, of course, is that contextual elements are lost when constant comparison inquiry is used. However, there are ways of dealing with this as will be shown in the chapters that follow. Finally, there is a brief discussion of the use of computer software, more specifically the Atlas.ti program in constant comparison inquiry, or other forms of thematic inquiry. The pros and cons are outlined with a cautionary note underscoring that all interpretation is really in the hands of the researcher. Computer software for field text analysis is a tool for managing and manipulating the material, not for doing the conceptual work of analysis. The chapter culminates in a discussion about quality issues and evaluation in constant comparison inquiry.

CONTRIBUTIONS OF GT

In 1967, sociologists Barney Glaser and Anselm Strauss produced their first book entitled *The Discovery of Grounded Theory*. It was a breakthrough for qualitative research because it provided a theoretical accounting to legitimize qualitative work at a time when positivism flourished and quantitative research was the norm. Given the background of these researchers, Glaser was trained in methodology steeped in positivism, while Strauss came out of the Chicago School tradition of pragmatism and symbolic interactionism, it is not surprising that the underpinnings of GT viewed with a present-day lens are somewhat contradictory in nature. Glaser brought to this mix a realist view of the world. He believed that there was a need for a linear and systematic analysis, and that a researcher can be unbiased and produce formal or 'grand' theory. Strauss, on the other hand, emphasized the importance of action and democratic processes, fieldwork traditions and emergent and contextual interpretations, beliefs that were consistent with his constructivist background (Charmaz, 2005: 508–509).

There is no doubt that the debut of GT gave a considerable boost to qualitative research, opening doors to research possibilities by providing a rigorous way to discuss and account for the work. It was used to undergird fieldwork studies in anthropology, sociology, and nursing, among others, and provided the basis for micro-ethnographies in education giving credence to studies that emphasized process instead of product and increasing the range and accessibility of research 'findings' (Bolster, 1982).

A mounting criticism of qualitative research based on GT occurred in the late 1970s through the 1980s with the steady and increasing interest in postmodern, feminist, and critical theories (Coffey, Holbrook, & Atkinson, 1996). This 'interpretive' turn embraced the notion of multiple realities, the complex, nonlinear, subjective and constitutive nature of research, the ethical implications of participant voice, research relationships and reflexivity. It emphasized the need for democratic research practices that produce social change. Even constructivist revisions of GT, such as those proposed by Seale (1999) and Charmaz (2005: 508–509), that are realigned with the Chicago School and emphasize process, fieldwork traditions, and possibilities for social change, thereby problematizing the positivist roots of GT, are treated skeptically. For many, the analytic tools that grew out of

GT and provided the basis for much of the naturalistic research of the 1980s, most commonly known as a type of thematic inquiry, or constant comparison inquiry, have remained suspect. Yet, rather than reducing it to an analytic coding strategy, there are many interesting and helpful ways of using constant comparison as a mode of inquiry to build understandings across phenomena, experiences, and/or cases while embracing a theoretical stance that acknowledges subjectivity and multiple realities, enacts ethical practices, and drives social action.

AN OVERVIEW OF CONSTANT COMPARISON INQUIRY

It is not surprising that time and again over the years graduate students have complained about the difficulty of finding examples of how to conduct qualitative inquiry using an emergent coding/thematic/categorizing/constant comparison perspective. It is difficult to respond succinctly to this because coding field texts is such a small part of what is entailed in implementing constant comparative inquiry, but is a very critical part of the work and not always transparently portrayed (Anfara, Brown, & Mangione, 2002). Knowledge of the history of qualitative research, the research traditions that inform the work, the situatedness of the work, and of the iterative nature of the work is needed. In addition, the terminology that is employed around the use of constant comparative inquiry varies considerably across research communities and makes for confusing reading. Often, qualitative research texts that attend thoroughly to research traditions omit needed analytic details even when examples are provided (Creswell, 1998; Yanow & Schwartz-Shea, 2006), or treat constant comparative inquiry as a toolkit of techniques (Hubbard & Shagoury, 1993) in isolation from the beliefs and values that guide research as a whole. What follows is a holistic overview of the general dimensions of inquiry, and a focus more specifically on the iterative practices involved in constant comparative inquiry, followed by some examples.

RESEARCH QUESTIONS

Research interests are often percolating inside of researchers unknowingly for many years (Butler-Kisber, 2005). The difficult step after identifying an interest is to translate it into actual research questions. Qualitative inquiry questions focus on what, how, and why, using participant voices and experiences to interpret and explain (or in other words to present a small 't' theory) about a phenomenon or what is happening in a certain context. Maxwell (2006) suggests that the strengths of a qualitative study are that it focuses on situations and/or experiences of people, it is inductive or emerges from these situations or experiences, and it emphasizes the use of words instead of numbers. Furthermore, he suggests (pp.18–32) that the initial components of a study are made

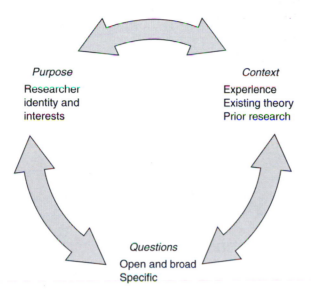

Purpose
Researcher
identity and
interests

Context
Experience
Existing theory
Prior research

Questions
Open and broad
Specific

FIGURE 3.1   INITIAL COMPONENTS OF A STUDY (BASED ON MAXWELL, 2006)

up of the purpose (researcher identity and interest), the context (experience, existing theory, and any prior research), and the research questions (broadly constructed to avoid eliminating aspects too early, and yet specific enough to help focus the work).

As indicated above, in order to be helpful, the overarching research question should be broad enough to avoid eliminating potentially important dimensions of a study, yet specific enough that it indicates what the study is about and what the context is. I often suggest to graduate students that the overarching question will ultimately be answered by what emerges in response to the subquestions plus the overall explanation that the researcher produces.

The subquestions should be created by fleshing out the dimensions of the overarching question. For example, Joanne Kingsley was for many years a classroom teacher of literacy, then a literacy consultant for a school board, and currently a language arts teacher at a university. She always has had a keen interest in literacy and lots of experience in the area. Her dissertation (Kingsley, 2007) focused on literacy learning. She was particularly interested in literacy based on social constructivist theory, so she sought out a classroom where the teacher, and others who knew her, claimed that she operated a constructivist classroom. Joanne's overarching question was: How does *literacy learning* occur in an espoused *constructivist,* grade 2/3 classroom in the greater Montreal area? (p. 5). It is broad because it does not eliminate any possible ways that literacy learning might take place (possibly ones that neither she had considered nor the literature had documented), and specific because it suggests the theoretical orientation of the classroom and the grade levels in which the study was to take place. To generate her subquestions she asked herself what are all the ways of getting at literacy learning in this classroom. She knew she had to look at what the children were doing, what the teacher was doing, and how the classroom context contributed to all of this. Her subquestions were:

- What kinds of *literacy activities* occur in this classroom?
- What role does the teacher play in the literacy learning?
- What aspects of the *context* play a part in this literacy learning, and how? (p. 5)

Joanne defined the italicized terms, that is, the terms literacy learning, constructivist, literacy activities and context, according to how she was using them for the purposes of her study. Ultimately, each subquestion was answered in different sections of her thesis by analyzing specific field texts. The overarching question was answered by integrating and interpreting what she found in response to each subquestion. In this way, her final explanation about how literacy learning was occurring in this setting was very grounded in her field text material and persuasive as a result.

LITERATURES AND INQUIRY

The delicate balance that every qualitative inquirer faces is to know what the relevant literatures are saying about the research topic, and to have a clear understanding about what she brings to the study in terms of identity and assumptions (as discussed in Chapter 2), while remaining open to what the field texts in the study reveal. Each qualitative research topic cuts across a number of fields and/or disciplines that can help focus the research questions and rationalize why a particular study is needed. An examination of the relevant literatures should go beyond a mere grocery list of articles. It requires choosing the literatures that are relevant to the study to limit its scope (Maxwell, 2006), and then analyzing critically and conceptualizing what others have said and done. At the same time it is necessary to provide some boundaries for what will be examined so that the work does not become an overwhelming project in itself. For example, in my thesis work on peer collaboration around educational tasks (Butler-Kisber, 1988), my overarching question was: *How do peers collaborate around educational tasks in a grade one and two multi-grade classroom?* More specifically my subquestions were: *How do tasks, working styles and friendships affect the collaboration? What role does the teacher play in collaboration? What contributes to effective collaboration efforts?*

To examine the literatures, I chose to look at a *decade* of literature, as well as some pivotal, earlier work, from the fields of cognitive psychology, sociolinguistics, cross-cultural and educational studies. I chose these areas because I was able to show that these literatures underscored

> the importance of peer friendships and relations and the social and cognitive benefits of peer collaboration. Not only do all learners benefit from the support derived from learning from others within the same peer culture, they also gain from the relatively equal status among peers, the exposure to many and varying viewpoints, and the negotiating involved in this process which requires understanding the perspective of others. (Butler-Kisber, 1988: 10)

I was able to categorize the studies on peer collaboration in classrooms and in play time into four main groups. They were: adult-imposed (i.e., teacher-imposed) collaboration with adult-defined tasks; adult-imposed collaboration with peer-defined tasks; spontaneous peer collaboration with adult-defined tasks; and spontaneous peer collaboration with peer-defined tasks. Unsurprisingly, the first of these was the most frequently discussed in the literatures, and the last very rare. It provided me with an initial way of thinking and talking about peer collaboration, and with a rationale for the need for further research. It should be emphasized however, that this grid did not become the lens for examining the field texts I constructed. Rather, the field texts informed the analysis and helped to push the boundaries of this initial conceptualization of peer collaboration and to discover new understandings.

CONSTRUCTING AND MANAGING FIELD TEXTS

Field texts (as explained in Chapter 1, the term 'field text' is being used instead of 'data' to underscore the fact that data are constructed, not entities in and of themselves) are what is usually generated from observations and/or interviews. As well, researchers frequently gather relevant documents, artifacts and other kinds of material that will contribute to the inquiry. What the researcher chooses to observe and record and/or emphasize in interviews is necessarily selective, even when she is trying to document everything. Field notes or observations that are recorded in the field are often cryptic because of the pace of what is transpiring. There is nothing that prevents the researcher from elaborating on these notes when transforming/transcribing them into complete sentences. The important thing is to make the transcriptions soon after the observations so that details can be remembered and included. It is helpful when recording the notes to document but separate interpretations and questions that arise from the running observations. This helps to prevent drawing premature conclusions about what is transpiring, but keeps track of important musings that may be helpful at a later time. It also helps to keep a running record of time as events unfold, by documenting the time every 10 or 15 minutes. Later, it is possible to calculate the approximate time spent on various activities, and this information can provide interesting insights.

One of the most helpful ways to document what is transpiring is to videotape (Erickson & Wilson, 1982). This preserves and permits the revisiting of the actions and communicative exchanges, both verbal and nonverbal, as well as the particular context at the time and can provide examples of rich, verbatim excerpts to include in the final product, adding to the persuasiveness of the work. The digital counter on the camera can document a more accurate estimation of time spent on various activities or events. There are trade-offs.

Transcribing videotapes is a long and arduous process (or a costly one if someone else does it), but provides an excellent 'close reading' of what is transpiring and helps the researcher to become very familiar with her field texts. It should be noted, however, that transcripts are not neutral texts that reconstruct as a carbon copy what has been recorded and/or observed. They are constructions, always partial and selective, and value laden and can represent potential power differentials that merit attention. Just the way a transcript is laid out on the page and the punctuation, pauses and silences are signified, or not, can suggest hierarchical differences (Mishler, 1986; Ochs,

1979). Researchers need to be aware of and sensitive to these dimensions and use a reflective and reflexive stance at all times.

It is often difficult to get permission to videotape, especially when children or other vulnerable groups are the participants. Furthermore, videotaping can be very intrusive, particularly if a technician is involved. Yet it is hard for the researcher to videotape and take notes simultaneously (a process I highly recommend to complement the videotaped data), and a static camera always misses some of the things that are transpiring.

One approach is to establish, from the outset, that videotaping will be a form of 'secondary field text' not transcribed in its entirety, but used as a way of revisiting and fleshing out or contextualizing the field notes (Mesher, 2006). Audiotaping can be used in similar ways to preserve and revisit what transpires. It is less imposing and intrusive, but loses some of the complexity that the visual documentation provides.

During individual or group interviews it is highly advisable at least to audiotape. It is almost impossible to ask questions and simultaneously keep notes. It is also less engaging and can be perceived as being rude for the researcher to redirect her gaze or create a pause in the conversation to make notes. And in dialogic exchanges, having verbatim text is invaluable. To generate rich field texts from conversational data, it is mandatory to transcribe interviews.

The scope of this chapter does not permit a full discussion about being in the field observing and/or conducting interviews. There are excellent sources that talk about researcher stance and reflexivity and the highly sensitive, relational dimensions inherent in these tasks. The ability to construct field texts that have both breadth and depth requires building trust and reciprocity with participants over time, being open to participant perspectives, and demonstrating a genuinely sensitive and caring attitude (Feldman, Bell, & Berger, 2003; Maykut & Morehouse, 1994; Seidman, 2006).

ANALYSIS

Researchers often refer to the research process in stages – being in the field, analyzing the material that has been amassed, and then writing up the report, article or thesis, etcetera. This, of course, is a false and linear depiction of what is an iterative and complex process. Analysis is going on from the outset – based on what the researcher brings with her to the inquiry, what she pays attention to and selects out of what she is hearing, seeing, and recording, and how the field texts are constructed. These are all part of the analytic process. Working with the field texts is another part of the analysis, as is the writing-up phase (Ely, Vinz, Downing, & Anzul, 1997). This section, however, will focus briefly on working with the field texts and then the next section will provide some detailed examples.

For ease of discussion, the working with field texts will be divided into the coarse-grained phase and the fine-grained phase. The coarse-grained phase is when the researcher really gets to know her field texts. It involves close readings and rereadings or listening and viewing, dialoguing with herself about what is being revealed, writing reflective and analytic memos and/or keeping a journal or log, and playing with some broad categories in which different portions of the field texts can be placed, at least temporarily. It includes assigning names to these categories, and working back and forth across the categories expanding and contracting them as the analysis proceeds. It may include going back to the participants to observe further and/or ask questions to help guide the process.

Fine-grained analysis is when the researcher looks even more closely. 'Chunks' of field texts are reassembled into more refined categories, and are broken down into others, and these are assigned, and reassigned names or codes. As explained below, this can be done either manually or electronically. This back-and-forth way, or accordion-like approach, expands and contracts categories and begins to reveal relationships across them. Rules of inclusion are written by the researcher that refer to what is required for a certain chunk of a field text to be placed in a particular category. These rules are based on what is contained in the chunk of each field text, not on some abstract idea in the mind of the researcher; the process is explained below in an example.

It is helpful in this process to give code names to the categories that come from the words of the participants. This can help push the analysis further and get at the insider/emic perspectives. When categories appear 'saturated' and cannot be broken down or added to any further, and most of the field text material has been accounted for, except for the outliers, the categories are reassembled into larger and more general themes based on the relational dimensions among the categories that emerge. The goal is to construct a plausible and persuasive explanation of what is transpiring from the emergent themes, recognizing again that all explanations are partial by nature, and there are always multiple ways that experiences and/or phenomena can be explained. Naturally, ongoing contact with the participants during this process is desirable and helpful.

The write–up is another analytic layer. Writing shapes the thinking and doing and gives nuances to the work. It is where the ethical dimensions of the study play themselves out as the researcher strives for transparency, inclusion of participant and researcher voices, aesthetic qualities, verisimilitude, and utility.

> Through imagination and craft, the researcher tries to penetrate the dimensions of experience below surface appearances and to represent these in compelling works that make the essence come alive … It is the ability to imagine how things are for others and how conditions might be improved, to identify the tension between the perception of reality and the vision, each needing to address and draw from the other. (Ely et al., 1997: 368)

Example 1

One of the most difficult aspects of implementing a constant comparison form of inquiry is in terms of moving from a descriptive categorization of the accessed field texts to a more conceptual and interpretive level. The following example traces the evolution of some categories in a constant comparison inquiry of peer collaboration in a multilevel grade one and two classroom that I conducted for my dissertation. I have found this example to be helpful to graduate students who are trying to understand the way to compare and contrast by unitizing the field texts and putting these units into categories and then, by an iterative process of expanding and reducing categories, ultimately produce themes that provide conceptual and interpretive understandings that are grounded in the data. Also, it is illustrative of how to write rules of inclusion (Maykut & Morehouse, 1994). These are propositional statements that the researcher creates based on the properties that are apparent in categorized units of the field texts. They provide a system for classifying the material that allows the researcher to decide whether or not a chunk of a field text fits into a certain category. Rules of inclusion can be modified to expand or exclude pieces of field texts as the analysis proceeds.

This example begins with an excerpt of field text that was typical of the kind of units that were initially put into a category called 'circle time'. It shows how the category was expanded into subcategories illustrative of different nuances/properties in the material, and how eventually the category was renamed to reflect a more grounded perspective. It describes how an outlier, or discrepant category of field text, was put aside until a more conceptual understanding emerged and a plausible explanation could be rendered.

FIELD TEXT EXCERPT: (N.B. ITALICIZED TEXT = OBSERVATIONS; BRACKETED TEXT = REFLECTIONS; M. = TEACHER)

After the children complete their calendars, they move and sit in a circle on the rug. (It is the first day back after a long weekend and the classroom is particularly quiet. Perhaps this is the result of weather coupled with the time away. Also, I'm not usually present on Day 1.) Caroline says she met Jason in the park, and quite a few eyes switch to Jason. Jason looks around to see who is noticing. (I couldn't get this on video.) She says how they played together with some friends but then had to go home because of lunch. Eric is next and tells how he went fishing with his father at a nearby lake. He didn't catch a fish. Naomi shares how she can't stand fishing because of the worms. M. looks at her watch and moves to her chair on the side of the carpet. (It is interesting to note how the children quickly change posture for the story when M. sits on the chair.) (Day 1, Tuesday, May 20: 8:35–9:00)

The initial code name for this pattern was 'circle time'. The rule for inclusion was:

Circle time: refers to an event that takes place almost every day for approximately half an hour after the children have entered the classroom, settled, and announcements have been made. The children and M. sit on the rug and share individual experiences, stories, and sometimes things of an academic nature. M. takes part as a listener and makes comments. Sometimes she intervenes to facilitate.

It should be noted that the term 'circle time' is descriptive and not conceptual, that is, it does not suggest how circle time functioned in this setting. Furthermore, it is very much linked to the literature on early childhood education. It is common practice to have children in the early grades gather together on the carpet each morning for some kind of sharing to start the day, and there have been numerous studies written about this practice. Therefore, it would be fair to say that this initial code name was an 'etic' or outsider one that had existing connotations which could influence and impose outside meaning on the field text material.

After examining, memoing about, and reflecting on the various 'chunks' that could be included according to the definition or rule of inclusion above, it became apparent that several different kinds of things were going on during these types of events and while they frequently occurred on the carpet, this was not always so. In other words, the gathering together to share served different functions at different times, and even took place in different locations. It was at this point that the pieces of text were fragmented further into subcategories and given descriptive code names. These codes were: 'personal sharing', 'topic sharing', 'product sharing', 'reading aloud', and 'scaffolding.'

The codes were given the following definitions, or rules of inclusion, that were used to decide, by comparing and contrasting the pertinent pieces of text, in which category chunks of the material should be placed.

Personal sharing: refers to the time when a large group of children gather with M. on the rug. The children share whatever they wish. Turn-taking occurs and the direction of the sharing flows with input from other children. Often there is a chaining of conversation within this flow, that is, someone initiates a topic and others follow with things that relate to the topic.

Topic sharing: involves a large group sharing and discussing thoughts and responses about a particular topic. It usually occurs on the rug. Turn-taking occurs between M. and the children. The children request turns, and M. selects, listens, and then responds.

Product sharing: involves a group of children, sometimes on the rug, sometime at their seats. There is an individual sharing of a product or something of an academic nature. M. takes part as listener, and facilitator. Everyone eventually gets a turn.

Reading aloud: occurs when M. reads a story or poetry to a group on the carpet. She sits in her chair facing the group. She puts on her glasses and commences to use a different teacher register that is a higher pitch than usual, and her speech is markedly more rapid than when she converses.

> Scaffolding: refers to the time M. picks up on something said during sharing and uses comments/input from the children to move the discussion to completion.

To visualize this process, one can think of creating folders (manually or electronically) with the code name and the rule of inclusion on the front. 'Chunks' of text from the field texts are separated and put in the folder according to the rule of inclusion. If a particular unit of text does not fit, then it is necessary to change the rule to make it fit, or to create another category and write a rule of inclusion for it.

After working with the chunks of field texts in subcategories of the larger category that was initially designated circle time, the code name 'circle time' was changed to *collaborative sharing,* which represented a more emic/insider and conceptual label. It emerged from my interaction with and memoing about the field texts and discussions with M. It did not arise from a preconceived notion from the literature. It allowed me to include chunks of field texts that had similar properties but were comprised of events occurring elsewhere in the room, not just on the carpet. It opened up possibilities about how I was understanding what transpired and made me aware of the nuances of collaboration that were occurring in this classroom that, at first glance, were not apparent to me and were not explicitly known to M.

A subcategory that no longer fit this definition was 'reading aloud'. I struggled with this and finally decided to put it aside as an 'outlier' (a category of discrepant field text material), about which I will say more below.

> Collaborative sharing: refers to the time at various points during the day that the children and M. sit on the carpet, or the children sit at their seats and M. stands, and share individual experiences, stories, and sometimes things of an academic nature. M. takes part as a listener and makes comments. Sometimes she intervenes to facilitate.

The scaffolding code name also had links to the literature (Wood, Bruner, & Ross, 1976). At first it may have prevented me from seeing beyond its etic/outsider definition. However, it did suggest to me that to understand what was going on I had to look more carefully at what M. was doing during these sharing activities. She did not direct these activities as she did in others, nor was she simply a facilitator as she was when they worked independently; there was more. Her role resembled that of a 'more capable peer'. While she did facilitate and scaffold when necessary, she mostly modeled, very carefully but unconsciously, the expected behavior for these types of events. The process of pushing analysis to a more conceptual level helped to reveal links across the field texts, to understand how things were functioning in this classroom, and to explain how and why these young 6- and 7-year-olds were such capable collaborators.

Teacher as more capable peer: occurs in collaborative sharing events and refers to when M. models collaboration for the children, not in a directive way that implies they should imitate her, but instead she becomes one of the collaborators, engaging in discussions and activities with them and helping them to go beyond what they are able to do in their peer collaboration activities.

For a long time it was impossible to find a place for the field text material categorized as 'reading aloud'. Although reading aloud resembled, in terms of time and space, some of the collaborative sharing events that took place on the carpet, the properties were different as described above in the rule of inclusion. Yet these reading aloud events did not look like other events in the classroom either. At one point I went to M. and worked with her to see if together we could shed some light on this outlier category. We decided it was most similar to 'teacher as more capable peer', but we were not totally satisfied. I would suggest, as others have, that the iterative nature of the interpretive analysis cannot be forced (Maykut & Morehouse, 1994). The process required more time and some deliberate probing on my part. By re-examining all the categories that had emerged and asking what function reading aloud events played in relation to this 'web of meaning' (Munhall & Oiler, 1986), a plausible explanation emerged. It is well documented that reading stories or poetry to young children is beneficial for literacy learning. However, this did not explain how these events that occurred early in the morning on the carpet, but did not fit in the category of collaborative sharing, were functioning in this particular classroom. In one of those 'eureka moments' that qualitative researchers talk about, it came to me. In addition to contributing to literacy learning, these events were acting as a transition from life outside the classroom to the work of schooling as explained in the excerpt below.

During these events M. always moved from her sitting position on the carpet to a chair that she kept in the area. Without instructions, the entire group of children re-oriented their positions to face her and became the audience for a portion of literature read by her. Sometimes it was a short story, at other times it was a continuation of a longer novel … or a poem. Within these events M. clarified things by asking questions or by offering an explanation. In a sense she got her turn at topic sharing when she read to them. At the same time she prepared them for the transition from the early morning personal sharing time in which they brought their experiences from home and elsewhere into the classroom … As she moved into her chair, she signaled this transition into the other activities of the school day. (Butler–Kisber, 1988: 189)

During personal sharing events the children talked about their experiences at home and at play. Outside life was valued by M. and brought into the classroom. The 'reading aloud' sessions implicitly indicated to the children that it was time to put these outside experiences aside and to move into the schooling work of the classroom.

In summary, this example shows how, in constant comparison inquiry, a category from a field text at first can be labeled in a way that is not conducive for understanding the emic/insider perspective of the context under study. As explained earlier, I unconsciously drew on my knowledge of the literature to create a code name, 'circle time,' that imposed outside meanings and understanding on the field texts, limiting my way of looking at what was happening. It was only through an iterative process of expanding and collapsing categories, and trying to explain how these different categories of events functioned, that a more conceptual understanding emerged as reflected in the evolving code names and the accompanying rules of inclusion. This, in turn, allowed me to make connections and see relationships across categories in the field texts, to account for discrepant categories, and create a plausible explanation about what was occurring in this classroom.

Example 2

Linda Furlini, a Ph.D. graduate from the Department of Integrated Studies at McGill University, recently completed a qualitative study of caregivers of persons with chronic dementia (2005) for her dissertation. After conducting interviews with 12 participants and creating a synopsis for each, she reduced her sample to a purposive one of five women that included a wide variation in the ages, experiences, and careers/roles of these participants. She used an adapted version of Seidman's (2006) approach to interviewing that necessitates meeting with participants for two to three interviews over time to build trust and allow for reflection in between.

After transcribing the interviews, she used both categorizing and connecting analytic approaches (Maxwell & Miller, 2008). The constant comparison approach was used to categorize her data across the interviews. A narrative (connecting) approach was used to create narratives for each participant to retain the contextual dimensions that are stripped away in categorizing and to provide portraits of each individual experience. Narrative inquiry produced interesting insights. It will be taken up in Chapter 5 and is not discussed further here.

Initially Linda categorized her field texts into four, broad, descriptive categories: care and medical activities, financial activities, legally related activities, and personal and family activities. None of these were particularly surprising given the limitations that result from chronic dementia, but these categories gave her a way of dealing initially with large amounts of data (Bogdan & Biklen, 1992). She has indicated that 'These categories gave me a better grasp of the types, variations, and purposes of the individual women's caregiving activities' (Furlini, 2005: 81).

From this point on she worked more conceptually, interrogating her field texts until three major themes emerged – multitasking, state of heightened alert, and interpreting the disease – that, while enacted differently in each woman's experience,

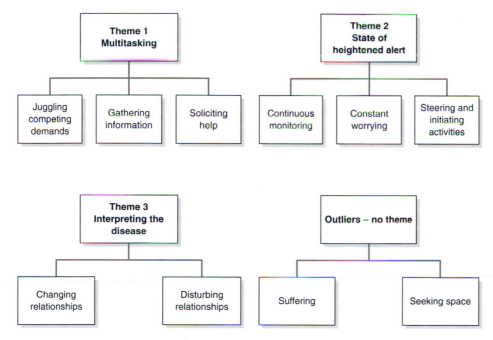

FIGURE 3.2   MULTITASKING, STATE OF HEIGHTENED ALERT, AND INTERPRETING THE DISEASE (FURLINI, 2007)

allowed Linda to talk about what was common across all experiences. Figure 3.2 illustrates the themes and their components (Furlini, 2005).

The connections between the subcategories and the three major themes made sense, but Linda was still confronted with two other subcategories, 'suffering' and 'seeking space' that did not fit anywhere, nor could they be subsumed into a larger category. For some time they remained as outliers. Then she began to discern some additional connections and was able to show how the three major demands on each of these women (that is, multitasking, being in a constant state of alert and the ongoing process of interpreting the evolution of the disease) were directly related to categories she had coded as 'suffering' and 'seeking space'. Suffering and seeking space were the outcomes of these demands. The immense suffering they experienced was largely silent, and the need for personal space produced a sense of guilt which remained repressed for the most part.

The use of the constant comparison approach in her inquiry provided Linda with a way of talking about commonalities across the participants' experiences and has contributed to her ability to advocate for caregivers and get the message out to broad audiences in the helping professions. The narratives she produced as a result of her connecting approach to analysis, not elaborated upon here, complemented and added a richness to the work, preserved the voices of the individual women, and have provided stories that resonate (Conle, 1996; Lofland & Lofland, 1995) with others, alleviating some pain and guilt among caregivers in similar situations.

Example 3

It may be useful at this point to provide one more example of how conceptual categories are developed by referring to an example from Strauss and Corbin (1990: 63–65). The example they give is that of a researcher observing a woman in a red dress who is working in a restaurant. Her activities include *watching* what is going on in the kitchen, *passing on information* to others, *monitoring* everything that is going on around her to ensure quality of service, *providing assistance* to wait people, *gathering information*, and *conferring* with the maître d'hôtel. These labels or codes are descriptive because they summarize what she does.

To move to a more conceptual understanding about her activities, it is necessary to ask why she is doing what she is doing, what function do these activities serve. The authors suggest that when looking across all the categories, it appears that they could be regrouped because they all help in *assessing* and *maintaining the flow of work* by watching, passing information, monitoring, offering assistance, gathering information, and conferring. They indicate that in this instance the woman in red is a 'food orchestrator'. I would add this broader and more conceptual category that includes the subcategories mentioned above could be labeled 'orchestrating'. A rule of inclusion might be: orchestrating (in this context) refers to watching, passing information, monitoring, offering assistance, gathering information and conferring to assess and maintain the flow of work. What is helpful for pushing thinking to a more conceptual level is to ask what the function is of a certain activity or interaction is, or to think metaphorically and ask what it reminds one of, or what else it 'looks like'.

THE USE OF VISUAL MAPPING FOR CONCEPTUALIZING FIELD TEXT MATERIAL

It was described above how Strauss and Corbin have suggested it is helpful to think metaphorically about patterns that are emerging in field texts to arrive at a more conceptual understanding about what is occurring. This process can suddenly illuminate connections that have remained elusive. Another approach that can be taken is to move from the linear understandings that are contained in written field texts to visual/spatial representations of the work. This, too, has the effect of seeing the patterns in new ways and discovering connections that were not obvious before. For the purposes of this chapter, two particular analytic tools – concept mapping and cartographic mapping – will be described with examples. Both of these also have representational possibilities for communicating the results of a study included in the vast array of display possibilities that are described in great detail by Miles and Huberman (1994).

Concept mapping

A concept map is a visual way of expressing ideas. 'Concept maps are created using hand-drawn sketches or virtual tools in a non-linear and visual format by drawing on paper or on the screen to show the thinking as it emerges, or to represent ideas in their embryonic stages' (Butler-Kisber & Poldma, 2009: 8). Concept maps were first used by psychologists at Cornell University in the 1970s. They were used as a tool for understanding and illustrating the evolving conceptions that children had about science, as a 'mind map' to get at their thinking and understanding. Since then they have been used across many academic disciplines and in the business sector to help groups of people to think together more effectively without losing their individuality, and to retain the complexity of the ideas that the group produces (Mertens, 2009: 266). When done as a group exercise the process is loosely structured around six steps: preparation, generation, structuring, representation, interpretation, utilization (Mertens, 2009: 267). The first step is the preparation done by the facilitator in conjunction with the funder or initiator of the work to establish the group composition. Then the facilitator works with the participants to delineate the focus for the work and the timeline for the process which can be scheduled quickly or more slowly over time. Second, the group produces, through brainstorming or other means, an array of statements that refer to the focus of the work. Third, the participants sort similar statements, either by hand or on the computer, into categories and name each of these with a short descriptor. These can be further sorted within categories in the order of importance. Fourth, the categories are mapped visually and links are made among the categories where appropriate. Fifth, the facilitator works with the group and they decide how to refine the categories and labels to represent the new understandings and interpretations emerging from this process. Finally, the maps are used to return to the original focus to address what has been conceptualized and how this can be communicated. While individual inquirers do not necessarily adhere to this precise series of steps, it does provide a useful way of thinking about concept mapping, in particular how groups of researchers might work together using collaborative mapping to help conceptualize their thinking.

> A concept map … is a picture of the territory you want to study, not the study itself. It is a visual display of your current working theory – a picture of what you think is going on with the phenomenon you're studying … a tool for … generating theory, and seeing implications … (Maxwell, 1996: 37). Concept maps are a way of 'thinking on paper' (Howard & Barton, 1986, cited in Maxwell, 1996: 37); they can show you unexpected connections or identify holes or contradictions …, and help you to figure out ways to resolve the latter (Maxwell, 1996: 37).

During the analysis of field texts, it is useful to use concept maps at a point when most of the material has been categorized and patterns have begun to appear. As described earlier in this chapter, this is at the time when the categories become more stable or 'saturated' and it becomes possible to create rules of inclusion for them. Because of the evolving nature of concept maps, Maxwell (1996) has suggested that using a blackboard is helpful because of the ease with which things can be changed. I have found that Post-it notes work very well. Each category is written on a Post-it and stuck on a large sheet of paper. Then the Post-its can be moved easily and reworked as the links and relationships become apparent and/or change. Maxwell

(1996) and others caution that when concept maps appear very 'elegant', more than likely they will not be too useful because this kind of map tends to emphasize the aesthetic of form rather than focusing on the content. Thinking and conceptualizing are messy and complex and the concept mapping process reflects this. Concept maps become refined after successive attempts over time (Butler-Kisber & Poldma, 2009).

Susan Kerwin-Boudreau, in her Ph.D. thesis (2008), examined the evolving perspectives on teaching and learning among a purposeful sample of six participants who were teaching at the college level and who had opted to enroll in a professional development program on the nature of teaching and learning. During this study, she included concept maps in yet another way. She used constant comparative inquiry to analyze the field texts she created from a series of ongoing interviews with her participants. However, she also obtained permission to access the journals they were keeping as part of the program and supplemented this process with concept mapping as a way of getting at the underlying reflective thinking in which her participants were involved. These maps also served to counteract some of the 'self-confirming inaccuracies' that can be an inherent part of reflective journals (Kerwin-Boudreau, 2008: 59). She had her participants construct concept maps at the beginning and the end of the first course they took in their program. This course focused on the issues and challenges of college teaching. By comparing the two concept maps and documenting the comments explaining the maps, she was able to see early on in this program that the participants' perspectives on teaching and learning were already changing. For example, she shared how Deana's concept maps and commentary showed a shift in her thinking about what it means to be an effective teacher. In Deana's first map (Figure 3.3), it can be seen that her focus was on the importance of having excellent knowledge of the subject matter, but paid little attention to how students learn. Only a few months later, in her second concept map, Deana's attention was much more focused on the details of how students can be helped in their learning (pp. 91–92). Clearly Deana was changing her perspectives on teaching and learning from a rather traditional, transmission model of teaching to a more learner-oriented one that pays attention to the necessary perspectives and strategies needed to facilitate learning among students. By using concept maps in this way, Susan was able to get new information about how her participants' perspectives were evolving. Furthermore, she was able to use this information to confirm and/or stretch her own thinking about some of the patterns that were emerging in her interview material.

Cartographic mapping

Cartography originating from the Greek words *chartis*, which means map, and *graphein*, which means to write, is the process of geographical map-making. It is built on the idea that certain phenomena can be understood and communicated most effectively when they are portrayed spatially. Cartography has been used around the world for many centuries and in interesting ways that have combined various dimensions of both science and art. Cartography uses maps in two ways. There are those that contain a variety of features designed for a general audience, and those that have specific themes that are intended for specific audiences. A whole field in the

Concept map 1 (Deana)

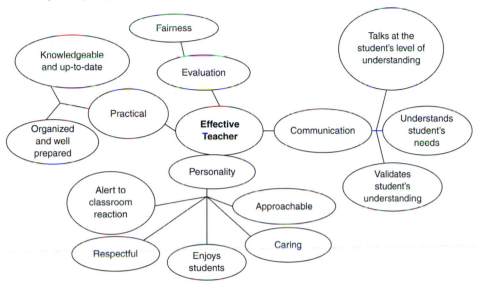

Concept map 2 (Deana)

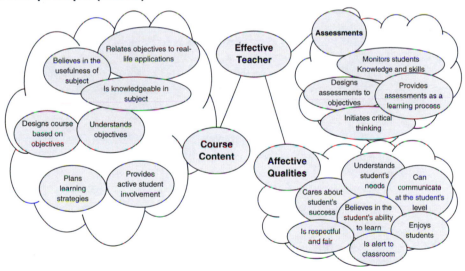

FIGURE 3.3   DEANA'S CONCEPT MAPS (KERWIN-BOUDREAU, 2008)

discipline of geography has developed from cartography in what is called a geographical information system (GIS) that captures, stores, analyzes, manages, and presents field text information that is linked to location, such as demographic information. Beyond the scope of this discussion, GIS technology has and continues to develop sophisticated software for mapping and presenting spatially material that represents real-world objects with digital data.

Cartographic mapping in qualitative inquiry is the process of translating thematic field text material onto some form of map or schematic in order to get a more holistic and conceptual understanding of it. It can help to push the analysis further and/or can be used effectively to communicate the ultimate findings to a wider audience. It requires that the researcher selects the appropriate kinds of categories of material that lend themselves to a spatial mapping process, reduces the complexity of what is to be mapped, and then organizes the material in an optimal way for understanding and/or communicating the work.

An example of cartographic mapping was included in a study of a campus safety audit conducted over a decade ago at McGill University (Butler-Kisber, 1995). Emanating from the work of the McGill Advisory Committee on Women Students' Issues, the purpose of the study was to involve women students, academic and support staff in examining the external and internal safety of 48 campus buildings. Participators in the audit took part in a preparatory workshop that familiarized them with a qualitative safety audit tool that had been developed by the Metro Action Committee on Public Violence against Women and Children (METRAC) used previously and successfully in Toronto. Then early in the evening on a designated date in March, 41 teams of four that each included two women students and two staff members, one of which came from the building(s) being studied by the particular team, went out and toured the buildings and surroundings. Then they collaboratively completed and returned the audit surveys, all within a three-hour period. The material was analyzed thematically and when distilled it revealed, not surprisingly, very specific themes about the need for signage, more lighting, security patrols, emergency phones, increased maintenance, and improved sightlines.

A recurring theme across the reports was the discomfort felt in and around specific dark and isolated areas on the campus. The importance of this theme was apparent both in the number of times it was mentioned and by the elaborated descriptions of these areas included in the audit surveys. The research team decided it might be useful to plot these areas on a map of the McGill campus to see what a holistic overview of this material would look like. Accordingly, the areas of perceived discomfort were shaded in on the map (Figure 3.4). What immediately and quite startlingly became apparent by this cartographic mapping exercise was that there were clearly ways of traversing the campus that were much brighter and had better sightlines than others. These ways ostensibly provided more comfort or a feeling of 'psychological safety', particularly for women and/or physically challenged members of the McGill community. The next step, using the same map of the campus, was to reciprocally chart a 'night route' that illustrated the more comfortable and recommended routes for traversing the campus after dark (Figure 3.5). A map of the night route was routinely given out in subsequent orientation sessions, and posted and distributed all over the campus. These two maps, the one of the dark and isolated areas and the one suggesting the recommended night routes, were used successfully to persuade the University to put additional resources into lighting and emergency telephones and to concentrate these along the night routes. They highlight the potential use and persuasive impact that this type of spatial mapping provides in qualitative inquiry.

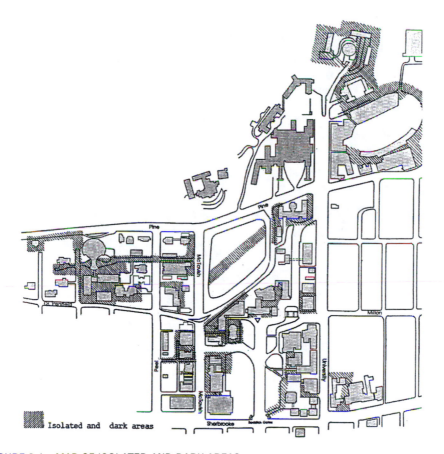

FIGURE 3.4   MAP OF ISOLATED AND DARK AREAS

COMPUTER SOFTWARE IN THEMATIC INQUIRY

It would be remiss not to discuss, albeit briefly, the use of computer software for thematic inquiry. Typically it is used to assist thematic analysis, and there are differing opinions about the merits of its use.

> The growing literature on computer assisted qualitative data analysis software (CAQDAS) expresses both hopes and fears. The hopes are that CAQDAS will: help automate and thus speed up and liven up the coding process; provide a more complex way of looking at the relationships in the data; provide a formal structure for writing and storing memos to develop the analysis; and aid more conceptual and theoretical thinking about the data … The worries are: that it will distance people from their data; that it will lead to qualitative data being analyzed quantitatively; that it will lead to increasing homogeneity in methods of data analysis; and that it might be a monster and hi-jack the analysis. (Barry, 1998: 2.1)

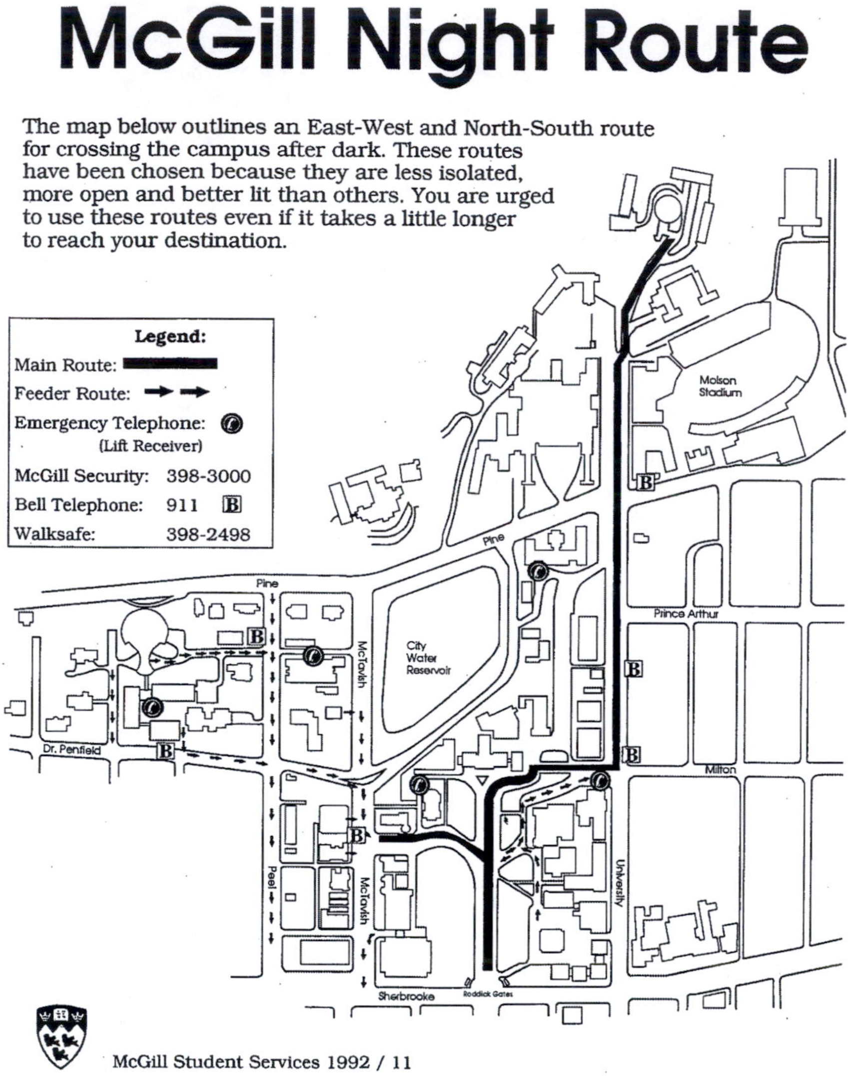
McGill Night Route
The map below outlines an East-West and North-South route for crossing the campus after dark. These routes have been chosen because they are less isolated, more open and better lit than others. You are urged to use these routes even if it takes a little longer to reach your destination.
Legend:
Main Route:
Feeder Route:
Emergency Telephone: (Lift Receiver)
McGill Security: 398-3000
Bell Telephone: 911
Walksafe: 398-2498
Molson Stadium
Pine
Prince Arthur
City Water Reservoir
McTavish
Dr. Penfield
Milton
Peel
University
Sherbrooke
Roddick Gates
McGill Student Services 1992 / 11

FIGURE 3.5 MAP OF NIGHT ROUTE

The scope of this section does not permit an in-depth elaboration of the points made above by Barry (1998). These are, however, important things to keep in mind when deciding to use or not to employ software in the analysis. As well, there is the question of which software to choose from an array of programs that include, among others, Ethnograph, Nudist, Nvivo, and Atlas.ti. It is most important to remember that software cannot perform the analysis. It is only a tool to assist the analytic process. It is the researcher that drives what happens, and to do this in a rigorous way she must be very deeply immersed in and very familiar with the field text material at all times. It is also important to avoid being seduced by some of the claims made about software packages. There is a danger that while programs may be offering the ability to categorize data, this is a capability that cannot be programmed. Categorizing produced by software would in fact be a quantitative variable analysis, and not the inductive process of categorizing that takes place in qualitative inquiry, and requires a 'human hand'. What software packages do offer are some very efficient and effective ways of storing, managing, manipulating and displaying field texts during the analytic process. It should be noted that even these tasks are selective and interpretive and have an effect on the research. Researchers need to consider and account for this (Weaver & Atkinson, 1994).

Atlas.ti has been most touted as a leader in the field of qualitative software along with Nudist (Weitzman & Miles, 1995). The brief discussion here will focus on Atlas.ti, not a comparison of the two. It is hoped this information will provide some parameters for making a decision about whether or not to use software, and some things to think about when deciding on what software package to choose.

Atlas.ti, which stands for *archive fuer technik lenenswelt und alltagssprache* and means 'technology, the life world and everyday language' ('ti' stands for text interpretation), was first produced in the late 1980s at the Technology University of Berlin and was made into a commercial product by Thomas Muhr in 1993 (Muhr, 2004). It has gone through a number of iterations, the most recent of which is Atlas.ti 6.0 which came out in February 2009.

> Atlas.ti's strengths are related to its immediacy, its visual and spatial qualities, its creativity and its inter-linkage. … The main strategic modes of operation can be termed 'VISE': Visualization, Integration, Serendipity and Exploration. Having all data and analysis on screen at once and being able to visually map out relationships between different parts of the data and theoretical ideas, and to form links between them and jump back and forth, all seem to encourage that creative process of sparking ideas and pattern recognition. (Barry, 1998: 8.2)

Atlas.ti is user-friendly, particularly in its most recent iterations. For researchers moving from a 'cut and paste' approach in thematic analysis, it is an easy transition because of the visual nature of the program, its ability to keep a wide range of activities on the screen simultaneously, and its 'drag and drop' capability (Hwang, 2008). Atlas.ti allows the researcher to import any size file of a field text, that can consist of written text, images, and audio or videotaped material, into what is called a hermeneutic unit (HU) that can be analyzed while always maintaining a file of the material in its original form. It is then possible to segment the material, code the material, write memos, and produce 'network views' or concept maps and conceptual statements/comments (rules of inclusion) about the relationships in the material. These 'conceptual network displays' can be manipulated and can include text segments and memos (Barry, 1998: 8.3). Hierarchical 'treeviews' keep track of the 'objects' created in the HU. By using what is called a 'code manager' the researcher can easily, with a double-click on a particular code, return to the primary document and see the segment of field text associated with this code. As well, the researcher can see the number of segments/quotations associated with a particular code.

Atlas.ti has been criticized for the uncertainty it creates because of its loose structure (Barry, 1998: 8.4). However, for those researchers who endorse a truly inductive and grounded approach to thematic inquiry described earlier in this chapter, this weakness conversely might be considered its strength.

EVALUATION AND QUALITY ISSUES IN CONSTANT COMPARATIVE INQUIRY

To reiterate, trustworthiness/credibility, the qualitative term for validity as mentioned in Chapter 2, is the cornerstone of all qualitative inquiry. Trustworthiness is a goal rather than a product. It is not something that can be proven or taken for granted. It has to be assessed in relationship to the goals and circumstances of the research (Maxwell, 1996). Transparency, persuasiveness and plausibility are what create trustworthiness. Factors that work positively for credibility are: prolonged engagement in the field or interviews that take place over time; persistent inquiry that produces rich field texts; triangulation or the convergence of field texts from different sources; the search for and explanation of negative cases or outliers; referential adequacy or interpretation that is grounded in the field texts; the inclusion of insider/emic perspectives; and participant checks and debriefings. Trustworthiness issues arise from: incompleteness of the field texts; the imposition of the researcher's framework on the interpretation; the ignoring of discrepant portions of field texts; the absence of reflexivity and accounting for researcher bias and influence; and the inability to posit other possible interpretations and then argue for the ones that have emerged in the inquiry.

While generalizability is not a goal of any type of qualitative inquiry, 'particularizability' is (Donmoyer, 1990). Then the question is whether the study shows rather than tells in compelling and helpful detail the particulars, that subsequently will be useful for thinking about similar situations or contexts.

Charmaz (2005: 528–529) suggests there are five major criteria for judging constant comparative inquiry: credibility or trustworthiness, originality, resonance, usefulness, and the nature of the writing. *Trustworthiness* includes whether the researcher has developed an intimate familiarity with the topic or context; whether there is sufficient field text material to merit the claims of the work; whether it is apparent that the researcher has made systematic comparisons between and across categories; whether the categories include field text material that has been constructed over a wide range of observations or over several interviews; whether there is clear and logical evidence that links field texts with interpretations; and whether there is sufficient evidence to convince the reader of the research claims.

Originality addresses whether the categories are grounded and insightful; whether the analysis provides a conceptual interpretation; whether the researcher includes the 'social and theoretical significance' of the inquiry and shows how the work makes a contribution.

Resonance refers to whether the richness and completeness of the research is portrayed; whether everyday or implicit understandings have been illuminated;

whether micro understandings have been linked to wider and more macro ones; and whether the interpretations make sense and contribute to participant understandings.

Usefulness includes whether the participants can make use of the work in their own lives; whether the analysis makes apparent the links to potential action and social change, and makes a contribution that initiates further research in other areas and generally contributes to a more just society.

Building on Richardson's (2000) work that suggests that *writing* itself is a form of inquiry and thus an important part of the constant comparison inquiry process, Charmaz echoes Richardson's appeal for personal and embodied texts that resonate with the real world and are aesthetic, reflexive, compelling, and for these reasons create an impact (p. 937).

CONCLUDING REMARKS

Constant comparison inquiry is a thematic form of qualitative work that uses categorizing, or the comparing and contrasting of units and categories of field texts, to produce conceptual understandings of experiences and/or phenomena that are ultimately constructed into large themes. These themes provide an explanation of the context under study that is grounded carefully in the field text materials. The categorizing removes portions of field texts from their exact contexts and so has a decontextualizing effect, but on the plus side allows researchers to make comparisons across individual experiences, events, and activities that can be helpful in inspiring social action and change.

REFERENCES

Anfara, V. A., Brown, K. M., & Mangione, T. L. (2002). Qualitative analysis on stage: Making the research process more public. *Educational Researcher, 31*(7), 28–38.

Barry, C. (1998). Choosing qualitative data analysis software: Atlas.ti and Nudist compared. *Sociological Research Online, 3*(3). Retrieved March 12, 2009, from www.socresonline.org.uk/3/3/4.html.

Bogdan, R., & Biklen, S. (1992). *Qualitative research for education: An introduction to theory and methods* (2nd ed). Boston: Allyn & Bacon.

Bolster, A. J. (1982). Toward a more effective model of research on teaching. *Harvard Educational Review, 53*(3), 294–308.

Butler-Kisber, L. (1988). *Peer collaboration around educational tasks: A classroom ethnography.* Unpublished doctoral dissertation, Harvard University, Cambridge, MA.

Butler-Kisber, L. (1995). Psychological safety of women on campus. A collaborative approach. *WILLA Journal, 4,* 5–8.

Butler-Kisber, L. (2005). Inquiry through poetry: The genesis of self-study. In C. Mitchell, S. Weber, & K. O'Reilly-Scanlon (Eds.), *Just who do we think we are? Methodologies for autobiography and self-study in teaching* (pp. 95–110). New York: RoutledgeFalmer.

Butler-Kisber, L., & Poldma, T. (2009). The power of visual approaches in qualitative inquiry: The use of collage making and concept mapping in experiential research. Proceedings of the *EKSIG Conference: Experiential knowledge, method and methodology*. London (June).

Charmaz, K. (2005). Grounded theory in the 21st century: Applications for advancing social justice studies. In N. K. Denzin & Y. S. Lincoln (Eds.), *The Sage handbook of qualitative research* (3rd ed.), (pp. 507–535). Thousand Oaks, CA: Sage.

Coffey, A., Holbrook, B., & Atkinson, P. (1996). Qualitative data analysis: Technologies and representations. *Sociological Research Online, 1*(1). Retrieved August 31, 2008, from www.socreonline.org.uk/1/1/4.htm.

Conle, C. (1996). Resonance in preservice teacher inquiry. *American Journal of Educational Research, 33*(2), 297–325.

Creswell, J. W. (1998). *Qualitative inquiry and research design: Choosing among five traditions*. Thousand Oaks, CA: Sage.

Donmoyer, R. (1990). Generalizability and the single case study. In E. W. Eisner & A. Peshkin (Eds.), *Qualitative inquiry in education* (pp. 175–200). New York: Teachers College Press.

Ely, M., Vinz, R., Downing, M., & Anzul, M. (1997). *On writing qualitative research: Living by words*. London: Falmer.

Erickson, F., & Wilson, J. (1982). *Sights and sounds of life in schools: A resource guide to film and videotape for research and education*. East housing, MI: Institute for Research on Teaching of College Education.

Feldman, M. S., Bell, J., & Berger, M. T. (2003). *Gaining access: A practical and theoretical guide for qualitative researchers*. Walnut Creek, CA: AltaMira.

Furlini, L. (2005). *Living with chronic dementia from the caregiver perspective: A case for educational support*. Unpublished doctoral dissertation, McGill University, Montreal, QC.

Furlini, L. (2007). *Living with chronic dementia: Complementary analytic approaches*. Paper presented at the School of Physical and Occupational Therapy Research Seminar Series, McGill University, QC (November).

Glaser, B., & Strauss, A. (1967). *The discovery of grounded theory*. Chicago: Aldine.

Hubbard, R. S., & Shagoury, R. (1993). *The art of classroom inquiry: A handbook for teacher-researchers*. Portsmouth, NH: Heinemann.

Howard, V. A., & Barton, J. H. (1986). *Thinking on paper*. New York: Morrow.

Hwang, S. (2008). Utilizing qualitative data analysis software: A review of Atlas.ti. *Social Science Computer Review, 26*(4), 518–527.

Kerwin-Boudreau, S. (2008). *The evolving practitioner: A qualitative inquiry into reflections on teacher perspectives in a professional development program in higher education*. Unpublished doctoral dissertation, McGill University, Montreal, QC.

Kingsley, J. (2007). *Literacy instruction in a constructivist classroom: A qualitative inquiry*. Unpublished doctoral dissertation, McGill University, Montreal, QC.

Lofland, J., & Lofland, L. H. (1995). *Analyzing social settings: A guide to qualitative observation and analysis* (3rd ed.). New York: Wadsworth.

Maxwell, J. A. (1996). *Qualitative research design: An interactive approach*. Thousand Oaks, CA: Sage.

Maxwell, J. A. (2006). *Qualitative research design: An interactive approach* (2nd ed.). Thousand Oaks, CA: Sage.

Maxwell, J. A., & Miller, B. (2008). Categorizing and connecting strategies in qualitative data analysis. In P. Leavy & S. Hesse-Biber (Eds.), *Handbook of emergent methods* (pp. 461–477). New York: Guilford.

Maykut, P. & Morehouse, R. (1994). *Beginning qualitative research: A philosophic and practical guide.* New York: RoutledgeFalmer.

Mertens, D. M. (2009). *Transformative research and evaluation.* New York: Guilford.

Mesher, P. (2006). *Documentation in an elementary classroom: A teacher-researcher study.* Unpublished doctoral dissertation, McGill University, Montreal, QC.

Miles, M. B., & Huberman, A. M. (1994). *Qualitative data analysis* (2nd ed.). Thousand Oaks, CA: Sage.

Mishler, E. G. (1986). *Research interviewing: Context and narrative.* Cambridge, MA: Harvard University Press.

Muhr, T. (2004). Atlas.ti 5.0 [Version 5:]. Berlin, Germany: Atlas.ti Scientific Software Development GmbH. Retrieved March 2009, from www.altasti.com.

Munhall, P. L., & Oiler, C. J. (1986). *Nursing research: A qualitative perspective.* East Norwalk, CT: Appleton-Century-Crofts.

Ochs, E. (1979). Transcription as theory. In E. Ochs & B. Schieffelin (Eds.), *Developmental Pragmatics.* New York: Academic Press.

Richardson, L. (2000). Writing: A method of inquiry. In N. K. Denzin & Y. S. Lincoln (Eds.), *Handbook of qualitative research* (2nd ed.), (pp. 923–948). Thousand Oaks, CA: Sage.

Seale, C. (1999). *The quality of qualitative research.* London: Sage.

Seidman, I. (2006). *Interviewing as qualitative research: A guide for researchers in education and the social sciences* (3rd ed.). New York: Teachers College Press.

Strauss, A., & Corbin, J. (1990). *Basics of qualitative research: Grounded theory procedures and techniques.* Newbury Park, CA: Sage.

Weaver, A., & Atkinson, P. (1994). *Microcomputing and qualitative data analysis.* Avebury: Aldershot.

Weitzman, E., & Miles, M. (1995). *Computer programs for qualitative data analysis: An expanded sourcebook* (2nd ed.). Thousand Oaks, CA: Sage.

Wood, D., Bruner, J. S., & Ross, G. (1976). The role of tutoring in problem-solving. *Journal of Child Psychiatry, 17,* 89–100.

Yanow, D., & Schwartz-Shea, P. (Eds.), (2006). *Interpretation and method: Empirical research methods and the interpretive turn.* Armonk, NY: M. E. Sharpe.

4

Phenomenological Inquiry

Phenomenology 'focuses attention on the deeply embedded frameworks of tacitly known, taken-for-granted assumptions through which humans make sense of their lives' (Yanow, 2006: 15). It is predicated on the work of Edward Husserl (1970), a transcendental phenomenologist, who theorized about how knowledge comes into being, and Martin Buber (1958), an existentialist, who believed that people cannot understand others the way they understand objects, but rather, human understanding requires a relationship of openness, participation and empathy. The use of phenomenology in research extends as far back as the 1950s, and it became increasingly popular in the late 1970s and 1980s (Giorgi, 1970; Van Manen, 1997) because it embraces within its perspective the ethical concerns that were emerging at the time in qualitative research. It requires that researchers state their assumptions and biases up front, and 'bracket' these, as they strive to understand the essence of the lived experiences of others. This chapter traces this evolution in more detail and then outlines the typical kinds of questions that researchers ask when interviewing participants about their lived experience(s). While phenomenologists are reluctant to outline a guide for inquiry for fear of making what is a nonlinear and imaginative process prescriptive (Sanders, 2003), this chapter provides some guidance for implementing phenomenological inquiry and describes a series of possible analytic steps. These include: extraction of significant statements; formulation of meanings; aggregating of formulated meanings into clusters of themes; validation of clusters with original descriptions; preparations of an exhaustive description of the phenomenon; final validation with participants. Some examples are provided both from the literature and from an exercise done by a graduate student. It suggests when a phenomenological approach can best be used and the challenges that researchers face.

HISTORY OF PHENOMENOLOGICAL INQUIRY

Phenomenologists believe that meaning-making and understanding takes place in the everyday world of the individual. Reality consists of objects and events as they are perceived in human consciousness, not independent of it. It is constituted by 'an intentional interpretation of our sense perceptions ... against a backdrop of preexisting conceptual categories derived from life experience in interaction with others' (Yanow, 2006: 12). These conceptual categories are shaped by 'consciousness, language, our cognitive and non-cognitive sensibilities and by our pre-understandings and presuppositions' (Adams & Van Manen, 2008: 614).

Phenomenology made its debut at the turn of the 20th century in the writings of philosopher Edward Husserl in what is known as *transcendental phenomenology*, or 'how knowledge comes into being in consciousness and clarifies assumptions upon which all understandings are grounded' (Adam & van Manen, 2008: 615). The emphasis is not just on what is known, but how it is known. *Existential phenomenology*, associated with Buber (1958), refocused inquiry from consciousness onto lived experience, about being in the world. *Psychological phenomenology* draws from both transcendental and existential phenomenology and is associated with the work of Giorgi (1970) in conjunction with the Dusquesne school, and members of the Utrecht school in Holland who endorsed a focus on lived experience and in so doing, the need to incorporate 'ethically and experientially sensitive practices' (Adams & van Manen, 2008: 615) into their research. Psychological phenomenology focuses more on describing and understanding the experiences of participants rather than the interpretations of the researcher (Creswell, 2007: 59). To do this, researchers use what is known as 'bracketing' or 'epoche' to set aside their preconceptions and assumptions and approach their studies with new, or fresh, eyes in order to grasp the uniqueness of the particular phenomenon. *Hermeneutical phenomenology* emanates from the work of Hans-Gorg Gadamer and focuses on the study of lived experience, and on interpreting the 'texts' of life (Van Manen, 1990: 4). The difference is the move beyond description to interpretation where the researcher actively takes a role in explaining participant meanings.

Creswell (2007) suggests, based on Stewart and Mickunas (1990), that regardless of the orientation there are four basic philosophical perspectives in phenomenology:

- The return of philosophy to the search for wisdom instead of a focus on science.
- The need to suspend all judgments about what is real.
- The understanding of intentionality, that reality is related to one's consciousness of it.
- The recognition that reality is perceived within the meaning of individual experiences. (pp. 58–59)

These perspectives underscore the work in phenomenological inquiry, which is a powerful way for 'understanding subjective experience, gaining insights into people's motivations and actions, and cutting through the clutter of taken-for-granted assumptions and conventional wisdom' (Lester, 1999: 1).

THE LANDSCAPE OF PHENOMENOLOGICAL INQUIRY

The basic tenets of phenomenology described above had an impact, for example, on the social phenomenology of Shutz (1962), the social constructivism of Berger and Luckmann (1966), Blumer's (1969) symbolic interactionism, and much of the work in ethnomethodology (Holstein & Gubrium, 2005: 483), as well as in ethnography, interpretive sociology, humanistic psychology, existential psychology, and education studies (Adams & van Manen, 2008: 615). The professional disciplines were attracted to phenomenological studies because of the focus on process, and because they provided an alternative to 'managerial, instrumental, and technological ways of understanding knowledge' and included more 'ethically and experientially sensitive epistemologies and ontologies of practice' (p. 615). In particular, phenomenological inquiry has had a longstanding history in nursing since the early 1980s, ostensibly to counteract the positivistic research orientation that dominated nursing research (Munhall & Oiler, 1986). It continues currently to be a popular mode of inquiry in the field (Pietersen, 2002; Sanders, 2003).

IMPLEMENTING PHENOMENOLOGICAL INQUIRY

> A powerful phenomenological text thrives on a certain irrevocable tension between what is unique and what is shared, between particular and transcendent meaning, between what can be thought and what remains unthought, and between the reflective and prereflective spheres of the lifeworld. (Adams & van Manen, 2008: 616)

Phenomenological inquiry shares with constant comparison inquiry a focus on reducing field texts to reveal some common features of shared understandings across experiences. It can be considered a categorizing approach to inquiry (Maxwell & Miller, 2008) for this reason. However, long before the issues of voice and reflexivity became an integral component of the postmodern and constructivist practices of constant comparison inquiry, the acknowledgment of researcher assumptions and the focus on understanding experience from the perspective of participants were absolutely basic to phenomenological inquiry. Thus there has been a longstanding awareness about the importance of the research questions, the need for empathetic understanding and trust-building with participants, and imaginative and ongoing reflection, in other words,

> the ability to enter into the lived experience and perspective of the other person, to stand not only in their shoes, but also in the emotional body – to see the world with their eyes. This requires not only empathy for the other, but the ability to make an imaginative and intuitive leap into their world. (Hawkins, 1988: 63)

Interviewing is the most frequent means used to get at not only the 'what,' but more importantly the 'how' of lived experience, since language is how we understand others (Miles & Huberman, 1994). This necessitates in-depth interviewing, preferably over time, and open-ended questions that draw out accounts of experience, their descriptions and explanations. However, as Adams and van Manen (2008: 618) suggest, depending on the nature of the phenomenon under study and the particular group of participants, it may be necessary to participate directly as a close observer and/or to explore other kinds of relevant, experiential material, such as diaries, journals, drawings, and other art.

Based on the work of Moustakas (1994), Creswell (2007: 60–61) posits the following general guidelines for conducting phenomenological inquiry:

- Decide if phenomenological inquiry is the appropriate approach for the study based on the focus of the work and arrange to work with several participants in order to generate understanding of 'common or shared experiences of a phenomenon' and a 'deeper understanding about the features of a phenomenon'.
- Specify the general phenomenological underpinnings of the study and 'bracket out' as much as possible personal experiences related to the phenomenon under study.
- Structure open-ended interview questions that relate to what the participants have experienced in terms of the phenomenon, and what 'contexts or situations have typically influenced or affected your experiences of the phenomenon'.
- Generate field texts about the experiences from the interviews, and other relevant materials.

At this point, it is helpful to map out what is an adapted version of Colaizzi's (1978) and Riemen's (1986: 94–95) guidelines for analysis. It is important to note that this linear depiction of analysis is contrary to what is really an iterative and reflective process. Analysis never just begins when the research material has been gathered together. Rather it is an ongoing, recursive process that starts well before a project is underway and certainly continues long after the work has been 'completed'. Nor are these guidelines suggested as a recipe for phenomenological analysis, but rather as a useful starting point, particularly for beginning phenomenological inquirers. These guidelines build on the general dimensions outlined above.

- Read and reread the field texts to get a feeling for what is contained in them.
- Extract 'significant statements' (sentences and phrases) from the field texts that relate to the phenomenon under study and eliminate duplications.
- 'Formulate meanings' about the significant statements that relate to the participants' contexts and that bring out hidden meanings, being careful not to lose the link to the significant statements.
- Cluster the formulated meanings into a series of themes to reveal common patterns across experiences.
- Write a detailed, 'exhaustive description' that reflects the participants' ideas and feelings about each theme. 'The exhaustive description of the phenomenon is as unequivocal a statement of the essential structure of the phenomenon as possible' (Riemen, 1986: 95).

To help in the close reading of the field texts, and reflecting and ultimately writing about the work, Adams and van Manen (2008) suggest that spatiality, temporality, relationality, and corporeality are useful constructs in the reflective process (p. 619). Naturally, it is important and appropriate to check back with participants at various points in the process to help confirm or disconfirm what has emerged.

Example 1

A summary of Riemen's (1986) study will help contextualize the guidelines above. Her overarching question was, 'What is the essential structure of a caring nurse–client interaction?' (p. 86). Five women and five men clients took part in the study and agreed to be tape-recorded in an interview of approximately one hour about their 'description of a caring and a noncaring interaction with a registered nurse' (p. 94). Following the guidelines above, she extracted the significant statements for both women and men from the point of view of caring and noncaring interactions (pp. 96–98). Next she formulated meanings of significant statements of caring and noncaring for both the women and the men. She clustered these into 'common themes of caring – *nurse's existential presence, client's uniqueness, consequences*,' and into 'common themes of noncaring – *nurse's presence, client's uniqueness, and consequences*' (p. 100). It should be noted that each of these themes had statements about their particular qualities not listed here.

Finally she constructed an 'exhaustive description of a caring nurse–client interaction' and an 'exhaustive description of a noncaring nurse–client description' (p. 101). These descriptions are as follows:

- *Caring interaction*: In a caring interaction, the nurse's existential presence is perceived by the client as more than just a physical presence. There is the aspect of the nurse giving of oneself to the client. This giving of oneself may be in response to the client's request, but it is more often a voluntary effort and is unsolicited by the client. The nurse's willingness to give of oneself is primarily perceived by the client as an attitude of behavior of sitting down and really listening and responding to the unique concerns of the individual as a person of value. The relaxation, comfort, security that the client experiences both physically and mentally is an immediate and direct result of the client's stated and unstated needs being heard and responded to by the nurse. (p. 101)
- *Noncaring interaction*: The nurse's presence with the client is perceived by the client as a minimal presence of the nurse being physically present only. The nurse is viewed as being there only because it is a job, and not to assist the client or answer his or her needs. Any response by the nurse is done with a minimal amount of energy expenditure and bound by the rules. The client perceives the nurse who does not respond to this request for assistance as being noncaring. Therefore, an interaction which never happened is labeled as a noncaring interaction. The nurse is too busy and hurried to spend time with the client and therefore does not sit down and really listen to the client's individual concerns. The client is further devalued as a unique person because he or she is scolded, treated as a child, or as a nonhuman being or object. Because of the devaluing and lack of concern the client's needs are not met and the client has negative feelings, i.e., frustrated, scared, depressed, angry, afraid, and upset. (p. 101)

It is interesting to note in this process some of the similarities that it has in common with creating rules of inclusion and themes in constant comparison inquiry discussed in Chapter 3.

The next example is from an exercise done by a McGill University M.A. graduate student, Kim Havard (2007), in an exercise using these guidelines.

The field text she was using was the transcribed, retrospective interview that I had conducted with Debbie and Ann discussed in Chapter 5. As mentioned earlier, Debbie and Ann kindly gave me permission to use this material in my classes and work. It should be noted that the numbers beside the extracted statements in the tables below relate to the numbered pages in the transcript.

Example 2
Phenomenological Inquiry: by Kim Havard

What is collaboration in academic research and how does it show itself? In phenomenology, you are looking for the essential characteristics of an experience across populations, but I only have access to data on one partnership, so I am really looking at collaboration within this partnership. I expect that some of the themes from this data would correspond to other people's experience of collaboration.

1. *Reading* – I first read the entire set of interview data. Because these were not my data, I had no idea even of what the general topic of discussion might be, or what the researcher was concerned with at the time. I decided that for me the key term (which only presented itself late in the data) was *collaboration*, and that this was the phenomenon I would attempt to analyze more systematically.

TABLE 4.1   SIGNIFICANT STATEMENTS: COLLABORATION

1. One terrible experience (5)
2. Wasn't the same type of person (5)
3. A little bit of negotiation already there (6)
4. Certain affinities (8)
5. I knew right away she wasn't doing that (taking advantage) (10)
6. The kinds of questions she was asking about it (10)
7. The kind of interest she had, and she was ready to say, 'No, I want adult, and not that' (10)
8. Very specific on certain things (10)
9. She wasn't going to be waiting for me to do anything (11)
10. She was comfortable (12)
11. She wasn't putting on airs (12)
12. One of the greatest things about it was finding our positions in the room (13)
13. Whether it was physically where we were, or if it was just our ways of seeing it (14)
14. We might have said, 'You focus in on Vicki and you focus in on the other thing, just because I think we were both feeling quite overwhelmed with, there's so much happening' (15)
15. We had no time to fool around anymore. We had to get in there now … That's when you started talking that way (17–18)
16. That's an evolution (18)
17. Roles in writing: synthesizer vs. verbose

(Continued)

TABLE 4.1 (Continued)

18. And I think that's where panic set in (19)
19. She's not going to like this. I know she won't (19)
20. There was tension (19)
21. We never sort of like, yelled or screamed at each other (20)
22. Frustration (20)
23. We had two more weeks, or whatever it was, and it's got to be done … It's got to be done, regardless (21)
24. Physically, how do we put these together? (21)
25. I didn't mind the cutting, but I wasn't quite sure why she was cutting (22)
26. That's where I really drew on your expertise … you were really good at that (23)
27. I'm not sure I would necessarily say there was tension. There was, with each other, during the trying to make sense of it. That was just the general frustration of trying to make sense of it (24)
28. It's not to say, you know, that either one is wrong. They're just two different styles and how do you put them together? (24)
29. We were trying to merge (25)
30. If we did this together, we're doing … I'm not doing two papers (25)
31. You're so used to trusting yourself to get papers in … and now and then that other paper would come back in my mind (25)
32. You DO have to please professors (26)
33. As the deadline grew nearer (26)
34. I'm a perfectionist when it comes to writing, and have a particular style, and can be quite authoritarian (26)
35. I did get intimidated a few times (26)
36. I DID try to write like her in some ways (27)
37. I would do it compared to this friend Cathy (27)
38. I think they were shifting roles (28)
39. I was so impressed (28)
40. So I started trying to do it (28)
41. I looked up to her as someone who had this knowledge and expertise that I could learn from (29)
42. I could draw on how you could just catch this global picture so well (29)
43. You can draw on other people too (29)
44. Trust yourself (29)
45. The Embellisher and the Slasher (30)
46. It was fun (30)
47. Driving, and hashing things, and laughing and thinking (31)
48. And then there were the phone calls (31)
49. I think in the humour a heck of a lot came out (31)
50. Whether that was a form of releasing, in those frustra–, in especially those frustrating times? (31)
51. We can cry or we can laugh, so we might as well laugh (31)
52. But it was funny, but it wasn't funny, you know (32)
53. Obviously something that helps me better see what I'm doing, and perhaps be more reflective on myself (33)
54. Provides another angle, to bounce around more ideas (33)
55. Trust (33)
56. Taking a leap of faith (33)
57. Consuming (33)
58. You want to be responsible (33)
59. That you're contributing, that your part is valuable (33)
60. You don't want to let your partner down (34)
61. Being very open, and willing to share what you have (34)
62. Respect that they have something to offer (34)
63. It's trust and faith in yourself, that you have something to contribute as well (34)

2. *Significant statements* – According to Riemen (1998), these are 'phrases and sentences that directly pertain to the investigated phenomenon' (p. 280). Since I was looking at collaboration, and the whole interview was about Debbie and Ann's experience of collaboration, I found that almost everything they said was significant and I came up with a lot of significant statements. I found it very difficult to eliminate any, even when they were saying the same thing in a different way.

TABLE 4.2   FORMULATED MEANINGS OF SIGNIFICANT STATEMENTS: COLLABORATION

1. The collaborators relate well to each other initially, communicate well and share common background and experiences (#4, 10, 11)
2. The collaborators are influenced by and drew on past experience, both positive and negative (#1, 2, 5, 31, 37)
3. The collaborators have clear goals and are motivated, remaining aware of goals and practical constraints throughout the process (#6, 7, 8, 9, 15, 23, 32, 33, 57, 58)
4. The collaborators remain committed to goals in the face of difficulty (#18, 24, 29, 30)
5. Collaborators believe that they have something important to contribute (#33, 63)
6. Collaborators act in good faith, willing to share what they have to contribute (#55, 59, 60, 61, 63)
7. Collaborators have respect for their partner's skills and expertise and learn from each other's strengths (#26, 39, 40, 41, 42, 43, 44, 62)
8. Collaborators trust that their partner will act in good faith, meeting commitments and respecting all contributions (#31, 55, 56)
9. Collaborators take advantage of different perspectives (#12, 13, 14, 53, 54)
10. Collaborators take complementary roles, drawing on their strengths and shift roles as environments change or new challenges arise (#16, 17, 38)
11. Collaborators recognize and are aware of tension and locate its source in the task (#20, 21, 22, 27)
12. Collaborators negotiate and compromise when they conflict, but may feel overwhelmed by their partners at times (#3, 19, 25, 34, 35, 36)
13. Collaborators use humor to deal with tension and cement their relationship with 'fun on the side' (#45, 46, 47, 48, 49, 50, 51, 52)

3. *Clusters of themes* – This is where I identified common themes from the formulated meanings. I had to constantly move back and forth from the original data to the themes to check that the themes were really grounded in the data. Riemen (1998) says to expect some themes to 'flatly contradict other ones or … appear to be totally unrelated to other ones' and that the researcher must then accept that 'what was logically inexplicable might be existentially real and valid' (p. 280). I thought this was very valuable, because it makes space for the contradictions and tensions that are the strength of qualitative research.

   – *Referred back to original descriptions*: I know that I haven't managed to include everything from the original descriptions, but how could I? I reread the original interview. Most of what I felt was important was included, but who is to say what is important? I did notice that I have a tendency to gloss over the parts of the partnership that I didn't see as working well. I think that I am looking more at characteristics of successful collaboration rather than anything else – but then, I am sure that any successful collaboration also has some of the problems that I've included. I went back and tried to include more of the problems.

TABLE 4.3   CLUSTERS OF COMMON THEMES

1. Shaped by the past

   a) The collaborators share common values or background, giving them a foundation that allows them to relate to each other and communicate well.
   b) The collaborators are shaped by their past partnerships, drawing on positive and negative experiences to guide and make meaning of their work together.

2. Commitment to goals

   a) The collaborators have a clear view of their initial goals and remain aware of goals and practical constraints as they work.
   b) They remain committed to goals in the face of difficulty.

3. Faith in each other, in yourself, and in the partnership.

   a) The collaborators have respect for their own and their partner's experience and strengths.
   b) The collaborators are willing to share what they have to contribute and learn from their partners in good faith, trusting that their partners will accept what they have to offer and do the same.

4. Complementary roles

   a) The collaborators take complementary roles, drawing on their own strengths and shifting roles according to the task and environment at hand.
   b) The collaborators appreciate and take advantage of the different perspectives they can contribute to the task, and of the opportunity those perspectives give for self-reflection.

5. Dealing with challenges

   a) The collaborators locate the source of tension in the task itself.
   b) The collaborators are willing to compromise in order to meet goals and defuse tension, but there is a fine line between compromise and capitulation that sometimes may be crossed.
   c) The collaborators use humour to defuse tension and have fun interacting beyond the bounds of the task, building a resilient relationship that can absorb some tension.

   – *Discrepancies noted:* There are conflicts or tensions between the themes, but not contradictions. I think that these conflicts or tensions reflect the conflicts and tensions within any collaboration. It may be that throughout the collaboration, more or less emphasis might be placed on any one of these characteristics. The constantly shifting roles and perspectives are the source of tension within collaboration, but may also be its great strength.

4. *Exhaustive description of phenomenon* – Riemen (1998) explains that this is 'as unequivocal a statement of the essential structure of the phenomenon as possible' (p. 280). This was a very difficult step for me, but I basically tried to rewrite, in very simple, accessible language and in the present tense, what I had seen in the themes.

5. *Conclusions and implications* – These interviews provide only a very small window on the experience of academic collaboration, but I think that was able to identify some essential characteristics that will resonate with other people's experiences. Identifying the significant statements and themes may also increase awareness of potential pitfalls in collaboration, including but not limited to:

   a)   Not sharing commitment/losing sight of goals.
   b)   Attempting to have both partners 'do it all' rather than capitalizing on strengths.
   c)   Not appreciating both partners' contributions, allowing one partner's perspective or strengths to overwhelm that of the other.
   d)   Neglecting to defuse the tension that the task will naturally generate.

TABLE 4.4   EXHAUSTIVE DESCRIPTION OF COLLABORATION IN AN ACADEMIC ENVIRONMENT

In a successful academic collaboration, partners are held together by shared background or values and commitment to shared and clearly identifiable goals. Drawing on past experience, expertise and individual strengths, partners adopt different perspectives and take different roles. These roles shift according to the environment and task at hand. The relationship between partners is characterized by mutual and self-respect regarding expertise and each partner's ability to make valuable contributions. Throughout the process and when confronted with challenges, the partners remain aware of practical constraints and committed to their goals. They employ a variety of techniques to defuse the tension associated with the task and with working as a team, developing a solid personal relationship, employing humour and compromise. When possible, they use negotiation and compromise rather than capitulation as a response to challenges.

Example 3

This final example does not go into so much detail. It is an interesting study done by Michael Angrosino (2003), in which he used the guidelines above for a phenomenological inquiry into 'L'Arche … a worldwide network of more than 100 communities designed as places of refuge for people with developmental disabilities … that sees itself as a countercultural witness in the midst of secular, materialistic, modern society' (p. 934). The goal was to identify 'the philosophical basis for the countercultural claims of L'Arche and … a descriptive analysis of how the L'Arche communities go about putting those claims into action' (p. 934). However, instead of basing the work on interviews with participants, he used the published writings of L'Arche as field texts for the analysis, claiming that is how this disparate community communicates with each other. He argues that while these documents of L'Arche are 'its idealized form rather than … the "lived experience" in the strictest sense of that term … given the fact that the Christian counterculture is explicitly about living up to a transcendent ideal, this focus is not entirely a distortion of the lived experience' (p. 936).

The documents were read to get a general feeling of them, significant statements were extracted, and then clustered into patterns, and an exhaustive description was written based on these previous steps. However, instead of using 'tabular summaries of the statements comprising the essential structure of the phenomenon' (p. 936), he presented this material in the form of narratives.

What this study suggests is that from a methodological perspective there is potential for using phenomenological inquiry with certain kinds of documents and texts and for dealing with far-ranging distances among participants. The current technology enhances these possibilities.

CHALLENGES FACING PHENOMENOLOGICAL INQUIRY

Over the years phenomenological inquiry, like other forms of inquiry, has been confronted with questions about validity, generalizability, and rigor. These are no longer substantive issues as postmodern forms of inquiry have shifted these positivist constructs to notions of trustworthiness, persuasiveness, and credibility as discussed in Chapter 2.

Researchers have recognized the value of studying the local and the particular. In fact, the early days of phenomenological inquiry no doubt contributed to the subsequent evolution in feminist and narrative research, and critical ethnography, among others, because of the emphasis on what we have come to call 'researcher reflexivity' (the need for a clear understanding of researcher assumptions and biases and an ongoing monitoring of these), and on empathetic and relational practices in interviewing.

Phenomenological inquiry continues to face questions, however, about whether 'bracketing' out presuppositions and assumptions is ever really possible to implement. It is a noble goal that all inquirers should keep up front during their work, but the current practice of acknowledging, explaining, and monitoring presuppositions and biases is perhaps more realistic than thinking that bracketing is possible. Based on the work of Le Vasseur (2003), Creswell (2007) has suggested that 'Perhaps we need a new definition of epoche or bracketing, such as suspending our understandings in a reflective move that cultivates curiosity' (p. 62). This merits further exploration.

Questions also arise about context and whether participants ever really experience the same phenomena given that each context, no matter how similar, is always unique and individual, as well as whether reduction, or a categorizing analytic approach, strips away needed context. The concerns can be countered by the slow and rigorous process with such attention to detail that phenomenological inquirers use, and can be outweighed by the need to acquire some general understandings about phenomena, understandings that are sometimes hidden or ignored, to enhance physical and psychological needs for different groups of people.

CONCLUDING REMARKS

Both constant comparison inquiry and phenomenological inquiry have roots that go back to the times when quantitative research reigned supreme. Many of the earlier practices in these two forms of thematic inquiry arose from an attempt to counteract quantitative research and gain legitimacy for qualitative inquiry. Postmodernism, feminism, and a much more critical stance that arose in the 1980s gave rise to the narrative turn in qualitative inquiry, which is the topic of Chapter 5.

REFERENCES

Adams, C., & Van Manen, M. (2008). Phenomenology. In L. M. Givens (Ed.), *The Sage encyclopedia of qualitative research methods*, Vol. 2 (pp. 614–619). Thousand Oaks, CA: Sage.

Angrosino, M. V. (2003). L'Arche: The phenomenology of Christian counterculturalism. *Qualitative Inquiry*, *9*(6), 934–935.

Berger, P. L., & Luckmann, T. (1966). *The social construction of reality*. New York: Doubleday.

Blumer, H. (1969). *Symbolic interactionism*. Englewood Cliffs, NJ: Prentice-Hall.

Buber, M. (1958). *I and thou* (2nd ed.). R. G. Smith (Ed. and Trans.), New York: Scribner.

Colaizzi, P. F. (1978). Psychological research as the phenomenologist sees it. In R. S. Valle & M. King (Eds.), *Existential-phenomenology: Alternatives for psychology* (pp. 48–71). New York: Oxford University Press.

Creswell, J. W. (2007). *Qualitative inquiry and research design: Choosing among five traditions* (2nd ed.). Thousand Oaks, CA: Sage.

Giorgi, A. (1970). *Psychology as a human science.* New York: Harper & Row.

Havard, K. (2007). *Phenomenological inquiry exercise.* Unpublished manuscript, McGill University, Montreal, QC.

Hawkins, P. (1988). *A phenomenological psychodrama workshop.* In P. Reason (Ed.), *Human inquiry in action* (pp. 60–78). London: Sage.

Holstein, J. A., & Gubrium, J. F. (2005). Interpretive practice and social action. In N. K. Denzin & Y. S. Lincoln (Eds.), *The Sage handbook of qualitative research* (3rd ed.), (pp. 483–505). Thousand Oaks, CA: Sage.

Husserl, E. (1970). *Logical investigation.* New York: Humanities Press.

Le Vasseur, J. J. (2003). The problem of bracketing in phenomenology. *Qualitative Health Research, 13*(3), 408–420.

Lester, S. (1999). *An introduction to phenomenological research.* Taunton: Stan Lester Developments.

Maxwell, J., & Miller, B. (2008). Categorizing and connecting strategies in qualitative data analysis. In P. Leavy & S. Hesse-Biber (Eds.), *Handbook of emergent methods* (pp. 461–477). New York: Guilford.

Miles, M. B., & Huberman, A. M. (1994). *Qualitative data analysis* (2nd ed.). Thousand Oaks, CA: Sage.

Moustakas, C. (1994). *Phenomenological research methods.* Thousand Oaks, CA: Sage.

Munhall, P. L., & Oiler, C. J. (1986). *Nursing research: A qualitative perspective.* New York: Appleton-Century-Crofts.

Pietersen, C. (2002). Research as a learning experience: A phenomenological explication. *The Qualitative Report, 7*(2). Retrieved October 2008, from www.nova.edu/ssss/QR/QR7-2/pietersen.html.

Riemen, D. J. (1986). The essential structure of a caring interaction: Doing phenomenology. In P. L. Munhall & C. J. Oiler (Eds.), *Nursing research: A qualitative perspective* (pp. 85–108). New York: Appleton-Century-Crofts.

Riemen, D. J. (1998). The essential structure of a caring interaction: Doing phenomenology. In J. W. Creswell, *Qualitative inquiry and research design methods: Choosing among five traditions* (pp. 271–295). Thousand Oaks, CA: Sage.

Sanders, C. (2003). Application of Colaizzi's method. Interpretation of an auditable decision trail by a novice researcher. *Contemporary Nurse, 14*(3), 292–302.

Shutz, A. (1962). *The problem of social reality.* The Hague: Martinus Nijhoff.

Van Manen, M. (1990). *Researching lived experience: Human science for action sensitive pedagogy.* New York: SUNY Press.

Stewart, D., & Mickunas, A. (1990). *Exploring phenomenology: A guide to the field and its literature* (2nd ed.). Athens, OH: Ohio University Press.

Van Manen (1990). *Researching lived experience: Human science for action sensitive pedagogy.* New York: SUNY Press.

Van Manen, M. (1997). *Researching lived experience: Human science for action sensitive pedagogy* (2nd ed.). London, Ontario: Althouse.

Yanow, D. (2006). Thinking interpretively: Philosophical presuppositions and the human sciences. In D. Yanow & P. Schwartz-Shea (Eds.), *Interpretation and method: Empirical research methods and the interpretive turn* (pp. 5–26). New York: M.E. Sharpe.

5

Narrative Inquiry

'Contemporary narrative inquiry can be characterized as an amalgam of interdisciplinary analytic lenses, diverse disciplinary approaches, and both traditional and innovative methods – all revolving around an interest in biographical particulars as narrated by the ones who live them' (Chase, 2005: 651). A narrative tells a short or extended story about something significant, or relates a life story from its inception (Chase, 2005). Narrative is a distinctive way of thinking and understanding that is unique and embodied, that is, it integrates the physical and psychological dimensions of knowing (Bruner, 1986). This chapter discusses narrative as the human enterprise, traces the roots of narrative from the life histories of the sociologists of the Chicago School in the 1920s, and the anthropologists of the same vintage who gathered life histories to understand experience in organizations and in other cultures. It discusses how feminist work in the late 1960s and 1970s used narratives to bring the previously silenced stories of women from the margins to the centre, and the questions and issues that arose as a result around voice, power, interpretation and representation. It suggests how the sociolinguistic work of the 1970s that examined narrative structures and the function of narratives in everyday life (Heath, 1983) opened the doors to the burgeoning interest in narrative in the 1980s, and beyond. This work has given credence to the value of personal, practical knowledge and the notion that narrative itself is a form of inquiry (Clandinin & Connolly, 2000). Finally, examples of narrative constructions are shared using Labov and Waletsky's (1997) structural analysis, Rhodes' (2000) ghostwriting approach, and Mishler's (1992) narrative analysis. This chapter concludes with a discussion about issues and quality in narrative inquiry.

NARRATIVE AS THE HUMAN ENTERPRISE

If we wish to understand the deepest and most universal of human experiences, if we wish our work to be faithful to the lived experiences of people, if we wish for a union between poetics and science, or if we wish to use our privileges and skills to empower the people we study, then we *should* value the narrative. (Richardson, 1995: 218–219)

Bruner (1986: 11–12) has described two general ways of thinking. The first is the paradigmatic or logico-scientific way that concentrates on similarity-based facts or clusters of thought used in thinking to create a form of argument through formal description and explanation. The second is narrative. It is the way humans account for their actions and events around them and shape their everyday experience. It is 'a dialectic between what was expected and what came to pass' (Bruner, 2002: 31). Bruner has suggested that '[b]oth can be used as a means for convincing another. Yet what they convince *of* is fundamentally different: arguments convince of their truth, stories of their lifelikeness' (1986: 11). The 'gift' of, or propensity for narrative is evident in very young children, and all languages have the essentials, or structures of grammar necessary for constructing narratives. This suggests that narrative is more than just an acquired way of thinking, and it is a universal one. In fact, in some cultural groups, narrative ways of thinking and doing have always been the way of communal life (Benham, 2007). There is extensive evidence of how, through the ages, stories have allowed us to 'redescribe' our experiences (Ricoeur, 1983) by intertwining action and consciousness, making the 'knower and known inseparable' (Bruner, 2002: 27), thereby fusing cultural life and identity. It is not surprising, therefore, that narrative ways of knowing and doing crept slowly and steadily into research in the late 20th century and revolutionized the nature of qualitative work.

THE ROOTS OF NARRATIVE INQUIRY

Chase (2005) has traced narrative research back to the sociology practiced by the Chicago School and its interest in personal life records that emerged during the 1920s and 1930s, and at the same time to the burgeoning anthropological interest in the life histories of people in other cultures. In the 1940s and 1950s these types of research were relegated to the margins as survey research and quantitative methods used to support and prove hypotheses eclipsed the 'mosaic' narrative work of the Chicago School (p. 653) and as discomfort arose in anthropology about the ethics of studying others. Chase suggests that the liberation movements of the 1960s and 1970s, and I would add at least from a North American perspective, particularly the women's movement, reignited interest in personal narratives. These were used to bring silenced voices to centre stage and to question mainstream and deficit notions of history, culture and society. Not only did narratives illustrate the poignancy and potential power of personal experiences, but this way of researching, which requires developing ongoing and trusting relationships, also brought to the surface unsettling questions about power, authority, voice, and representation in research (p. 655). At the same time, a major shift occurred in the study of language. Linguists had carefully documented the structural aspects of language and had shown how language is acquired universally by young children because of their natural predisposition for it

(Chomsky, 1965). Sociolinguists, educators, sociologists and anthropologists (Cazden, John, & Hymes, 1972; Cook-Gumperz, 1977; Heath, 1983) then became interested in the functional or pragmatic aspects of language, and turned to the study of everyday language in interactions. They were able to show that oral narratives have a structure of their own and are worthy of study (Labov & Waletsky, 1997), and that they are constructed dialogically in context, are recounted with intentionality to accomplish a purpose, and are always partial and told from a particular perspective (Chase, 2005: 656). The stage was set for the narrative turn in qualitative research.

THE NARRATIVE TURN

The historical roots of narrative provided the context for narrative to flourish. Pinnegar and Daynes (2007: 9–28) have delineated four basic themes that contributed to the narrative turn. The first and most important of these was the change in the nature of the research relationship. No longer was it possible to think of research as a process that takes place in a controlled, objective and decontextualized space existing outside of time where facts can be examined, hypotheses tested and principles/theories generated as typically is done in the physical sciences. There was dissatisfaction with this type of a research stance. Researchers demanded that the human element in their work warranted recognition by acknowledging the subjective, relational, contextual, and constitutive nature of inquiry. The second of these was the change from using numbers as a vehicle for research to using words. It became apparent that it is impossible for numbers to portray the complexity of human experience, and the 'rules that govern counting highlight the limits of numbers in accounting for the particular, local, and contextual in human relationships' (p. 18), while narrative structures 'provide ways of holding meaning together in more complex, relational, and therefore more nuanced ways' (p. 20). The third theme was a change of focus from the general to the particular. There was a realization that 'particularizing' about a phenomenon (Donmoyer, 1990), that is, sharing in great detail the complexities and nuances of something being studied, has as much, or even greater value for understanding and contributing to change than 'generalizing'. In fact, narrative researchers question whether anything can truly be generalized when context plays such an important role in understanding. Pinnegar and Daynes (2007) credit the work of Rorty (1986), Latour (1979), and Harding (1991), among others, for the final theme entitled 'blurring knowing'. It came as a result of a concerted critique of the scientific hold on the social sciences that demanded proof of valid knowledge and the search for 'single truths'. In actual fact, laboratory work is always heavily imbued with largely unaccounted for assumptions and biases that researchers bring with them (Latour, 1979). Not only was a single way of knowing held suspect, but the raced, classed and gendered lenses that tinted such work were also revealed and criticized. In a sense it was a return of the social sciences to their historically and largely narrative roots, claiming ownership for multiple, subjective, and contextual ways of knowing and doing that blurred the boundaries of what counts as knowledge (p. 28).

CURRENT APPROACHES IN NARRATIVE INQUIRY

Chase (2005) suggests that there are five major approaches to narrative inquiry closely aligned with fields of research. There are narrative psychologists who examine how stories affect people's lives (Rogers, 2007). There are narrative sociologists who examine the content and process of storying and identity construction who are interested in 'the narrative practices by which storytellers make use of available resources to construct recognizable selves' (p. 658). There are other sociologists who use intensive interviewing to examine how interviewees use language to construct meaning and make sense of their personal lives (Mishler, 1992), and there are anthropologists who have merged life history approaches with traditional and more current, critical practices of ethnography. They engage for extended periods of time in a particular context with individuals or small groups to co-construct an explanation of what has transpired (Myerhoff, 1994). Finally, there are those researchers who are not particularly aligned with a single field but call themselves 'autoethnographers'. Individually or collaboratively they use narrative dialogue, self-study/autobiographical and memory work to construct stories of their own experiences (Butler-Kisber & Borgerson, 1997; Ellis & Bochner, 1996).

As might be expected, this classification scheme is not exhaustive, and the boundaries among these different orientations are much fuzzier than the categories suggest. In fact, there is a whole category of educators not mentioned by Chase who define themselves as 'narrative inquirers' (Clandinin & Connolly, 2000; Clandinin, 2007). They align themselves with Deweyan pragmatics and the belief that experience/thought results from ongoing and continuous interaction with all aspects of the environment. Experience then is transactional, 'it is a changing stream that is characterized by continuous interaction of human thought with our personal, social, and material environment ... [i]n this pragmatic view of knowledge, our representations arise from experience and we must return to that experience for their validation' (Clandinin & Rosiek, 2007: 39). Knowledge generation, therefore, is spatial, temporal and selective. It comes directly from perceptions of experience, and is social and constitutive. Furthermore, Clandinin and Rosiek argue that narrative is the perfect vehicle for inquiry because it illustrates the selectivity of experience, uses the narrative mode to represent the iterative and continuous aspects of experience, and emphasizes the social and contextual aspects of understanding (pp. 39–42).

> Narrative inquiry is a way of understanding experience. It is collaboration between researcher and participants, over time, in a place or series of places, and in social interactions with milieus. An inquirer enters this matrix in the midst of living and telling, reliving and retelling, the stories of the experiences that make up people's lives, both individual and social. (Clandinin & Connolly, 2000: 20)

Implicit in this approach to narrative inquiry is the importance of reflexivity, that is, the researcher must examine carefully what she brings to and contributes to the process. Also, there is the importance of 'living the story', which is the beginning point of inquiry rather than a beginning point that starts with the telling of the story (Clandinin & Caine, 2008: 542). Narrative inquirers who live the story with their participants are interested in improving individual and social conditions, but not at the expense of abandoning local experiences or using them solely as stepping-stones for more macro and ideological explanations of oppression (Clandinin & Rosiek, 2007). Above all, these narrative inquirers do not shy away from tensions that occur in their work. Instead, they always honor the personal and local and participate in the continuous stream of experience using the natural structure of narrative for co-constructing understanding with their research participants.

NARRATIVE ANALYSIS

Initially, one of the most difficult notions to internalize about narrative work is that, depending on the author/creator, virtually the same experience can produce different narrative accounts, and all stories are always partial and perspectival (Bruner, 2002). Part of this comes from positivist notions that are still heavily ingrained in our ways of thinking and make us unconsciously receptive to the possibility of an absolute way or 'truth'. Added to this is the historical privilege that has been accorded to print and continues to influence what we accept and internalize from written texts. An interesting exercise to emphasize the partial and multiple renderings and interpretations that can emerge from narrative inquiry is what I have come to call the 'Owl Moon Exercise'. It is an exercise I have used with graduate students and other researchers to illustrate these points. The participants are given a 'field text' of the award-winning Owl Moon story written by Jane Yolen (1987). In this instance, this means that the entire text of the story is compressed by using smaller print and columned pages so that the 'field text' can be seen in its entirety quite easily. No changes are made to the story itself.

The story is about a young girl who accompanies her father into the woods one cold winter evening in search of owls. They have to be exceedingly quiet so as not to frighten any owls in the vicinity. The story is written in the voice of the child and the reader is privy to both the anguish and excitement in the silence, the walk and the wait that is suddenly rewarded with the appearance of an owl. While directed to children, adults can find resonance with it on many levels, and always respond to it very positively. After reading the story aloud, participants are asked to work in pairs to reread the text and then to use Labov and Waletsky's (1997) narrative structural analysis, mentioned earlier, to take excerpts from the story and create a shorter narrative account of it. Because Yolen's story already has a coherent plot and is written in an appealing literary style, participants do not have to be concerned with anything other than selecting the most appropriate sentences to create their shortened versions. They complete the exercise using Labov and Waletsky's narrative structure below to tease out a shortened version of Owl Moon:

NARRATIVE STRUCTURE

1. **Abstract or** summary of the story
2. **Orientation** of the story (that is, the time, place, situation, participants)
3. **Complicating action**(s) in sequence
4. **Evaluation** (the significance of the meaning of the actions and/or the attitude of the narrator)
5. **Resolution** (what finally happened)
6. **Coda** (a return to the present)

Abstract or summary
It was late one winter night long past my bedtime when Pa and I went owling. (Yolen, 1987: 2)

Orientation (time, place, situation, participants)
We walked toward the woods, Pa and I. Our feet crunched over the crisp snow, and little gray footprints followed us. (Yolen, 1987: 3–5)

Complicating action(s) (sequence)
I had to run after him to keep up … I could feel the cold, and the tops of my cheeks … felt cold and hot at the same time … But I never called out. If you go owling you have to be quiet. (Yolen, 1987: 5–6)
All of a sudden an owl shadow … flew right over us. (Yolen, 1987: 21)
Pa turned on his big flashlight and caught the owl just as it was landing. For one minute, three minutes, maybe even a hundred minutes we stared at one another. (Yolen, 1987: 23–26)

Evaluation (significance & meaning of action, attitude of narrator)
We watched silently with the heat in our mouths, the heat of all those words we had not spoken. (Yolen, 1987: 21)

Resolution (what finally happened)
Then the owl pumped its great wings and lifted off the branch like a shadow without a sound. (Yolen, 1987: 28)

Coda (return to the present)
I knew then I could talk, I could even laugh out loud. But I was a shadow as we walked home. (Yolen, 1987: 28)

FIGURE 5.1   'OWL MOON' NARRATIVE SUMMARY

The results are always the same. Each pair has a different version of the original story, and when read aloud they are all credible versions of the original with slightly different emphases. The exercise illustrates poignantly how multiple versions of experience are the norm. As well, it shows how each version of an experience and the perspectival nature of a shared experience do not lessen the plausibility of the representation if comprehensive and coherent. One such summary is provided in Figure 5.1.

Another example that used Labov and Waletsky's structural analysis to create narratives was implemented in a large, initially quantitative, longitudinal study on high-school drop-outs. It was based on questionnaires given to 808 high-school students over a five-year period. One of the researchers, Anne Lessard, from the Université de Sherbrooke, Québec, persuaded her colleagues that it would be worthwhile to interview a group of the participants over time to try to get a more phenomenological and insider perspective on what precipitates dropping out of high school. In the sixth year, participants in the larger study were contacted, and once it was ascertained that indeed they had dropped out of school, they were invited to 'tell their story' (Lessard, Butler-Kisber, Fortin, Marcotte, Potvin & Royer, 2008). To assist in this work, I was invited to participate as a qualitative inquiry consultant.

Eighty former students (36 females and 44 males) between the ages of 17 and 21 ultimately agreed to be interviewed. Anne conducted all the interviews using semi-structured protocols based on the previous work, as well as more open-ended questions to encourage descriptions and stories of their schooling and experiences after dropping out. Following the interviews, the transcript material was reduced by eliminating the words of the interviewer and re-placing these with italicized words that changed each question into a statement. This was done to preserve the meaning and flow of the exchanges while indicating that these words came from the question posed by Anne.

Next Labov and Waletsky's structural approach, as described above, was used to produce a shorter and synthesized narrative account of sequential and non-repetitive language. This included

> an abstract (a summary of determining events in the life of a participant), an orientation (a description of events which contributed to shaping the educational journey), the complicating action (events which directly contributed to dropping out), a resolution (elements which helped make sense of dropping out), an evaluation (elements presented by the participant describing the participant's evaluation of the resulting situation) and a coda (elements pertaining to the participant's outlook on the future, considering past events). (Lessard et al., 2008: 30)

Then these condensed stories were written in the third person to illustrate the presence of the researcher in the account (p. 32). The synthesized narratives were examined further by the team of researchers to elicit common and more conceptual themes across the narratives using an adapted version of constant comparison inquiry described in detail in Chapter 3. The themes that emerged such as 'living invisibly', 'navigating the edge', 'never being in the game', and 'swamped in family turmoil' gave poignant, contextualized, and deeper understandings about the complexity of factors that contribute to dropping out of high school, not all of which are connected to lifestyle and family life as is often suggested. This work was able to show that dropping out of school is not an event, but rather a process, and often a long one, in which students experience various 'shades of disengagement' in a journey that includes factors which 'set the stage', those that have the students 'teetering' where things might go either way, and finally come to a point where the student just gradually 'fades out' of school, or experiences a 'pivotal moment' that ultimately precipitates an abrupt withdrawal from schooling. It was by starting with and shaping these narratives that the team was able to nuance these complex journeys grounded in the everyday experiences of the participants.

LIVING THE STORY WITH PARTICIPANTS

Narrative inquirers, who 'live the story' (Clandinin & Connolly, 2000) with their participants, record personal and social interaction through detailed field notes, available documents, artifacts produced in the context, and interviews. They also keep extensive personal journals to interrogate their assumptions, note reflections, and experiment with interpretations. In addition to emphasizing the relational and ethical aspects of the research from the outset, as outlined previously in Chapter 2, they look for continuity in experience – past, present, and future, and how this experience relates to the contextual dimensions. They talk about living in a 'three-dimensional inquiry space' made up of the temporal, the personal, the social, and place (p. 50). They may note stories that occur as they 'work alongside' their participants, but more often they document 'doings, happenings, all of which are narrative expressions' (p. 79).

As in any inquiry, the analysis is ongoing, iterative, and fluid in an inward and outward motion from the first day in the field. It includes transcribing field notes and interviews into field texts to construct a 'chronicled account' of what is taking place. Coding is done less inductively than described in Chapter 3. Rather, broad 'brush strokes' (Bodgan & Biklen, 1992) are used to 'code narratively' the field texts and other material to establish the names of the actors, the contexts where actions and events occur, the storylines that connect, the gaps that exist, the tensions that arise, and the tone of the narrator (p. 131). 'This sense of continually moving back and forth between being in the field, to the field texts, and research texts is always present as we negotiate the inquiry' (p. 135). The ethics in this kind of inquiry, the relational responsibilities, the tone and transparency of the research texts, the dangers and potential risks inherent in the work are attended to by a constant 'wakefulness' (p. 182). This quality helps to create research texts that are thorough, honest, sensitive, and ultimately useful to others.

Space does not permit sharing some of the narrative inquiries in doctoral theses in which the researcher has 'lived the story' with her participants. However, excellent examples can be found in the work of Huber (1999), Steeves (2000), and Vaselenak (2006).

STARTING WITH THE STORY

Other narrative researchers generally use interviews as their prime way of eliciting life histories, stories of identity, or narrative accounts about a certain facet of experience as mentioned above. They may also collect relevant documents and artifacts, and may spend time in a participant's context to observe the activity and interactions related to the focus of the study. Rich and detailed accounts of lived experience are highly dependent on trusting relationships developed between the researcher and participants. This necessitates a prolonged and sustained interaction. Also, it requires attention to reflexivity and a great deal of sensitivity exercised by the researcher.

For example, Linda Furlini (2005), who studied 'living with chronic dementia from a caregivers' perspective' mentioned in Chapter 3, based her work on the narrative principles described above. Not only had she been an insider as the caregiver for both her parents over a 20-year period, but also she had been part of a quantitative study on caregivers and experienced first-hand how her voice and experience, and that of fellow caregivers, had been 'smoothed over' (Clandinin & Connolly, 2000) in the results of the study. This gave her the impetus to conduct an inquiry that would honour the voices of her participants and share their experiences narratively. She worked with her five participants over the course of a year, interviewing each of them several times with sufficient time in between for reflection and reshaping her questions based on what was emerging. She developed long-term relations with them, became their confidante, and received helpful correspondence and documents from them at their initiative. At the same time, she carefully and consistently interrogated her assumptions and biases that she brought to the work:

> After twenty years of caregiving I need to gain introspection about my desire to conduct this study, particularly since I had already completed a Master's thesis on caregivers' experiences with chronic dementia. I questioned why, at this point in my life, I wanted to pursue research on caregivers and on what the impact of my life experiences would be on the research process. As I began my doctoral work, I took a course on autobiography and wrote about my own multi-layered caregiving experiences as part of my course work. I present portions of my autobiographical writings in this chapter to provide transparency about my position as a researcher, and to demonstrate that the documentation of my unique caregiving experiences can be used to construct new knowledge. (Furlini, 2005: 50)

As explained in Chapter 3, Linda approached her analysis from two, complementary vantage points. She used a categorizing (Maxwell & Miller, 2008) or constant comparison approach, described in Chapter 3, to code and create themes across the five caregivers' experiences and a connecting or narrative approach to construct and 'represent a holistic understanding of the women's stories' (Furlini, 2005: 73). The field texts were vast and dense, with stories within stories, so she revisited all the interviews with an eye for uncovering 'recurring symbols or other expressive motifs that are the basic constructive units of narrative flow' (Cándida-Smith, 2002: 721) and realized that their central stories all revolved around an inherent dilemma and that '[t]hese dilemmas represented unique but significant themes of individual caregiving experience' (Furlini, 2005: 74). With a dilemma as the core of each story, Linda constructed short, compelling narratives (narrative summaries) or (re)presentations using an adapted version of Rhodes' (2000) autobiographical ghostwriting approach. Rhodes defines (re)presentation as follows:

> A (re)presentation is both a presentation (i.e., a simulacrum) and a representation (it refers to something outside of itself and is born out of a

historical critique of referentiality); the connection between the signifier and signified may be severed, but its shadow remains. (Re)presentation then enacts an approach to writing that professes a profound agnosticism toward the relationships between writing and reality. (p. 515)

Ghostwriting, then, constructs a portrayal of a participant's experience that is 'sanctioned' by the participant in which the researcher is 'explicitly absent' (p. 519). However, the

ghostwriting approach … both recognizes the researcher's role in the co-construction by his or her adoption of the identity of a ghostwriter and deprivileges the researcher's position by excluding him or her from the outward (re)presentation of the narrative. The researcher is both in and out of the text. (p. 520)

To begin her process, Linda prepared an outline of the dilemma of each participant by taking selected portions of the transcribed texts that were scattered across the transcripts and making a note of how each excerpt pertained to the particular dilemma. She extracted these and 'reordered them to include their contexts and poignant representations of their experiences so as to make these dilemmas coherent' (Furlini, 2005: 75). She inserted her own words when needed to help integrate the text, and '[b]y including only sections of the selected texts extraneous details were eliminated, narrative contiguity was enhanced and contexts were preserved' (p. 75). She struggled with whether or not to make editorial changes and decided for the sake of fluidity and coherence to do so. She suggests that autobiographical narratives that she ultimately created helped 'to tease out the central elements of each caregiver's dilemma, represent them powerfully and preserve the contextual dimensions' (p. 76). By writing in the first person, and adhering as closely as possible to the words and sense expressed by the participants, Linda was able to foreground their voices and perspectives. For validation and ethical reasons, Linda shared each narrative with her participants for input and ultimate approval. She reports that the women felt the narratives were cathartic and validating, and provided more distant and helpful lenses for understanding their experiences (p. 115). The excerpt below from the introduction of one of Linda's narratives gives a sense of what a caregiver faced with her ill mother:

My parents are Holocaust survivors but never worked through their trauma. It's heavy stuff and very sad. When my father met my mother she became his life. Later, within the space of 10 years, my brother and I grew up and left, and my mother's two sisters, her brother–in–law and best friend passed away. She had always been depressed but now she was different. My father didn't tell his GP (general practitioner) about my mother's symptoms, perhaps because he didn't know, or he was in denial. So I wrote down my observations and sent them to the GP, who referred her for an assessment. My mother was diagnosed with Alzheimer's. She was unmanageable but I had no time to deal with her. I worked hard to coordinate home care services for my mother, but my father was irrational and refused them all. So I was always dealing with a crisis. (2005: 121)

Linda's narratives are compelling and poignant. They have served to reach different audiences, and have ignited response and action.

FINDING THE STORY

Not all narrative inquiry clearly starts with living alongside the participants or starting with the story. An example of this is what began as a self-study or practitioner inquiry (Cochran Smith & Lytle, 2008) that I conducted over a decade ago (Butler-Kisber, 2008). I was intrigued at the time with the burgeoning literature on teachers-as-researchers and wanted to turn the lens on myself to examine in some detail my teaching and interaction with students, to understand more fully what I did, and at the same time to model teacher-researcher practices that I advocated for education students.

The graduate course I was teaching was a seminar on trends and issues in literacy learning predicated on the literature of multiliteracies and the sociopolitical nature of literacy learning. There were nine women in the course, several from different countries. All had varying backgrounds which encompassed some form of teaching. In addition to readings, small presentations and ongoing discussions, the students were required to conduct an inquiry in an educational setting and were encouraged to work collaboratively.

The classes were videotaped and a research assistant who had taken the course previously scripted what was transpiring during classes, as well as in the 'action room', a place set up for students where they could meet and work between classes. I provided extra material resources there, and made myself available for individual help. Work constraints prevented all but two of the students from pairing up. Debbie and Ann, the only two full-time students, ended up becoming the most frequent users of the action room, and were featured the most in the field notes and videotapes that documented interaction there. As a result, their collaboration became another compelling focus of the study. Space does not permit a full recounting of the nature of their collaboration. Suffice to say it illustrated some important facets of collaboration not usually accorded much attention. What is important for this discussion is how Ann's story, an under-the-surface story, of her experience of silencing and loss of voice, emerged in her work with Debbie during the course. I became interested in pursuing this story for both pedagogical and methodological reasons.

It was not a matter of living the story from the beginning, although many of the features of narrative inquiry described above were present, nor was it a matter of starting from the story as Linda's example illustrates. Rather, it was a slow realization that something important was percolating beneath the surface of things; these tiny threads of evidence that were sprinkled across months of videotape transcripts, field texts, discussions, documents, etcetera, needed to be pieced together. I turned to Mishler's (1992) 'chained narrative' approach. Mishler has used chained narrative to show the dialectic between narrative and identity formation, and how personal narratives provide a way of giving coherence and continuity to one's identity. It allows one

> to tell his life story as a series of temporally ordered episodes in which transitions can be 'explained' as efforts to resolve conflicting motives and pursue certain aims.

Discontinuities … do not disturb the coherence because they are 'chained' … to both prior and succeeding episodes by adequate 'reasons'. (Mishler, 1992: 35)

I used this approach to distil the episodes of Ann's story from across the field texts, and then arranged these temporally from the origins, to the turning point and conclusion, to provide an explanation (Figure 5.2) of Ann's story (Butler-Kisber, 2002: 222). The ellipsis insertions in the text indicate Ann's pauses as she spoke.

---

1. **Origins**
   I, well, there … well, I don't know if this comes into it, but I grew up on a farm. And at night after milking and all of that stuff, neighbors would drop in and sit around the fire and tell stories. And I could sit up all night listening to those stories, just listening … to Dan stories. And old Hanna, she had a few drinks, you know, for medicinal purposes, and all of these stories. This guy, old people, and all these old stories. And the horse ran away, you know, somebody cut somebody's sleigh up, and there's hundreds of them. And I used to sit …

2. **Use other's words**
   That's like my problem. I, I'm so used to using all the books in the literature, I find it so hard to use myself … I'm so used to, everything I say, I have to back up because I can't use myself 'cause I'm not an authority. You know, that whole idea … my experience is just my experience and what's awfully hard for me is saying, 'Well, I've got to write my stuff, and not somebody else's.'

3. **Write what professors want**
   I don't care how great, you know, how wonderful the system is, what do they want? Well, this always worked before now, this … Well, there, what they want is this way, so that entered into my mind, too, 'cause I've done enough of them, you know, to know you do have to please professors.

4. **Recognizes her ideas are present but her voice is not valid**
   And they're just fly-by-night things to me. I don't see them as valuable for writing down, you know. Like I just go by feeling a lot … I do that for all kinds of things.

5. **Turning point**
   And it's nice when you get things that can break the ice, and, and get you in because I, I freeze in groups. Okay? And I cannot think. I just cannot think. But when I'm driving I the car, I mean, I could be Einstein. You know, I think of these great things … this, this is not senseless talk, this small talk that often we don't allow kids to do in the class because they're just disturbing someone else or they're not doing what you want them to do … that could be detrimental to the rest of their lives, maybe. Sometimes these little humorous things that … their true stories, also, are, are help to people to get over things. That helped me, too, to see for my own personal … I find it very difficult to talk in groups, I mean, I can't believe I did the Springboards thing (the conference presentation), never mind … I just can't believe I did that.

6. **Personal reflections are valid**
   And then, how did we start writing our reflections? And how, why we decided to do that? I don't know, I have no clue … all of a sudden we just, that was a whole big thing, our … cooked notes and we had just as many reflections. And that was how we were feeling and thinking throughout the process … I went to those an awful lot for answers. I know that.

7. **Personal voice is acceptable and credible**
   Teachers all have their power to build their own theory based on fact. I see it as a natural evolution. So there's nothing wrong with being intense, and messy and nervous, and all that. That's part of I think, as human beings. That's part of … so I don't worry about that type of thing that much anymore, even when I write other papers.

FIGURE 5.2   EXPLANATION OF ANN'S STORY

In this analysis (Figure 5.2), I was able to use Mishler's narrative structure to pull together the threads of Ann's story as mentioned. I have discussed elsewhere (Butler-Kisber, 2002) my reasons for distilling the story further into found poetry (see also Chapter 6 for a rationale and ways to conduct poetic inquiry) because I believed the rhythm, pauses, and musicality in poetry allowed me to give a sense of the auditory subtleties and poignancy of Ann's story that would resonate with other women's experiences in academia, and retain the signature of her voice.

In a sense this story emerged, or was 'found', because Ann was 'working alongside' Debbie and their relationship developed and deepened over time. It was also because they realized the assignment for the course placed a value on what they discovered and learned as inquirers. As a result of both, Ann began to trust her own intuitions and thoughts. Furthermore, the consistent interaction I was able to have with them over time, particularly in the action room, deepened our relationship and allowed extended discussions to occur. The field texts, particularly the videotapes, preserved these and allowed me to 'discover' Ann's story. Perhaps I was 'wakeful' about what was transpiring (Clandinin & Connolly, 2000), but more probably my own experiences that had repressed my voice in certain educational contexts made me alert to the seeds of this story as I did 'close readings/viewings' of the field texts (Butler-Kisber, 2005).

The chained narrative helped to construct the story. When I shared it with Ann and Debbie, they felt it resonated deeply with what had transpired, and provided a compelling portrayal of how Ann had previously lost and then regained her voice in her academic work. It was a story to which Ann responded with a feeling of validation and appreciation. She expressed her desire for it to be shared with others, yet she did not want to tell it herself. It suggests strongly the need to know and understand the diversity of learners in all classrooms at all levels, and to revisit issues of ownership/appropriation, or who tells what story. As will be suggested later, it is not so much about who tells the story, but how it is told, and why.

Another way of constructing a narrative to make sense of interview material is commonly referred to as 'case synopsis', which first made an appearance in the work of Fischer & Wertz (1979; 2002). Their process is based on a phenomenological perspective. However, instead of going through a series of steps to produce a cluster of themes that are subsequently incorporated into an 'exhaustive description' of a particular phenomenon, as outlined in Chapter 4, they use a connecting process of familiarizing and demarcating the field text, then ordering and condensing it while staying very close to the verbatim material to keep the process transparent. Then they produce a series of narrative synopses, and a final, 'general condensation' illustrative of the various dimensions across cases of phenomenon under study.

An example of this is a small study that I conducted with a graduate student after teaching one of my first qualitative research courses in 1995 (Butler-Kisber & Borgerson, 1997). As part of the course requirements, each student had to produce a mini-proposal for a research project and then carry out the project during the semester. At the time, I had recently become excited about and influenced by the early work of Eisner (1991) on arts-informed inquiry. As well, I could not help but believe that, just like young children, graduate students must have different propensities for communicating their work (Gardner, 1983; 2000), even if these are stifled during their schooling because of the emphasis on reading and writing. Therefore, I encouraged students to explore different ways of presenting their work if they felt comfortable doing so. When the projects were submitted, only one student had taken up the invitation. This peaked my curiosity, and after the course was over and the grades submitted, I invited John Borgerson to engage with me in an audiotaped, retrospective and dialectic interview (we interviewed each other over several hours) to try to understand what made him take up the invitation, how the process of doing this work unfolded, and what I might have done to encourage this work. We collected artifacts from the course to help confirm and/or disconfirm what emerged from our interview. John also interviewed a few of his colleagues to see where they stood on the matter. Their explanations varied from needing more time and direction for the work, feeling more secure in using a conservative approach for the paper, to having a firm belief that art has to be kept separate from science and inquiry. These responses heightened my interest in what prompted John to incorporate the visual representation and poetry into his research assignments.

In the interest of time, the audiotapes were transcribed by an outsider. Then the resulting field text was analyzed to shape the material into the relevant narratives. We based our approach on that used by Fischer and Wertz mentioned above, with some adaptations. We started by culling from the transcript all the material that related to John's experiences prior to beginning graduate work to get a sense of what he brought to the course that perhaps others did not. From this we created an individual case synopsis that resonated with our discussions and foreshadowed some of the thematic elements that emerged to help define how he approached his work in the course. We distilled this into a distinct and representative paragraph highlighting in bold the words that were taken verbatim from the text and we felt were salient to this synopsis:

> John had been a **high school mode** and a **band director mode** for 23 years while he taught English and music. **His 'colour' came from his travels.** When his job was cut as itinerant band director, **he spent all his time retraining to teach 7-year–olds.** That became a **renaissance** for him, **the re-discovering of schooling and education.** He **discovered with the children the importance of journaling with drawing and writing, finding things they were doing fascinating** and doing them himself. He continued **orchestrating his class,** not minding that they were **all doing different things.** Not wanting to be **locked in one spot,** he took his **grade two children out often into the larger community, broadening their horizons** but with a purpose. When his school principal indicated **sabbaticals** were **going to people who had to retrain,** he thought about it for a week or two, submitted a proposal and ended up for a year at McGill. (Butler-Kisber & Borgerson, 1997: 4)

We used the same approach to build an individualized case synopsis to portray what was relevant and salient about why I was encouraging arts–informed work in my course:

> **I was very influenced by Howard Gardner's work,** for it propelled me **back to my own teaching practice in an elementary classroom. One**

student who was having difficulty with literacy and numeracy was very talented in art. In a transportation project where the children constructed their findings instead of writing them, **he really blossomed by building a Viking ship with three other children**. This talent generally went unnoticed in his schooling and **he ended up in special class**. Later I used and explained this story **in conjunction with Gardner's work** and encouraged different kinds of representation in teacher preparation courses. **When I got interested in teaching qualitative research, and saw Eisner's work, this started to make another connection for me**. I realized that for **graduate students doing qualitative research, we were really talking about the same thing** as classroom inquiry and **therefore, there should be multiple forms of representation** in this work, too. **Eisner was the first step that I came across that was actually delving into that**. So I became **seriously interested in that a few years ago and have been pursing that ever since. I think we penalize students at every level if they're not allowed to explore alternate forms**. (Butler-Kisber & Borgersen, 1997: 6-7)

Next, after close readings of the transcripts, we demarcated the material in to units where 'the criterion for a unit was that its phrases require each other to stand as a distinguishable moment in the overall experience' (Fischer & Wertz, 1979: 144). The lines of the transcript were numbered to allow an easy return to the transcript from where the phrases were taken and to tease out the temporal aspects of the experience, and then to order these units accordingly. There was repetitiveness about certain units that suggested patterns across them. For example, the notion of 'invitation' emerged and how these invitations were a starting point for John in preparing his assignments and how invitations emerged for John from different contexts, such as in his readings, his conversations with peers, and his daily observations that he often recorded visually in his journals:

Invitation in class: (transcript lines are numbered)

33: You'd mentioned … creativity was a possibility

47: … you (Lynn) would like this to be exciting and engaging

21: … Eisner and … Gardner were mentioned if you were interested in creativity

22: … in art and interested in that type of thing and my ears perked up

58: I'm going to see if she really means what she says

Invitations from other contexts:

456: … it could be anywhere that I am

455: It could be in a newspaper

456: It could be a section of art

457: A piece of artwork that I'll see will inspire me

461: ... something that's important to me

458: ... so I will take note

In a similar fashion his process emerged in units that included 'invitation', 'direction', 'orchestration', and 'representation'. It would be naïve to suggest that John's arts-informed process that he used for his work in the course, and for other creative endeavours in which he was involved, was a linear one that followed these four steps. However, when John retrospectively and unconsciously organized and communicated his experiences as he did in our interview, it gave us both a better understanding of what was involved in his process:

> It appears that John is very receptive to, and constantly receives, stimuli from around him that 'invite' pursuit. He seems to be able to balance what might otherwise become frenetic activity by prioritizing and establishing goals and reminding himself of these to keep directed and efficient. This occurs once something has engaged his interest and perhaps helps him to remain open to suggestion. In the orchestration phase he enjoys engaging with 'many voices', including books, friends, media, and his everyday environment. He keeps track of these in his journal and/or on readily accessible material such as placemats, coasters, newspapers, napkins, etcetera. When faced with the task of creating a representation, such as an assignment, he returns to all of this material and produces his message through a combination of expository and other expressive means requiring him to attend to different levels and dimensions of what he wants to communicate. (Butler-Kisber & Borgerson, 1997: 6)

It became apparent through this process that John came well primed to embrace the invitation to delve into artful representation, while the others in the class perhaps were not. As well, when using Fischer and Wertz's approach to examine what signals I gave to the class, in what we came to call 'fanning interest', I was tentative in my messages. I wanted to encourage artful inquiry, but not mandate it for democratic reasons and because of the various levels of skill students brought with them. This approach to narrative inquiry gave John new insights into his creative process and how he might shape this in future work. For me it provided the impetus to move beyond talking and encouraging students to explore artful inquiry by showing and integrating artful approaches into the course curriculum.

ISSUES AND QUALITY IN NARRATIVE INQUIRY

In Chapter 3, some basic criteria were discussed for evaluating constant comparative inquiry that can be helpful in evaluating any qualitative or interpretive inquiry. These will not be repeated here. Instead, this section will focus more specifically on narrative inquiry, some of the issues narrative inquirers face, and how narrative inquiry can be evaluated.

A repeated question that arises in narrative inquiry is about the veracity of the stories, how 'accurate' they are. Mishler (1990) suggests that 'Focusing on trustworthiness rather than truth displaces validation from its traditional location in a presumably objective, non-reactive, and neutral reality, and moves it to the social world – a world constructed in and through our discourse and actions, through praxis' (p. 420). In narrative work, the dichotomous distinction between fact and fiction is not a pressing issue. The boundaries of fact and fiction blur when we think of the constructed nature of narratives. In fact, some narrative researchers turn to fiction in the most traditional sense to work through different ideas emerging from the work (Leavy, 2007; Murphy, 2004), to write more autobiographically (Dunlop, 2000), and/or to reach broader audiences. Of more concern is the observance of ethical practices throughout the research process that attend to the relational nature of the work, the positioning of the researcher in the inquiry, and that focus on issues of power and voice (Clandinin & Connolly, 2000). Also, it is extremely important to make the research process transparent, to show by example and help other researchers in their work, and to contribute to change in lived social conditions (Mishler, 1990).

By virtue of the extended time spent with participants, the close relationships that develop between the researcher and participants as a result, and the detail that is included in narrative accounts, anonymity can become an issue for either of two reasons. First, it is difficult to retain anonymity and comply with the institutional review demands required for ethical research. Second, some participants do not want their anonymity protected. Rather, they want their stories to be shared and to be identified. It is the careful, respectful, and delicate balancing and negotiation of ongoing relationships that can help to ensure that ethical practice is carried out and no harm is done (Clandinin & Connolly, 2000).

Lieblich, Tuval-Mashiach, and Zilber (1998: 173) suggest the following criteria for evaluating the quality of a narrative inquiry. The first is 'width', or the comprehensiveness of the evidence. By this they mean how well the researcher shows, or makes transparent, her entire research process so that the quality of the field texts, analysis and interpretations can be examined and how well the researcher has 'walked around' her interpretations positing other possibilities and then persuasively ruled them out. The second is 'coherence', or how well the parts of the work fit together, and how well the inquiry is shown to relate to, or work against, existing research and theory. The third refers to the 'originality' and 'insightfulness' that is demonstrated in the work, and whether it resonates with others and adds insights to their lived experiences. The fourth is 'parsimony', or whether the inquiry concisely and 'elegantly' has an 'aesthetic appeal'. I would add from the work of Barone and Eisner (1997) whether the author has used 'contextualized and vernacular language' (p. 76) to enhance the utility of the work, and has shown clearly her 'personal signature' (p. 77), indicating the constructed nature of the account and the ethical underpinnings of the research. As well, it is worth considering whether the work addresses the tensions that emerge, or just provides a 'smoothed over' account of the inquiry (Clandinin and Connolly, 2000).

CONCLUDING REMARKS

Narrative inquiry has grown exponentially in the last 25 years. It has become a hallmark of qualitative inquiry and a basis for how researchers shape their studies, carry out the work, and represent it. It has paved the way for the next wave of inquiry that began to make an appearance in the early 1990s, and has been steadily growing and flourishing since then. It is known as 'arts-informed inquiry'. Some possibilities are explored in the next four chapters.

REFERENCES

Barone, T., & Eisner, E. W. (1997). Arts-based educational research. In R. M. Jaeger (Ed.), *Complementary methods for research in education* (pp. 73–98). Washington, DC: AERA.

Benham, M. K. P. (2007). Mo'ōlelo: On culturally relevant story making from an indigenous perspective. In D. J. Clandinin (Ed.), *Handbook of narrative inquiry: Mapping a methodology* (pp. 512–534). Thousand Oaks, CA: Sage.

Bogdan, R. & Biklen, S. (1992). *Qualitative research for education: An introduction to theory and methods.* Boston: Allyn & Bacon.

Bruner, J. (1986). *Actual minds, possible worlds.* Cambridge, MA: Harvard University Press.

Bruner, J. (2002). *Making stories: Law, literature, life.* Cambridge, MA: Harvard University Press.

Butler-Kisber, L. (2002). Artful portrayals in qualitative research: The road to found poetry and beyond. *The Alberta Journal of Educational Research, XLVIII*(3), 229–239.

Butler-Kisber, L. (2005). Inquiry through poetry: The genesis of self-study. In C. Mitchell, S. Weber, & K. O'Reilly-Scanlon (Eds.), *Just who do we think we are? Methodologies for autobiography and self-study in teaching* (pp. 95–110). New York: RoutledgeFalmer.

Butler-Kisber, L. (2008). Collaboration in student-oriented teacher inquiry. In B.M. Shore, M.W. Aulls, & M. A. B. Delcourt (Eds.), *Inquiry in education, Vol. II: Overcoming barriers to successful implementation* (pp. 129–147). London: Routledge.

Butler-Kisber, L., & Borgerson, J. (1997). Alternative representation in qualitative inquiry: A student/instructor retrospective. Paper presented at the *Annual Meeting of the American Educational Research Association*, Chicago, IL (March) ED 420 680.

Cándida-Smith, R. (2002). Analytic strategies for oral history interviews. In J. F. Gubrium & J. A. Holstein (Eds.), *Handbook of interview research: Context and method* (pp. 711–731). Thousand Oaks, CA: Sage.

Cazden, C. B., John, V., & Hymes, D. (1972). *Functions of language in the classroom.* New York: Teachers College Press.

Chase, S. E. (2005). Narrative inquiry: Multiple lenses, approaches, voices. In N. K. Denzin & Y. S. Lincoln (Eds.), *The Sage handbook of qualitative research* (3rd ed.), (pp. 651–679). Thousand Oaks, CA: Sage.

Chomsky, N. (1965). *Aspects of the theory of syntax.* Cambridge, MA: MIT Press.

Clandinin, D. J. (2007). Preface. In D. J. Clandinin (Ed.), *Handbook of narrative inquiry: Mapping a methodology* (pp. ix–xvii). Thousand Oaks, CA: Sage.

Clandinin, D. J., & Caine, V. (2008). Narrative inquiry. *The Sage encyclopedia of qualitative research methods*, Vol. 2 (pp. 541–544). Thousand Oaks, CA: Sage.

Clandinin, D. J. & Connolly, F. M. (2000). *Narrative inquiry: Experience and story in qualitative research.* San Francisco: Jossey-Bass.

Clandinin, D. J. & Rosiek, J. (2007). Mapping a landscape of narrative inquiry: Borderlands spaces and tensions. In D. J. Clandinin (Ed.), *Handbook of narrative inquiry: Mapping a methodology* (pp. 35–75). Thousand Oaks, CA: Sage.

Cochran Smith, M. & Lytle, S. (2008). Professional inquiry. Paper presented at the *Annual Meeting of the American Educational Association*, Chicago, IL (April).

Cook-Gumperz, J. (1977). Situated learning: Language socialization of school-age children. In S. Ervin-Tripp & C. Mitchell-Kernan (Eds.), *Child discourses* (pp. 103–121). New York: Academic Press.

Donmoyer, R. (1990). Generalizability and the single case study. In E. W. Eisner & A. Peshkin (Eds.), *Qualitative inquiry in education* (pp. 175–200). New York: Teachers College Press.

Dunlop, R. (2000). *Boundary Bay: A novel as educational research.* Doctoral dissertation, University of British Columbia, Vancouver, BC.

Eisner, E. W. (1991). *The enlightened eye: Qualitative inquiry and the enhancement of educational practice.* New York: Macmillan.

Ellis, C. & Bochner, A. P. (Eds.), (1996). *Composing ethnography: Alternative forms of qualitative writing.* Walnut Creek, CA: AltaMira.

Fischer, C. T., & Wertz, F. J. (1979). Empirical phenomenological analyses of being criminally victimized. In A. Giorgi, R. Knowles, & D. Smith (Eds.), *Duquesne studies in phenomenological psychology* (pp.135–158). Pittsburgh, PA: Duquesne University Press.

Fischer, C. T., & Wertz, F. J. (2002). Empirical phenomenological analyses of being criminally victimized. In M. Huberman & M. B. Miles (Eds.), *The qualitative researcher's companion* (pp. 275–304). Thousand Oaks, CA: Sage.

Furlini, L. (2005). *Living with chronic dementia from the caregiver perspective: A case for educational support.* Unpublished doctoral dissertation, McGill University, Montreal, QC.

Gardner, H. (1983). *Frames of mind: The theory of multiple intelligences.* New York: Basic Books.

Gardner, H. (2000). *Intelligence reframed: Multiple intelligences for the 21st century.* New York: Basic Books.

Harding, S. (1991). *Whose science, whose knowledge: Thinking from women's lives.* Ithaca, NY: Cornell University Press.

Heath, S. B. (1983). *Ways with words.* Cambridge, England: Cambridge University Press.

Huber, J. (1999). *Negotiating the interface of embodied knowledge within the professional knowledge landscape.* Unpublished doctoral dissertation, University of Alberta, Edmonton.

Labov, W. & Waletsky, J. (1997). Narrative analysis: Oral versions of personal experience. *Journal of Narrative Life History*, 7, 3–38. (Original work published in 1967)

Latour, B. (1979). *Laboratory life: The social construction of scientific facts.* Beverly Hills, CA: Sage.

Leavy, P. (2007). Fish soup. In P. Leavy (Ed.), *Method meets art: Arts-based research practice.* (pp. 45–46). New York: Guilford.

Lessard, A., Butler-Kisber, L., Fortin, L., Marcotte, D., Potvin, P., & Royer, E. (2008). Shades of disengagement: High school dropouts speak out. *International Journal of Social Psychology of Education, 11*(1), 25–42.

Lieblich, A., Tuval-Mashiach, R., & Zilber, T. (1998). *Narrative research: Reading, analysis, and interpretation.* Thousand Oaks, CA: Sage.

Maxwell, J., & Miller, B. (2008). Categorizing and connecting strategies in qualitative data analysis. In P. Leavy & S. Hesse-Biber (Eds.), *Handbook of emergent methods* (pp. 461–477). New York: Guilford.

Mishler, E. G. (1990). Validation in inquiry-guided research: The roles of exemplars in narrative studies. *Harvard Educational Review, 60*, 415–442.

Mishler, E. G. (1992). Work, identity, and narrative: An artist-craftsman's story. In G. C. Rosenwald & R. L. Ochberg (Eds.), *Storied lives* (pp. 21–40). New Haven, CT: Yale University Press.

Murphy, S. (2004). *Understanding children's knowledge: A narrative inquiry into school experiences.* Unpublished doctoral dissertation, University of Alberta, Edmonton.

Myerhoff, B. (1994). *Number our days: Culture and community among elderly Jews in an American ghetto.* New York: Meridian/Penguin.

Pinnegar, S. & Daynes, J. G. (2007). Locating narrative inquiry historically: Thematics in the turn to narrative. In D. J. Clandinin (Ed.), *Handbook of narrative inquiry: Mapping a methodology* (pp. 3–75). Thousand Oaks, CA: Sage.

Rhodes, C. (2000). Ghostwriting research: Positioning the researcher in the interview text. *Qualitative Inquiry, 6*(4), 511–525.

Richardson, L. (1995). Narrative and sociology. In J. Van Maanen (Ed.), *Representation in ethnography* (pp. 198–221). Thousand Oaks, CA: Sage.

Ricoeur, P. (1983). *Time and narrative, Vol. I.* Chicago: University of Chicago Press.

Rogers, A. G. (2007). The unsayable, Lacanian psychoanalysis, and the art of narrative interviewing. In D. J. Clandinin (Ed.), *Handbook of narrative inquiry: Mapping a methodology* (pp. 99–119). Thousand Oaks, CA: Sage.

Rorty, R. (1986). Science as solidarity. In J. Nelson, A. Megill, & D. McClouskey (Eds.), *The rhetoric of the human sciences* (pp. 38–52). Madison: University of Wisconsin Press.

Steeves, P. (2000). *Crazy quilt: Continuity, identity and a storied school landscape in transition: A teacher's and a principal's work in progress.* Unpublished doctoral dissertation, University of Alberta, Edmonton.

Vaselenak, L. (2006). *Search for visual creativity: Visual narrative inquiry.* Unpublished doctoral dissertation, University of Alberta, Edmonton.

Yolen, J. (1987). *Owl Moon.* New York: Philomen.

6

Poetic Inquiry

Poetry has forever had the power to attract humankind because of its ability to convey poignancy, musicality, rhythm, mystery and ambiguity. It appeals to our senses and opens up our hearts and ears to different ways of seeing and knowing.

> Poetry's work is the clarification and magnification of being. Each time we enter its word-woven and musical invocation, we give ourselves over to a different mode of knowing: to poetry's knowing, and to the increase of existence it brings, unlike any other. (Hirshfield, 1997: vii)

In poetry, so much can be said and revealed in compelling and contracted forms.

> Poetry concisely registers on the nerves the whole skein of human emotions. It harrows, enthralls, awes, dazzles, confides … The soul is the depth of our being and poetry is one means of sounding that depth … A poem doesn't wile away time; it engages our fleetingness and makes it articulate. It seizes and shapes time. (Wormser & Cappella, 2000: xiii)

It is almost certain that poetry predates literacy since many of the ancient works such as the *Odyssey* were written in poetic form. Because of the original prominence of oral cultures and the rhythm and musicality in poetry, it was a way to narrate and memorize cultural stories, and to preserve them by transmitting them through the generations of ancient cultures.

The use of poetry in qualitative research is not particularly new. As early as 1982, anthropologist Toni Flores was using poetry in her work, at first as a form of self-therapy and reflexivity to help quell the feelings of doubt she had about living and researching in another culture. Subsequently, she realized that her poems served to 'add to one's observation of the process of observation' and added 'a dimension to our study of our own methods, by turning the subject into an object, by turning the observing *I* into the observed *me*' (Flores, 1982: 18). The use of poetry in qualitative research has taken root across many disciplines that now include, among others, anthropology (McConochie, 1986; Madison, 2008), medicine (Carr, 2003; Shapiro & Stein, 2005), nursing (Souter, 2005), social work (Furman, Lietz, & Langer, 2006; Shafer, Maxwell, Strauss, & Knopp, 2007), and most particularly education (Butler-Kisber, 2002; Leggo, 2008; Finley, 2000; Glesne, 1997; Neilsen-Glenn, 2008; Prendergast, 2006; Sullivan, 2004; Thomas, 2008).

Poetry, however, got a real boost in qualitative circles in the early 1990s when sociologist Laurel Richardson used 'found' poetry, words extracted from sociological interviews and crafted into poetic form, to depict the poignant stories she heard from her participant (Richardson, 1992). This was at a time when many qualitative researchers, in particular feminists, were grappling with ethical issues of voice and representation in their work (Personal Narratives Group, 1989). They turned to 'experimental writing' to retain the voices of their participants, and to communicate more evocatively and accessibly. Since then, others have built on this work to counteract the hegemony inherent in more traditional texts, to evoke emotional responses that bring the readers closer to the work, and to permit silenced voices/stories to be heard (Butler-Kisber, 2002: 230). This body of work has demonstrated how form mediates understanding (Eisner, 1991), and that 'experimental' texts bring new and unexpected insights into the world of everyday experience.

Since the early 1980s, poetry in research has been described variously as 'field poetry' (Flores, 1982), 'ethnographic poetics' (Brady, 2004), 'poetic transcription' (Glesne, 1997; Reissman, 1993; Richardson, 2002), 'data poems' (Sullivan, Butler-Kisber, Commeryas, & Stewart, 2002), 'autoethnographic poetry' (Furman, 2003), 'investigative poetry' (Hartnett, 2003), 'research poetry' (Langer & Furman, 2004; Stein, 2003), and as 'poetic inquiry' (Butler-Kisber, 2004). Poetry has been used reflectively and reflexively by researchers in their work, as well as for field text analyses, and/or as representational forms. These various approaches to poetic inquiry have served to bring together, in what has proven to be fertile ground for exchanges and learning, researchers who have discovered the possibilities in poetry and poets who have realized the 'research' in their poems.

This chapter suggests that two helpful ways for framing and thinking about poetic inquiry are as 'found poetry', when words are extracted from transcripts and shaped into poetic form, and as 'generated', or more autobiographical poetry, when the researcher uses her own words to share understandings of her own and/or others' experiences (Butler-Kisber, 2005). Found and generated poetry can also be classified as either narrative, poetry that tells a story, or lyric poetry, the goal of which is to 'stress moments of subjective feeling and emotion in a short space' (Faulkner, 2005: 6). It should be noted, however, that these are false dichotomies as it is not always easy to specify exactly what is found and what is generated, and as Faulkner (2005: 16) points out, narrative and lyric dimensions are often mixed. I am using the terms 'found' and 'generated' poetry here as a way of thinking about this work. Examples are included to show how researchers have been able to transform their work into poetic form. The chapter discusses how generated poetry can be used as an effective reflexive strategy, and how poetry clusters (Butler-Kisber & Stewart, 2009) around a particular topic or theme can tease out nuances that give greater depth to the work. Finally, it discusses the criticisms of poetic inquiry, issues of quality, and when and where poetic inquiry might/should be used. Suggestions are provided for how researchers who are interested in this genre of research and do not have literary backgrounds can develop their ability to do this kind of work.

FOUND POETRY

Found poetry is the rearrangement of words, phrases and sometimes whole passages that are taken from other sources and reframed as poetry by changes in spacing and/or lines (and consequently meaning), or by altering the text by additions and/or deletions. The resulting poem can be defined as 'treated' (changed in a profound and systematic manner) or 'untreated' (conserving virtually the same order, syntax and meaning as in the original) (see Wikipedia: www.answers.com/topic/found-poem).

One of the earliest examples of found poetry was in the work of 19th-century poet Isidore Ducasse (aka Conte de Lautréamont) entitled *Poésies*. He appropriated words found in popular texts, encyclopedias and even in existing poetry and shaped them into poetic form. A forerunner to the Surrealist Movement, he believed that compilations of found words and phrases become more specific and useful when they represent a collective of multiple voices (Hadlock, 1997).

Laurel Richardson is considered to be the first social scientist to include found poetry as a form of representation in her work by using words and phrases from taped interviews conducted with her participant, Louisa May. Her rationale for her work is that 'poetic representation offers … researchers an opportunity to write about or with, people in ways that honor their speech styles, words, rhythm and syntax' (Richardson, 2002: 880). She suggests that poetic representation is integral to both oral and written traditions and, as such, makes research 'findings' accessible to diverse audiences. As well, it is 'a practical and powerful … method for understanding the social, altering the self and invigorating the research community that claims knowledge of our lives' (Richardson, 2002: 888).

Corrine Glesne (1997) built on Richardson's work. After interviewing an octogenarian professor of education, Dona Juana, from the University of Puerto Rico and beginning her analysis of the taped interviews, Glesne realized that linear and progressive coding were not revealing the links and subtleties she saw within her data. She began to move back and forth across the pages of the transcripts underlining salient words and phrases and putting these together in stanzas in a process that she has referred to as 'poetic transcription' mentioned above. She illustrates how she remained close to the field texts by showing an excerpt from the transcript and underlining the found words she used in the poetry, giving transparency and credibility to her work. Her attention to and explication of her process have made her work very helpful to others experimenting with poetic inquiry.

Glesne suggests how poetic transcription represents an amalgamation of both the participant's and the researcher's voices rather than the single, authorial voice of the researcher that appears in traditional work. Furthermore, she discusses how the careful and close readings that are part of the process give the researcher new insights about the participant and her experiences (1997: 215). The portrait of Glesne's participant comes alive in her poetic renditions and provides the reader/listener with a nuanced and multi-layered understanding of this fascinating woman and her Puerto Rican context.

That Rare Feeling

I am a flying bird
moving fast
seeing quickly
looking with the eyes of god
from the tops of trees.

How hard for country people
picking green worms
from fields of tobacco,
sending their children to school,
not wanting them to suffer

as they suffer.
In the urban zone,
students worked at night
and so they slept in school.
Teaching was the real university.

So I came to study
to find out how I could help
I am busy here at the university,
there is so much to do.
But the university
is not the island.

I am a flying bird.
moving fast, seeing quickly
so I can give strength,
so I can have that rare feeling
of being useful.

(1997: 202–203)

There is no template or prescribed approach for creating found poetry. Some researchers start with the transcribed interviews and approach the work by categorizing and coding (Maykut & Morehouse, 1994), and then they choose the most salient words within a particular theme/experience and work with these to re-create the rhythm and speech patterns of the participant. Others (Butler-Kisber, 2002; Madison, 1991) use forms of narrative or poetic transcription/analysis (Mishler, 1992; Reissman, 1993) to maintain and/or pull together the contiguous dimensions as well as the aural aspects of rhythm, pauses and emphasis of a particular story or experience from the outset, and then work with these field texts to craft a poem or poems.

Melanie Stonebanks, an M.A. student at McGill University, combined both the use of found poetry augmented with some of her own words for an exercise she produced for a class assignment on poetic inquiry. She was using a transcript of an interview I had conducted with Ann and Debbie after they had worked closely together in a graduate class on literacy, as discussed in Chapter 5. The purpose of the interview was to examine their collaborative experience. Subsequently they gave permission to use this interview as field text material in my qualitative inquiry course, so that students without material of their own are able to carry out the class exercises. Figure 6.1 below shows the phrases she extracted from the field text material with which she worked.

88:	I thought, Oh, I'd really like to do it with somebody, but I didn't know anybody – and Ann was there
96:	but we ended being there and I just seized the moment, and I said, Ann would you like to do this with me?
130:	but the more I thought about it, and the more I **listened** to you…
133:	whether I asked you first and just said, Look, do you want to do this together? Would you consider it? And I remember there was a little bit of **negotiation** already there
147:	That was it, because you had already made the offer.
182:	and we started chatting and so on … this is what was the clincher for me – 'cos I think I was feeling insecure …
189:	But even before that, I think we were just … **Talking** … talking before class started
196:	It was like all of a sudden – Okay then, she's doing this. I can do this. This will be great fun. And I just relaxed
203:	but I think maybe certain **affinities**.
277:	the kind of vibes that are the positive vibes that you got from Debbie … is that she had some direction already? [ ]she wasn't waiting …
288:	It just felt that she was **comfortable**.
292:	You know [ ] comfortable. She wasn't putting on airs.
296:	I felt she was looking for, as much as I was looking for.
298:	Yeah. And she felt comfortable – the nicest way of putting it.
302:	What kind of role, were there roles, or, or, you know, more static roles?
306:	It felt great at the beginning.
378:	And you know, there's two of us!
385:	(Ann) Detailed things, and I think it came from all my reading,
398:	(Debbie) Oh yeah. It was like a wide-angled lens.
406:	(Debbie) I have a very difficult time, to go in really narrow. And I, inevitably I just, I widen out, I widen out and get frustrated at times,
421:	She wants *the essence*. (Ann)
429:	I think because you can't talk about the essence if you're just looking at one particular part of it. (Debbie)
449:	That's an evolution … she's the synthesizer, and I'm the verbose one.
474:	That was when it was difficult.
481:	That was hard.
491:	Well, there was **tension**.
496:	But you knew it was there.
497:	Visible sort of **frustration**.
540:	and we had two sets of writing. Yeah. **Very different**. And it was like, physically, how do we put these together?
572:	No, we were still scrambling.
588:	But that's where I really drew on your expertise

614:   I said, We have two different styles, so HOW do you do this?
620:   but it's not to say that, you know, that either one is wrong. They're just two different styles and how do you put it **together**? And so, I think what it was, was we were trying to **merge** …
631:   Somehow I'm going to learn how to do this with another person, and do it properly.
637:   There's a complimentarity about your styles that seem to work really well, and yet when you go to merge, those different styles in the writing, that makes it a little frustrating
644:   it's, not lack of **trust**,
671:   Just relax about this, sweetheart, you know.
712:   I think they were **shifting roles**.
758:   I'm just going back – I, just the roles – I could be the Slasher, when it comes to writing … and you could be the Embellisher.
766:   There we go, **the Embellisher and the Slasher**.
771:   there are moments when, quite often when I think I see **humour**.
801:   We've got two choices: we can cry or we can laugh, so we might as well laugh.
808:   There was a lot of laughing.
809:   I don't know if you do collaboration if you don't have … humour.
842:   How would I define collaboration. Uh, the first word that came to mind was **TRUST**. You know – out of the blue … And taking a **leap of faith**, in a way … it's uh, **consuming** … you're always thinking about it. And you want to live up to your part of it. You want to be **responsible**. You want to be, to show that you can do it too, that you're **contributing**, that your part is valuable. **You don't want to let your partner down**.
860:   Being very **open**, and willing to **share** what you have, but also when you say there's the element of trust, but there's also the element of **respect**.

FIGURE 6.1   EXCERPTS FROM TRANSCRIPT WITH WORDS AND PHRASES HIGHLIGHTED (REPRODUCED WITH KIND PREMISSION BY MELANIE STONEBANKS)

Melanie became very engaged in the work and outlined her process as follows: (Personal communication, May 2009)

- Conduct a close reading of the transcript to allow themes to 'pop out' and to keep in mind certain elements to muse about while letting the writing possibilities 'cook' inside.
- Pull out the phrases and words that will 'breathe life into the poem', highlighting any words that might help to shape the poem (see below).
- Immerse oneself in the world and words of experience and successful attempts of writing poetry. (In this instance she read some poetry by Georgia Heard, Langston Hughes, Eloise Greenfield, and particularly Naomi Shihab Nye who suggests that poetry hides, in this case, in the transcript. Melanie found resonance in this idea.)
- Combine phrases from the transcript, adding words to help with the flow and rhythm to portray, in this instance, Ann and Debbie's views on collaboration.
- Use poetic license to help to craft the text.
- Use key words from the transcript in the title to help give meaning to the poem.

The result of this process was Melanie's poem about Ann and Debbie's collaborative experience:

Ode to the Embellisher and the Slasher

Collaboration hides in listening,
in talking even before you begin.
It hides in certain affinities that draw us to one another.
It is in the positive vibes that exist without being seen.
It doesn't put on airs.
It is simply that feeling of being comfortable.
It just feels right.

Collaboration hides in the roles we take on.
It hides in the carefully considered details found
when you go in really narrow.
It hides in the wide-angled lens where you widen out,
widen out, so far that
you get frustrated at times.

Collaboration hides in the tension of difference.
In the scrambling, the merging, and
in the shifting roles.
It hides in the complementarity of styles
that seem to work really well
together.

Collaboration hides in the knowledge of choice –
to cry or to laugh,
humour wins out every time.
It hides in the openness of wanting to share,
in not only the element of trust but also in that of
respect.

Collaboration hides in the all consuming
need to be responsible and contributing.
It hides in never wanting to let your partner
down.

It hides in the essence.
It hides in the evolution.
It comes bounding out of the blue
and forces you to take a
leap of faith.

(Melanie Stonebanks, 2009)

Another M.A. student, Gail Fairbank, used a transcript from a project she was working on with a research group who, with university professors as participants, were looking at 'reflection on teaching.' She described this work as follows:

In this final interview we ask the professors questions about their overall goals and how they reached them or not in the course and what changes they would make the next time they teach it. We also ask them if they feel the interviewing and videotaping (of them) affected them in any way. (Gail Fairbank, Personal Communication, May 2003)

Gail had chosen this particular transcript because the professor documented on this videotape had a significant reaction to seeing herself on film. Gail indicated that she and another graduate student talked at some length about the participant's response because it resonated with their initial experiences they had when taking on teaching commitments as graduate students in their department. They identified with the participant's feeling of vulnerability and diminishing self-esteem because they had had the opportunity to see themselves teach. They were actually somewhat comforted to know that they were not alone in these feelings; that they can exist as well in the experiences of veteran professors.

Gail outlined her approach as follows:

I tried, in this found poem, to stay as loyal to her words as I could. I cut out a chunk [of the transcript] at the end because I found it was redundant. I also cut out her references to how much the students said they liked her lectures. I decided I would put that it another poem. For this poem, I truly wanted to represent her feelings. Poetry was the perfect medium for this. I cannot think of any other way to represent her feelings so powerfully. In the transcript itself, her feelings get lost in a bunch of 'ums' and 'uhs' and ellipses. When I read the poem, I can hear her talking. (Gail Fairbank, Personal Communication, May 2003)

By My Own Light

The idea of watching myself on videotape
was just pure agony.
I keep saying to myself
'Well listen, be objective,
learn from this.'
But I was just squirming. I don't know why.
I *hated* my own voice.
I felt I had this sort of awful teacher voice,
in the worst sense of that term.
I was boring.
It wasn't perhaps my best day.
I think on my better days, I can do better …
at least by my own light.
I've never actually liked looking at photographs of myself.
When you look at yourself in the mirror,
you see yourself reversed.
When you look at a photograph,
you see yourself as you are.
You never see things

like the back of your head
for example,
or yourself in profile.
And ... you know, I looked so very different
than I thought I looked
and sounded so very different than I thought I sounded
that it made me all sort of squirmy
and self-conscious.
I'm surprised how unpleasant an experience it is
to look at me the way other people do
and to see and hear me
the way other people do.
I was boring and sententious ...
contrived.
There's something a little posture-y about it
that I didn't like.
And I really don't know how to change it.
Maybe I should just forget about it.
I don't have to watch videos of myself every day.

(Gail Fairbank, 2003)

Glesne, Stonebanks, and Fairbank all recognized the 'occasions for poetry' (Sullivan, 2009) in the field texts with which they were working. Not all transcripts lend themselves to found poetry. When they do not, the results can appear flat and contrived. This does not mean that researchers should shy away from working poetically. The insights and new perspectives that can be gained from just working with this genre without 'going public' are worth it.

Audio or videotaped interviews, because they closely approximate everyday conversation, and preserve the auditory and/or visual aspects of the exchanges, work best. Observational field texts, particularly if videotaped, where sights and sounds of language and gesture can be revisited, also lend themselves to poetic form (Butler-Kisber, 2001). A close and ethical researcher/participant relationship most often produces the richness and poignancy in what is conveyed. Then it is the delicate convergence of what emerges because of this relationship, and the creativity and sense of craft that is brought to the work, that give resonance, appeal, and usefulness to this type of inquiry.

There are other researchers who have created found poetry from existing texts rather than transcripts. For example, Prendergast (2006) appropriated words from the literatures that she was examining for her dissertation to represent a literature review of aesthetic philosophy and performance theory in order to derive understandings about the role of audience in performance (p. 369). She rationalizes her work based on the long history that exists among poets who have used found poetry in their work and her desire to express her 'own view of the thoughts and words of others through the re-creation of their texts' (p. 372). Sullivan (2000) has used a similar approach to succinctly and saliently portray

Dewey's poignant messages about the importance of art in education and society. These forms of 'experimental' writing, used to summarize and represent salient ideas taken from longer texts, offer interesting possibilities for both research and curriculum.

GENERATED POETRY

Generated poetry, as mentioned earlier, is when researchers use their own words to describe an interpretation discovered in research with others (Furman, Lietz & Langer, 2006), or write autobiographically about personal experiences that may be 'metaphorically generalizable' (Stein, 2003) because the work 'may speak *about* one' but also 'speaks *to* many' (Furman, 2005: 35). Percer (2002) has discussed how difficult it is to make this process apparent, even when asking seasoned poets to elaborate. She concludes that it is 'impossible to separate poetic language and form from an understanding of the phenomena' (p. 3). And perhaps it is not even desirable or advisable to try. Yet, it is difficult in the research world to ignore clarification and explication even in these current times that embrace much more fully arts-informed work, in this instance, poetic inquiry. Moreover, for novice researchers, wishing to experiment and explore, or more seasoned ones venturing into poetic inquiry, some sort of scaffolding can be helpful.

I have described elsewhere (Butler-Kisber, 2005: 105) how I have found it helpful to re-imagine a pivotal memory or event as vividly as possible, recalling the visual and auditory context, and then to brainstorm a series of words, phrases and metaphors that become the kernels for a poem. In summary, this 'visualizing process' for poetic portrayals is as follows:

- Identify an event/experience or phenomenon on which to focus.
- Picture the context(s).
- Use the 'mind's eye' almost like a camera to scan the context from different vantage points noting sensory details, zooming in to visualize specifics and to 'hear' the auditory details.
- Brainstorm and record concrete and evocative words or phrases and/or metaphors.
- Begin arranging the words in poetic form, going back and forth to the mental images and sounds to experiment with 'exact' word(s) to express the salience of the event/experience or phenomenon.
- Add and subtract words and phrases and play with rhythms, line breaks, pauses and syntax to bring the memory to life.
- Read aloud to fine-tune.
- Revisit the piece as needed after putting it aside.

Charlotte Hussey, a poet, researcher, and colleague at McGill University, 'free writes' in her journal daily and then 'nuggets' words and phrases, choosing those that are concrete, vivid, salient, and poignant. She repeats this process until a direction or theme emerges, and then she shapes these nuggets into poetic lines and stanzas. In her workshops she emphasizes short, free-writing 'sprints' using different kinds of elicitations such as a memory, a story, a photograph, or another poem. The process of doing a sprint consists of the following moves:

- Brainstorm with your neighbour about some interesting images of your childhood or adolescence.
- Make a list of these.
- Pick one image and free write about it for 2 minutes, non-stop. Punctuation is not necessary.
- Read through it and mark passages, phrases, words that seem energized and compelling.
- Reflect upon the image and free write about your emotions, how you felt.
- Read through it and mark passages.
- Copy those nuggets onto a fresh page. (Hussey, Personal Communication, January, 1999).

Hussey finds it helpful to direct participants to fold their pages in half before free writing to break up the initial tendency to write discursively rather than freely (Personal Communication, January 2000).

To illuminate the research process in her dissertation, Hussey (1999) used a number of heuristic devices, like the free writing described above. Heuristic devices are deliberate techniques that help to structure and shape thought processes (Hussey, 1999: 356). A heuristic device does not supply a recipe or a step-by-step model for a particular process. Rather, it serves as a 'scaffold' to help the writer find material that is filed away in memory, suggest new material that can be obtained through reading and/or observation, and to help order whatever is being generated by the writer (Hussey, 1999: 357).

One such heuristic device was an epistolary format composed of letters and generated poems that she exchanged with her imaginary muse and modernist poet, H.D., and other letters directed to her dissertation committee. This letter-writing format enabled Hussey to communicate with an audience and express her thoughts about her work as it unfolded. It got her reading and communicating with H.D. about these readings, and imagining and composing H.D.'s reply (1999: 360–361). Hussey explained that, 'not unlike a two-voiced response journal, it helped me sift through texts to glean out their essentials' (p. 361). The third form of letter writing that she employed was entitled 'Dear Reader', in which she used expository writing to communicate 'a close reading of my own composing procedures' (p. 362) to her committee. Moving back and forth across her musings with H.D., her explanatory letters to her committee and the creation of poetry that marked her journey, the result was a very artful, compelling and transparent portrayal of the complexities of her poetic inquiry process.

Mary Stewart (2003), a researcher first, who came to poetry, initially used found poetry in her dissertation to deal with an ethical dilemma she faced. She was studying literacy in a grade one classroom taught by a teacher who was loved by the children and parents alike for her constructivist approaches, her sense of humour and fair play, and her overall expertise and enthusiasm. After interviewing a number of parents who all lauded the teacher, she came across one parent who spoke highly of the socialization experience her child was receiving, but was less enthusiastic about the language arts instruction. As a result, she was home schooling her daughter to make sure she was getting the 'basics' in language. To avoid eliminating these discrepant ideas she had in her field texts, and putting the parent on the spot, Mary created found poems that included the conflicting information but left room for interpretation, as poems do. When checking back with this participant and sharing the poems, the parent indicated she was very satisfied that the poems accurately reflected her view of the classroom. Mary was able to sensitively convey the contradiction ethically and transparently.

Subsequently, while working regularly with Charlotte Hussey in a poetry workshop, Mary turned to generated poetry (Butler-Kisber & Stewart, 2009). An example emerged in a poetry exercise that used photographs as an elicitation/heuristic device. Participants brought photographs to the class and shared with each other why these pictures held significance. The poetry writing process was facilitated by a heuristic strategy outlined by Hussey in her dissertation (1999: 50–51) which suggests that the writer should 'narrate the photograph' as follows:

- Speak the poem as the photographer.
- Speak the poem as someone or something in the photograph addressing the photographer.
- Address the poem to someone you know who has not seen the photograph.
- Address the poem to someone in the photograph.
- Address the poem to the photographer.

Furthermore, Hussey (1999) suggests a heuristic device for 'hatching the words' (p. 127) ultimately used in a poem as follows:

- Circle the key words of a given text.
- Free write about these key words and any others as well. Start this writing off by answering the following questions about each word:

  1. What does this word have to do with my past?
  2. With my present?
  3. With my future?
  4. What strong emotions does it express?

- What would someone real or imagined, dead or alive, have to say about this word?
- Quickly write 10 metaphors for your word.
- Go to the thesaurus and look up your word, and free write phrases that come quickly to mind as you scan the word lists of which your word is a part.
- Now from all these verbal broodings, start nuggeting, or extracting, the authentic, energized bits and see if you can make a poem, or add a metaphor, a vivid memory or vignette …

With these devices in mind, Mary's poem was generated from a picture of herself with her father who was no longer alive. Her free writing and subsequent nuggeting took her back to the last few days of her father's life and the poignant and mixed emotions these memories held for her. The result was the following:

Putting My Father Down

Propped up
in the velvet wing chair
in my parents' bedroom
my father looks like a fevered child waiting
in the principal's office
to be taken home.

Quietly, knowing
my role I slink to the basement
and make the call.
Bring him in
I am told
his numbers
are way off.

As if luring
a puppy into a cage
I offer half truths
and help him pack the old razor, the one
that won't get stolen,
into his soft-sided
luggage next to
seven hundred pages of Serum
and crosswords.

He jokes about the cute nurses
at the General
And I, laughing,
follow his shortcuts there.

(Mary Stewart, 2001)

Poetry, like any art, requires practice ... But since we consider ourselves fluent in language, we may imagine that talent is the only requirement for writing poetry. Talent certainly is essential, but so are curiosity, determination and the willingness to learn from others ... most poets would argue ... that the aspiring poet must apprentice ... herself, must master the elements of language, the complexities of form and its relation to the subject, the feel of the line, the image, the play of sound, that make it possible to respond in a voice with subtlety and range when he hears that music in his inner ear, or she sees in the world that image that's the spark of a poem. (Behn & Twichell, 1992: xi)

There is no doubt that immersing oneself in reading poetry and participating in poetry instruction and exercises are very valuable experiences and contribute to the craft and literary dimensions of poetry (Butler-Kisber, 2002, 2005; Percer, 2002; Richardson 2002). There are also many useful texts and Internet sites on producing poetry. It is not within the scope of this chapter to examine these in any detail, but two that might be useful are *Teaching the Art of Poetry* by Wormser and Cappella (2000), and *The Practice of Poetry* by Behn and Twichell (1992).

Found poetry can be restricting because the researcher tries to adhere to the words that are present in the transcripts or field texts. In fact, in instances when researchers deviate slightly from the found words, there are those that feel it is important to acknowledge the degree of liberty that they have taken with the found words (Glesne, 1997). The restrictions that result from using found words can be alleviated somewhat by constructing interview questions that elicit metaphors and imagery which enrich the language of the responses (Richardson, 2000). On the other hand, using found words can be somewhat reassuring. The researcher does not feel the pressure of finding the perfect word and/or phrases to convey a specific thought. The flip side of this is that while generated poetry is very open and liberating, the onus is on the writer to find that special mix of words to make the work compelling.

What remains elusive in poetic inquiry, as with any kind of creative process, is the ability to really demonstrate how the poet moves from thoughts, images and sensations to the actual shaping of the words on the page. This creative process, to some extent, will always remain impervious to an articulation that is largely intuitive, and individualistic. To add to knowledge about poetic inquiry specifically and in qualitative inquiry generally, however, it is imperative that researchers try to find ways to share our processes with each other.

POETRY CLUSTERS

The Merriam-Webster Dictionary defines cluster as 'a number of similar things that occur together'. I/we have suggested elsewhere (Butler-Kisber, 2001, 2005; Butler-Kisber & Stewart, 2009) that a themed 'cluster' of poems, or a 'series' of poems (Richardson, 2000: 881), is a powerful and compelling way of getting a prism-like rendition of the subtle variations of a phenomenon, while at the same time giving a more complete overview. They produce the particular and the general simultaneously, and help to show the tentativeness of individual interpretations.

Poetry clusters are not new. There are many well-known poetry collections that are created around a particular theme, and much of the poetry from antiquity retained constant, thematic threads while being performed orally with improvisation by different performers over time. In research, poetry clusters can be created as found poetry (Myer, 2008; Wells, 2004) or as generated poetry (Butler-Kisber & Stewart, 2009). I would suggest that, for example, Stewart's poem above, 'Putting my Father Down', when clustered with the following two poems all on the topic of death show the cycle of life, the irony of death, the interconnectedness between life and death, the everyday nature of death, and the reluctance to name it. Clusters give nuances that are not apparent in a single poem. They provide a closer 'reading' of the topic while at the same time a more 'general' one.

Walking My Mother

Like a large insect
moving toward its prey
the chair rolled steadily
through the bland corridor
only her small silver head
peeked above
the handles hard
between my hands.
Careening thoughts
resounded noisily
love, sorrow
fragility, finality
questions …
She said, 'I used to push you.'
We laughed
at life's irony.

(Butler-Kisber, 2005)

Fani

You sat
diminished
breathless on the couch.
The cough
a ripple that interrupted
erupted
wracking every sinew.
Your luminous gaze
chided my inner thoughts
bathed me in warmth.
Gently, you said,
'I thought
I would be
one of those miracles,
I won't.'
Like giving birth
taking death is slow
an arduous argument
between spirit and body.

(Butler-Kisber, 2008)

EVALUATION AND QUALITY ISSUES IN POETIC INQUIRY

The 1990s marked a change in how qualitative research was received and evaluated. The huge increase in narrative work and the burgeoning interest in arts–informed inquiry necessitated thinking and talking differently about qualitative studies. Lincoln (1995) articulated what had been part of the feminist research agenda for some time. She defined this 'new paradigm' as one that embraced the need for ethical and deep relationships between researchers and participants, one that committed to research activity that would engender change and make participant lives better, and that would be oriented to social justice and equity for all. She suggested that these new commitments in research necessitated new standards for research writing that demonstrate the positionality of the researcher, the reciprocity between researchers and participants, the reflexivity in the work, and the inclusion of voices, particularly those that are typically marginalized or silenced. Far less effort was directed to answering questions about validity and generalizability as notions of trustworthiness, persuasiveness and credibility (Reissman, 1993) and belief in the value of the particular (Donmoyer, 1990) became accepted ways of talking about qualitative inquiry.

When these new forms of writing increased and moved from prose to other forms of writing such as poetry, discussions about the quality of the art form and who should write poetry became a hot topic. The polarized versions of this discussion were equally unsettling. Should there be researcher poets, or only poet researchers who engage in this kind of work? The former had the potential of hampering the progress of arts–informed work when a representation lacks aesthetic qualities, and the latter smacks of elitism and formalist notions of art that many have tried to counter (Butler-Kisber, Yi, Clandinin with Markus, 2007).

Work by Richardson and Finley have been helpful. Richardson (2000) suggests generally that good qualitative research and/or work that includes experimental writing should 'contribute to our understanding of social life … succeed aesthetically …' and include '… reflexivity … [have] impact [and] express a reality' (p. 254). Finley (2003) acknowledges that she is not overly interested in the qualities of 'craftsmanship, artistry, and expertism' but rather in whether the research has utility in the community. She suggests that meritorious work must clearly include participant voices, and show a caring and ethical relationship with the participants. In addition, it should experiment with form, create an open space for subsequent dialogue, induce questions rather than answers, demonstrate passion, and move others to action (p. 294).

Others have written more specifically about how to discern quality in poetic inquiry (Faulkner, 2007; Piirto, 2002). Perhaps the most helpful attempt has been by Sullivan (2009). As a poet first, who then came to qualitative inquiry, she talks about the 'occasions for poetry' (p. 111) as mentioned earlier. When summed, these occasions provide the architectural dimensions of a poem. One of these is *concreteness* that brings the image to life and provides the reader/listener with a sensory and embodied experience. Another is *emotion*. Descriptions, memories and experiences that evoke emotion contribute to the aesthetic quality of poems. Still another quality of poetry is the presence of '*ambiguity*, open-endedness, paradox, mysteries, unresolved complexity…' (p. 119). Sullivan suggests, too, that poems must have *associative logic* or 'a set of complex principles related to web-like relations' (p. 120) that provides a type of coherence that is different from that found in linear texts. Finally she discusses how the associative logic found in poetry comes from a 'nexus of tensions' that are integral to the logic (p. 122). Her work provides a way of talking about the aesthetic elements of the craft that should be particularly useful to researchers creating poetry. A compilation of the qualities suggested by Lincoln, Richardson, Finley and Sullivan should be helpful to both the researchers and those evaluating this type of work.

CONCLUDING REMARKS

My use of the term 'poetic inquiry' to describe the various approaches and occasions for poetry in qualitative research is not an accident. I believe it encompasses a form of work that includes much more than 'experimental' writing and the production of poetry; it is an artful way of being as a researcher. This means developing research questions and programs that have utility and social consciousness. It means living an ethic of care that includes sensitivity and reflexivity. In addition, it requires attending carefully to people, places, events, and contexts, engaging in the pursuit of an aesthetic craft, and sharing our processes and supporting the work of others in interest of the greater good.

REFERENCES

Behn, R., & Twichell, C. (Eds), (1992). *The practice of poetry.* New York: HarperCollins.

Brady, I. (2004). In defense of the sensual: Meaning construction in ethnography and poetics. *Qualitative Inquiry, 10*(4), 622–644.

Butler-Kisber, L. (2001). Whispering angels: Revisiting dissertation data with a new lens. *Journal of Critical Inquiry into Curriculum and Instruction, 2*(3), 34–37.

Butler-Kisber, L. (2002). Artful portrayals in qualitative research: The road to found poetry and beyond. *The Alberta Journal of Educational Research, XLVIII*(3), 229–239.

Butler-Kisber, L. (2004). Poetic inquiry. In L. Butler-Kisber & A. Sullivan, A. (Eds.), Poetic inquiry in qualitative research. *Journal of Critical Inquiry into Curriculum and Instruction, (Special Issue), 5*(1), 1–4.

Butler-Kisber, L. (2005). Inquiry through poetry: The genesis of self-study. In C. Mitchell, S. Weber, & K. O'Reilly-Scanlon (Eds.), *Just who do we think we are? Methodologies for autobiography and self-study in teaching* (pp. 95–110). New York: RoutledgeFalmer.

Butler-Kisber, L., Li, Y. & Clandinin, J., with Markus, P. (2007). Narrative as artful curriculum making. In L. Bressler (Ed.), *International handbook on research in arts education* (pp. 219–233). Dordrecht, Netherlands: Springer.

Butler-Kisber, L., & Stewart, M. (2009). The use of poetry clusters in poetic inquiry. In M. Prendergast, C. Leggo & P. Sameshima (Eds.), *Poetic inquiry: Vibrant voices in the social sciences* (pp. 3–11). Rotterdam: Sense.

Carr, J. M. (2003). Poetic expressions of vigilance. *Qualitative Health Research, 13*(9), 1324–1331.

Donmoyer, R. (1990). Generalizability and the single case study. In E. W. Eisner & A. Peshkin (Eds.), *Qualitative inquiry in education* (pp. 175–200). New York: Teachers College Press.

Eisner, E. (1991). *The englightened eye: Qualitative inquiry and the enhancement of educational practice.* New York: Macmillan.

Faulkner, S. L. (2005). *How do you know a good poem? Poetic re-presentation and the case for criteria.* Paper presented at the 1st International Conference of Qualitative Inquiry. University of Ilinois at Urbana-Champaign (May).

Faulkner, S. L. (2007). Concern with craft. *Qualitative Inquiry, 13*(2), 218–234.

Finley, S. (2000). 'Dream child': The role of poetic dialogue in homeless research. *Qualitative Inquiry, 6*(3), 432–434.

Finley, S. (2003). Arts-based inquiry in QI: Seven years from crisis to guerilla warfare. *Qualitative Inquiry, 9*(2), 281–296.

Flores, T. (1982). Field poetry. *Anthropology and Humanism Quarterly, 7*(1), 16–22.

Furman, R. (2003). Autoethnographic poems and narrative reflections: A qualitative study on the death of a companion animal. *Journal of Family Social Work, 9*(4), 23–38.

Furman, R. (2005). Autoethnographic poems and narrative reflections: A qualitative study on the death of a companion animal. *Journal of Family Social Work, 9*(4), 23–38.

Furman, R., Lietz, C., & Langer, C. L. (2006). The research poem in international social work. *International Journal of Qualitative Methods, 5*(3), 24–34.

Glesne, C. (1997). That rare feeling: Re-presenting research through poetic transcription. *Qualitative Inquiry, 3*(2), 202–221.

Hadlock, P. G. (1997). *Lautreamont and the poetics of indeterminacy.* Unpublished doctoral dissertation, University of Pennsylvania, Philadelphia.

Hartnett, S. J. (2003). *Incarceration nation: Investigating prison poems of hope and terror.* Walnut Creek, CA: AltaMira.

Hirshfield, J. (1997). *Nine gates: Entering the mind of poetry.* New York: HarperPerennial.

Hussey, C. (1999). *Of swans, the wind and H. D.: An epistolary portrait of the poetic process.* Unpublished doctoral dissertation, McGill University, Montreal, QC.

Langer, C. L., & Furman, R. (2004). Exploring identity and assimiliation: Research and interpretive poems [19 paragraphs]. *Forum Qualitative Sozialforschung/Forum Qualitative Social Research [On-line Journal], 5*(2), Art. 5. Retrieved August 24, 2008, from www.qualitative-research.net.fqs-texte/2-04/2-04langerfurman-e.htm.

Leggo, C. (2008). Imagination's hope: Four poems. *LEARNing Landscapes, 2*(1), 31–34.

Lincoln, Y. (1995). Emerging criteria for quality in qualitative and interpretive research. *Qualitative Inquiry, 1*(3), 275–289.

Madison, D. S. (1991). 'That was my occupation': Oral narrative, performance, and black feminist thought. *Text and Performance Quarterly, 13*, 213–232.

Madison, D. S. (2008). Narrative poetics and performative interventions. In N. K. Denzin & M. D. Giardina (Eds.), *Qualitative inquiry and the politics of evidence* (pp. 221–249). Walnut Creek, CA: Left Coast Press.

Maykut, P., & Morehouse, R. (1994). *Beginning qualitative research: A philosophical and practical guide*. London: Falmer.

McConochie, R. P. (1986). Three poems from the Alps. *Anthropology and Humanism Quarterly, 11*(1), 15–16.

Mishler, E. G. (1992). Work, identity, and narrative: An artist-craftsman's story. In G. C. Rosenwald & R. L. Ochberg (Eds.), *Storied lives* (pp. 21–40). New Haven, CT: Yale University Press.

Myer, E. (2008). 'Who we are matters.' The phenomenology of teacher identities: Representation in found poetry. Paper presented at the *Annual Meeting of the American Educational Research Association,* New York (March).

Neilsen-Glenn, L. (2008). Second hand philosophy. *LEARNing Landscapes, 1*(2), 215–216.

Percer, L. H. (2002). Going beyond the demonstrable range in educational scholarship: Exploring the intersections of poetry and research. *Qualitative Report, 7*(2). Retrieved August 2, 2008, from wwwnova.edu/ssss/QR/QR7-2/hayespercer.html.

Personal Narratives Group (Ed.), (1989). *Interpreting women's lives: Feminist theory and personal narratives*. Bloomington: Indiana University Press.

Piirto, J. (2002). The question of quality and qualifications: Writing inferior poems as qualitative research. *Qualitative Studies in Education, 15*(4), 431–445.

Prendergast, M. (2006). Found poetry as literature review: Research poems on audience and performance. *Qualitative Inquiry, 12*(2), 369–388.

Reissman, C. K. (1993). *Narrative inquiry*. Newbury Park, CA: Sage.

Richardson, L. (1992). The consequences of poetic representation: Writing the other, writing the self. In C. Ellis & M. G. Flaherty (Eds.), *Investigating subjectivity: Research on lived experience* (pp. 125–137). Newbury Park, CA: Sage.

Richardson, L. (2000). Introduction – Assessing alternative modes of qualitative and ethnographic research: How do we judge? Who judges? *Qualitative Inquiry, 6*(2), 251–255.

Richardson, L. (2002). Poetic representation of interviews. In J. F. Gubrium & J. A. Holstein (Eds.), *Handbook of interview research: Context and method* (pp. 887–891). Thousand Oaks, CA: Sage.

Shafer, A., Maxwell, B., Strauss, R., & Knopp, V. (2007). I must tell you in a poem: Poetry and commentary. *Journal of Medical Humanities, 28*(2), 173–180.

Shapiro, J., & Stein, H. (2005). Poetic license: Writing poetry as a way for medical students to examine their professional relational systems. *Families, Systems, & Health, 23*(3), 278–292.

Souter, J. (2005). Loss of appetite: A poetic exploration of cancer patients' and their carers' experiences. *International Journal of Palliative Nursing, 11*(10), 524–532.

Stein, H. F. (2003). The inner world of workplaces: Accessing this world through poetry, narrative, literature, music and visual art. *Consulting Psychology Journal: Practice and Research, 55*(2), 84–93.

Stewart, M. (2003). *Literacy instruction in a cycle one classroom: A qualitative study*. Unpublished doctoral dissertation, McGill University, Montreal, QC.

Sullivan, A. (2000). The necessity of art. Three found poems from John Dewey's 'Art as Experience'. *International Journal of Qualitative Studies in Education, 13*(3), 325–327.

Sullivan, A. (2004). Poetry as research: Development of poetic craft and the relations of craft and utility. *Journal of Critical Inquiry into Curriculum and Instruction, 5*(2), 34–37.

Sullivan, A. (2009). Defining poetic occasion in inquiry: Concreteness, voice, ambiguity, tension, and associative logic. In M. Prendergast (Ed.), *Poetic inquiry: Vibrant voices in the social sciences* (pp. 111–126). Rotterdam: Sense.

Sullivan, A., Butler-Kisber, L., Commeryas, M., & Stewart, M. (2002). Constructing data poems: How and why – A hands-on experience. Extended pre-conference session at the *Annual Meeting* of the *American Educational Research Association*. New Orleans, LA (April).

Thomas, S. (2008). Riding the waves, reading the sea. In J. G. Knowles, S. Promislow & A. Cole (Eds.), *Creating scholartistry: Imagining the arts-informed thesis or dissertation* (pp. 209–213). Halifax, NS: Backalong.

Wells, K. (2004). Safe in my heart: Found poetry as narrative inquiry. In J. McNinch & M. Cronin (Eds.), *I could not speak my heart: Education and social justice for gay and lesbian youth* (pp. 7–18). Regina, SK: University of Regina.

Wormser, B. & Cappella, D. (2000). *Teaching the art of poetry: The moves.* London: Erlbaum.

7

Collage Inquiry

The term 'collage', which refers to a genre of art, is derived from the French verb *coller*, which means 'to stick', and refers to the process of cutting and sticking found materials onto a flat surface. The roots of papier collé, or collage, date back to at least 1000 years ago when Japanese calligraphers used scraps of torn paper to adorn their written texts. There are instances of collage in folk art, as in the work of Mary Delany (1700–88). She created paper mosaics by cutting petals from colored paper and pasting them onto black paper backgrounds (Hayden, 1980). Families in the Victorian era frequently made scrapbooks of collages depicting their everyday experiences. However, collage became acknowledged as art during the early part of the 20th century when artists such as Picasso and Braque used this medium to challenge the traditional conventions of art, the elitist nature of art, and the notion of a single reality. These collagists pushed the boundaries of representation and initiated the postmodern tendencies that were to follow (Butler-Kisber, 2007, 2008).

Unsurprisingly, it is because qualitative researchers have been dissatisfied with traditional forms of representation, and because our world has become increasingly visually oriented, that attention has been turned to visual approaches in inquiry. Collage happens to be one such genre and has attracted attention because it is a user-friendly medium, one in which the basic skills of cutting and sticking that are acquired early in life can be used. While this does not ensure a quality product, it does entice researchers to experiment more readily. Moreover, collage evokes embodied responses, and uses the juxtaposition of fragments and the presence of ambiguity to engage the viewer in multiple avenues of interpretation.

This chapter examines collage production that uses found images from popular magazines as a reflective process, as an elicitation for thinking, writing, and/or discussion, and as a conceptualizing approach. It should be noted that in terms of elicitation, I do not mean 'to draw out or evoke an admission' (Pink, 2001: 68), but rather to elicit multiple perceptions, interpretations, and possibilities (Schwartz, 1992: 13). This chapter shows with examples that by working in this nonlinear and intuitive way, implicit assumptions can surface and/or be countered. It also discusses how collage clusters can help to conceptualize dimensions of understanding that were previously unconscious, and how collage creation can be a way of making thoughts concrete, facilitating the thinking, writing and talking about the inquiry. Finally, the challenges that researchers face when conducting collage inquiry are discussed.

THE 'BIRTH' OF COLLAGE

In the spring of 1912, Picasso pasted a piece of oilcloth printed with a trompe l'oeil chair-caning pattern to the surface of a small, oval canvas representing a café still life. This work, which he framed with a coarse rope, has acquired legendary status in the history of art as the first deliberately executed collage – the first work of fine art, that is, in which materials appropriated from everyday life relatively untransformed by the artist, intrude upon the traditionally privileged domain of painting. The use of these materials ... challenged some of the most fundamental assumptions about the nature of painting inherited by Western artists from the time of the Renaissance. The invention of collage put into question prevailing notions of how and what works of art represent, of what unifies a work of art, of what materials artists may use; it also opened to debate the more recent Romantic definition of what constitutes originality and authenticity in the work of art. If the *Still Life with Chair-Caning* remains [an] enigmatic and powerful work even now ... it is because of the audacity with which it raised these questions, which continue to be of importance to artists and theorists today. (Poggi, 1992: 1)

Brockelman (2001) posits that the Cubist intentions were to 'represent the intersection of multiple discourses' (p. 2) and that this is what differentiates them from the earlier folk art mentioned above. He suggests that work of the Cubists initially sparked the beginning of the 'postmodern condition' which is 'collage-like' (p. 184). It is a form of 'collage hermeneutics' in that 'knowledge no longer answers uncertainty with certainty, but rather with more uncertainty' (p. 186). A collage itself is allegorical because each element in the work belongs to a previous world from which it was taken, and a new one into which it is pasted. Thus, collage speaks with two voices (p. 31). In collage, the 'disruption of aesthetic unity underscores the fundamentally *relational* nature of visual representation and does so by maintaining the structural elements of such representation while denying any ontological attribution of them' (p. 33). In other words, 'collage reflects the very way we see the world with objects being given meaning not from something within themselves, but rather through the way we perceive how they stand in relationship to one another' (Robertson, 2000: 2).

COLLAGE IN INQUIRY

The postmodern tendencies have driven researchers to find new ways of making meaning and enabling understanding to deal with the 'crisis of representation'

(Denzin & Lincoln, 2005) that has plagued the research field for at least two decades. This search plus the increasingly visual world have led to increasing experimentation with collage. This has not remained solely in the area of research. Collage is used across the grades and curricular areas as a pedagogy for scaffolding writing (Oshansky, 1994), as a way of visually synthesizing a process, and as a way of examining identity and values (McDermott, 2002) because the 'images enable meaning to travel in ways that words cannot' (Burns, 2003: 9). Collage has been used extensively in the health sciences as one of the vehicles for art therapy, in part for efficiency of time (McNiff, 1998; Sturgess, 1983). It has been used in the business world to tease out relational dimensions of what is experienced by employees or the public in terms of business environments and/or the marketplace, and to help translate inner thoughts into public representations (Ozawa & Osumi, 2002). It is when the language of texts or speech interacts with a 'visual language' such as that of collage that new meaning and understanding occur (Norris, 2008).

In terms of arts-informed inquiry, collage can contribute in several important ways. First, because of the sensory or embodied response it engenders, collage can help the viewer respond very concretely. A single or linear thought 'gives way to relations of juxtaposition and difference' (Rainey, 1998: 124) and the fragments both work together or in opposition to produce new connections and illuminating ideas. Second, the use of metaphor (similarity or comparison) and metonymy (contiguity or connectedness) and the gaps and the spaces within a collage reveal both the intended and the unintended. The process itself lessens 'conscious control over what is being presented, contributes to greater levels of expression, and in turn greater areas for examination and subsequent clarification' (Williams, 2000: 275). Third, in linear, written texts the author works from the ideas to the feelings or from the 'head to the heart'. In collage the opposite is true. The creator seeks the fragments and glues them together to express a feeling or sense of an experience or phenomenon rather than a particular idea. She works from the 'heart to the head', and in this way permits 'reseeing, relocating, and connecting anew' (Mullen, 1999: 292). The tacit, or what has remained unconscious, bubbles to the surface. Finally, in written texts there are typically many iterations or drafts to hone the final form and articulate the message as precisely as possible. In collage, there may be various 'tries' and or changes to the images until they are glued down, but once stuck, the images cannot easily be altered. The allegorical and relational qualities, however, provide various ways of interpreting conscious and unconscious ideas, and there is sufficient residual ambiguity for different interpretations and successive ones over time (Butler-Kisber, Allnutt, Furlini, Kronish, Markus, & Stewart, 2005).

I have discussed in some detail elsewhere (Butler-Kisber, 2002) how I became interested in arts-informed inquiry after attending the first American Educational Research Association Arts-based Institute under the direction of Elliot Eisner in 1993. My work had remained within the textual boundaries of arts-based research until working with John Borgerson (Butler-Kisber & Borgerson, 1997) and Donna Davis (Davis & Butler-Kisber, 1999), two graduate students both of whom were artists, when I became aware of the possibilities of using collage in inquiry. Since then, I have ventured into the genre myself, and by working with graduate students and colleagues I have developed some ways of thinking about and using collage as inquiry. Three ways that are particularly useful, though certainly not exhaustive, nor mutually exclusive, are as a reflective process, as a form of elicitation, and as a way to conceptualize ideas.

COLLAGE AS REFLECTION

Memoing, journaling, and concept mapping have been discussed in previous chapters as ways for the researcher to keep track of queries, to ponder emerging ideas, reflect on relationships and linkages in the field texts, and to attend to researcher reflexivity. Collage can be used in the same way, and like concept maps, has the advantage of producing a web of connections instead of linear ones. At the same time, as mentioned above, the joining of disparate fragments can produce associations and connections that bring unconscious thoughts to the surface.

An interesting way to try out the power of collage as a reflective tool is to pick a focus, collage it, pick a title for it and then write a paragraph describing what the collage is about. When done in the context of a graduate class or workshop, the individual collages can be displayed without titles and the participants can circulate to view the collages while jotting down two or three adjectives on Post-it notes which are attached to the back of each collage. I have named this the 'Markus Approach' after Pamela Markus, an artist and former Ph.D. student (see below) who suggested letting the viewers make these 'comments' prior to sharing the titles and paragraphs about each collage. When sharing takes place, the adjectives are read aloud followed by the original description and title. This moment is poignant. Inevitably there are some wonderful surprises. In some instances it is remarkable how the adjectives echo what the researcher has intended. This validates the work. In others, some aspect is highlighted in a way that was not intended and brings new meaning to the work. The whole exercise underscores the ambiguities and multiple interpretations that are inherent in visual work.

For example, Ramona Parkash (2007), a current Ph.D. student at McGill University, created her collage based on her proposed study. Her focus is on the educational journey and the implications that young adults from a small Caribbean island face when there is no post-secondary university system. They must seek tertiary education elsewhere. Having taught on the island and remained in ongoing contact with a group of about 20 high-school graduates, Ramona intends to illuminate their stories and explain their choices for tertiary education and uncover issues they confront in leaving, accessing other institutions, and in returning to the island. Many of the descriptors she received about her collage from her classmates suggested 'freedom' in the journey and 'opportunity', 'fun', and did not reflect what she had hoped to signify. Several other colleagues focused on light-providing descriptors such as 'inspiration' and 'scrutiny'.

Ramona explained her work as follows:

FIGURE 7.1   COLLAGE BY RAMONA PARKASH, *PATHWAYS*

Initially, when I began looking for images that appeared to resonate with my interest in exploring the educational and occupational decision making of young people from this Caribbean island, I gravitated to pictures of landscapes. I liked the metaphor of long, winding roads as representational of the numerous pathways students take to achieve their aspirations and career goals. As I layered images of mountains and roads, I sensed the physical exhaustion that typically comes with decision making – the sleepless nights of exploring all options, weighing the positives with the negatives, and trying to ensure a sense of satisfaction in the outcome. The inclusion of the different facial expressions of the man on the top of the page represented the various emotions that young people must feel while trying to figure out their post-secondary lives. The blurred crowd in the top left-hand corner simulated the confusion. The last image that I snipped out of a magazine was of four children, arm in arm, which I pasted as if walking down a long road.

  When my colleagues viewed my collage I was surprised to see how many of them had extracted a different interpretation and feeling of the images posted. While I had tried to portray confusion and imbalance, many of my classmates interpreted freedom in the journey and opportunity. Some viewed the jet on the top-right corner as a symbol of success and adventure (travel).

After several days, I revisited my collage and thought about the comments, particularly about the light. I experienced somewhat of a 'eureka' moment. In all of my previous writing about my proposed study I had mentioned how local islanders and expatriate youth were the primary participants for the study. I emphasized the difference in career conceptualization of these two groups. Yet when I looked at my collage and how the illumination focused on the four youths making their way down the road, local and expatriate youth of this island were not these children. It was at this point when I realized that I had forgotten to include a very important population on the island – the Haitian refugees and new immigrants. The image of the four children represented the forgotten participants – an important group of young people who are considered 'outsiders' on the island. (Parkash, 2007)

Whatever the original intention or idea of the collagist may be, the multiple levels of processing frequently assure that the result will be made 'strange,' opening up the possibility for the emergence of tacitly or intuitively known content and the appearance of unexpected new associations (Davis & Butler-Kisber, 1999: 5).

The collage process and exercise created these associations and helped Ramona to rethink her proposed study in a very important way.

In another example, Michele Pinard, a Ph.D. candidate at McGill University, used her self-study as a focus for her collage. She is studying critical incidences in her life and in her experiences visiting and working in other countries to understand how these have influenced her as a person and teacher of multicultural education. She hopes her study will contribute to developing the best possible ways for serving those whose lives are less fortunate than hers.

In the following excerpt Michele traces her thought processes as she produced her collage for the exercise:

I found as I collected magazines from the coffee table at home in preparation for the collage workshop that I was staring at myself: confronting my political positions, my leisure interests and aspirations, my avenue for collecting 'news' from the world, my tendrils for retaining connections with 'home', my professional updates, organizations that are my beneficiaries. I couldn't help but ask again the question initially scratched in the Identity Memo: Who am I? Sub-questions I asked myself included: Whom or what do I care about? What roles do I play? What topics attract or repel my energies? Where do I place myself in the world? Where am I most at peace?

When I actually began searching for images in class, I began by selecting one image of an outdoors woman. She actually looked something like me in my

(Continued)

(Continued)

younger years. I remember worrying that my collage would be too transparent, not symbolic enough. It was as if my nameplate, the one that indicated that I was 'Michele', would scream out at my classmates, unmasking me and identifying that I was unable to create artistic based representations.

My thoughts drifted for a while as I thumbed through the magazines and I thought about how parents have power when they name their children. No one in class knew (and I did not explain in the interview exercise) that my name is a modification of my father's middle name, Michael. Ironically, I reminded myself, my husband's name is also Michael and we gave one of our daughter's my name as her middle name. I wondered if that had deeper meaning … I knew that Michael means archangel for Christians. I also recalled, painfully, how I was raised in a very Catholic home but reminded myself that I have safely distanced myself by eschewing its label and rituals since I was very young. I found the beliefs too constricting. Labels in general I find constraining and I knew my life had been far from angelic.

Nevertheless, I have been Michele for nearly a half century. I let this thought settle as I cut out the first image. Nicknames have come and gone and the essence of who I am has evolved. I was raised to be politically aware, influenced by my mother's relatives' tendency to pride themselves on two counts: religious faith and political activism. Kitchen table debates were incessant and one was valued for how skillfully one could argue a political point. Regrettably, I sighed, the more conservative the view, the more legitimate it was considered to be.

A sense of pain was awakened in me as I recalled that bias has caused perpetual conflict for me. I was raised in the 1960s–1970s when women's rights and anti-establishment fervor were ripening. Influential males, such as my uncles who were only a few years older than I was, delighted in confronting me and my desire for liberation by slamming doors rather than holding them and refusing to allow me special treatment because I was (I often reminded them) a female. Eventually, my parents gave up on legislating my religious practice, though they have never formally accepted the fact that I have strayed from the flock. Femininity is not so easily obscured.

Education is (and still continues to be) what separates me from my family most. Few of my extended relatives have been formally educated beyond high school; I was the first to go to a four-year college. They were proud that I was awarded a scholarship to attend an exclusive liberal arts university. Later, we both discovered that this opportunity was a double-edged sword. I was able to travel and study abroad but this led me to pointedly question US politics and the economic system. I had witnessed how our country privileges itself to utilize far more than its 'fair share' of natural resources at the expense of the majority of the world's people. When I verbalized these feelings around the kitchen table, my opinions were scorned. I was labeled 'Michele the radical', 'Michele the unappreciative', 'Michele the unpatriotic', 'Michele the rebel', 'Michele the weird', 'Michele the liberal, bleeding heart, do-gooder'. Although I had been raised in a religious tradition to share, to value the earth's fragility, to love 'the family of God', I found that overseas experiences drove me to confront the realities of our 'family values' in a global context. I confused and threatened my family by raising issues of equity and social justice that reflected upon the goods on their kitchen table. This disconnection from my family has affected my ability to harbor inner peace.

All of these thoughts were flooding my brain as I sat selecting images for the collage. As if to calm myself, I immediately was drawn to the land and water images. Time I spend near water and in the woods is restorative for me. Next to water, my mind is soothed and I am able to sort out my thoughts more clearly. (Even now as I write, the sound of water outside is washing over me.) Cruelly, however, I recalled that it was water that struck me most obtusely as a political symbol for economic injustices when I returned from my first trip to Africa. Water is in such precious supply there. Whereas I had grown up on Long Lake and water was synonymous with my 'place' in the world, in Africa, I found that its presence was a matter of life and death. Lack of clean water literally contributed to more deaths (either through dehydration, illness, infectious diseases, or – war) than any other problem faced by people on the continent. When I returned to the Adirondacks from Kenya, I was struck by how much green and how much water there was in the mountains in contrast to the red ochres of Africa. I had taken the natural resources of my homeland so for granted. Including the water and woods as a backdrop to my collage and the issues overlaid was essential in my life story at this moment.

As I embellished my collage, I accentuated this love of and appreciation for water. The lake, water birds, bamboo, globe with oceans, and even the bubble bath (though I don't indulge in those often) reflect my keen awareness of life's vital connection to water. However, the sick child with an empty bowl, the African continent with no rivers, and a child planting in very dry earth stand in contrast. I respect the power of water. When swimming (my sport of choice), I feel free to think and wipe away tensions in my life. I remember thinking when I chose the background that perhaps I was rooting myself too deeply in this image, considering how many people lack the luxury of water. I felt that we were being instructed to let images select us but this huge chunk of my life would not let go. The peaceful surface glossed over the impending reality that inequitable distribution of water is predicted to be a probable cause of the next world war.

Focusing back on the identity question, I became attracted to quirky symbols of the various roles I play in life: student, mother, teacher. The monkey at the school desk was an odd image and I am still not sure why I chose it, except that the desk reminded me of when I was in primary school, dutifully doing my schoolwork. I have always been drawn to learning more and it is a position in which I feel quite alive. The nearby image of the pregnant woman sitting upright in a chair with the 1970s deco symbol reflected a period in my life when I was forced to leave frivolity behind. I did have long hair at the time and, though I was never very fashionable, I interpreted the drawing as a time in my life prior to having children that was more glamorous and free. Directly below are two stark images of families, one with a pitchfork, likely chosen to symbolize my agrarian roots, and the other a white-collar family, more reflective of my contemporary reality. I have straddled those two

(Continued)

FIGURE 7.2   COLLAGE BY MICHELE PINARD, *WHO AM I?*
(IT SHOULD BE NOTED THAT THIS IS A RE-CONSTITUTED VERSION OF THE COLLAGE TO HELP
TO SHOW WHAT TRANSPIRED AFTERWARDS; SEE BELOW.)

(Continued)

worlds all my life. Education has been the vehicle separating my family from the
farming life of my ancestors.

The images of the Asian tree, African acacia, and the sticks on top of the little
African girl's head all remind me of the ties I have to the land. I still have a physical
scar on one of my ankles from a time I was challenged to carry a heavy load of firewood by a Kenyan woman. When I dropped the load, it scraped my ankle, forever
reminding me of how hard the average female there works to acquire sustenance for
the family. The idea of the bubble bath I find to be absolutely ludicrous. The cande-
labra suggests the amount of leisure that I have compared with people in most of
the world, although I honestly don't feel like I have time for self-indulgence of that
sort. Finally, the dominant image of a young woman with binoculars implies gathering information from the world to share with others, something teachers do. The
child's hand placed on 'my' back represents the duty I feel to press points of social
justice and equity with those who, like me, do indeed have privilege.

Two other images in the collage require explanation: the hats and the flags. Hats
have a purpose: to shield our eyes from the harsh realities of the sun, which can
damage our eyes. The sun, however, can painfully illuminate realities in the shadows
of life; the sun can also toughen or sicken our skin, as can the truth. The young
lady's hat is custom fit to her lifestyle. The baseball cap symbolically portrays how

her eyes are protected while she concentrates on a leisurely activity. The straw hat implies the opposite: providing shade while the oppressed child works. The ill-fitting hat suggests that the burdens this young girl carries are too large for her innocent position in life. Behind the firewood collector is a planting girl. Our view of her is almost completely recessed. She appears absorbed beneath the hat. The infant child is not benefiting much from the hat, either. She remains exposed to the weather's elements in all her nakedness.

The flags are symbols of national pride, developed and imbued with subtle messages that supposedly equate with the nations' histories or values. When we see a chain of flags, we may think of an organization that promotes global unity – the United Nations, for instance. The collective is supposed to take responsibility for problems that affect all. I fractured the unity by not framing the entire picture with flags and by disconnecting them at points along the perimeter to show that the approach to reconciling these two realities is disjointed. I also extracted the flag of Israel and placed it off-center, along the divide between the Adirondack and African sections of the collage. I did this because I believe it is one of the central problems that the US does not know how to address, although it is so obviously one of the largest driving issues behind world violence. It is obscured, most likely, from all but the most discerning individual's view.

I have been very disturbed … about the war in Iraq. At the time it started in 2003, I was attending the School for International Training (SIT). World Learning, the school's umbrella organization, has as its mission promoting world peace through intercultural understanding. I had enrolled after becoming fed up with what I thought was an inconsequential career. I had been teaching in public schools for 14 years and I did not think I was making much of a difference in life. My daughters were nearing college age and I felt it was time to do something significant with my life, before it was too late. Discussions about the merits of going to war were muted by outrage against going to war on the SIT campus and very informed individuals accurately predicted that the motivations were trumped while the consequences would be dire. I learned there that teachers can and should be agents of social change. Although I am now working toward effecting this change, I suspect the tension I feel about my effectiveness, given the huge challenges, is imparted by the arrangement of images in the collage. (Pinard, 2007)

For the final course submission, Michele decided to re-visit her collage exercise as follows:

Thinking back to the various exercises we did, I realized that a pivotal exercise was the collage-making workshop. I literally felt all thumbs and wondered whether I could allow ideas to emerge as instructed. This required an act of self-trust, as well as trust in the medium. When I read what peers wrote on their 'sticky' messages,

(Continued)

FIGURE 7.3   COLLAGE BY MICHELE PINARD, *HOPEFUL*

(Continued)

I found that the two themes that had spoken through me also resonated consistently in the minds of those who viewed my 'work'.

These ideas were explored in Barone and Eisner's (1997) article. Distinguishing 'art' from 'science', they have outlined seven criteria that should be integral to arts-based educational inquiry, including the ability to create a virtual reality, leave ambiguity, use 'thick, contextual "language"', promote empathy, and create a new vision that draws the audience in, thereby provoking new ways of looking at situations. Well-done collage does draw the viewer in, leave room for interpretation, show imagery that is 'rich' in color and symbolism, cause the viewer to either negatively or positively identify with the images, and skew how people are used to viewing ordinary images when they are in a more standard context.

For the final project, I decided to take my collage and 'play' with it – massage the contents a bit more, as I expect we should do with any field text material. I turned it upside down and looked at the images from a different perspective. I decided to attempt something I had seen an art class do several years ago, called a 'pleating technique'. I cut duplicates of the original collage into one-inch strips. Then I glued them in an alternate pattern: the first strip right side-up, the second upside down. I continued with the 22 strips, separating them into two 8.5' × 11' pages. Then, with the aid of a local Office Max employee, we scanned the image into Photoshop, connected them, and printed a poster. I folded the seams between the strips into an accordion fashion and decided to literally 'frame' the 3-D images to represent symbolically the question I was asking myself while I was creating

FIGURE 7.4   COLLAGE BY MICHELE PINARD, *PESSIMISTIC*

the original collage: 'How can I best serve those whose lives are so in contrast to mine?'

Interestingly, during the process of putting together the final work, I happened to invert the entire accordion. Besides being able to view the overall collage from two different directions, I noticed that the result was that I viewed the issues represented in the original with a very different viewpoint. Whereas the original drew my eye down to the right hand corner where the African child sat with an empty bowl (perhaps eliciting the 'despair' comments from peers), when viewed the other way, the picture led my eye upwards. I felt more hopeful viewing the image from that perspective. Experiencing this made me think of the 'pentimento' (Hellman, 1973), where an artist changes her mind and 'repents', or paints over the original way she conceived the thought to reflect a fresher thought. I also felt that I had shifted the overall dominance from a 'Northern Hemisphere' viewpoint to a 'Southern' one and had given the African child more 'voice'. As opposed to being seated waiting for the stereotypical hand-out, it seemed the child's needs were more dominant than the woman's leisurely pursuits. Thinking about this was an exhilarating moment for me.

I suspect quantitative researchers or qualitative writers also experience epiphanies when they reach a fresh conclusion or, after having re-examined the field text material posit differently than they originally had. Therein lies the excitement in doing research and the necessity for explaining one's intentions, processes, and biases. For me, the journey has been full of such moments. I feel I'm just beginning to explore this path. (Pinard, 2007)

Michele's focused reflection using collage, and subsequent revisiting and experimenting with her visual image helped her to articulate memories and feelings and provided her with ways to move her research proposal further.

COLLAGE AS ELICITATION

The use of pictures, photographs and/or art to elicit conversation and/or writing has been used extensively in education, in art therapy, and research for a long time. In education in particular, other art forms such as poetry, music and drama have been used as an impetus for further thinking, discussion, and writing. In much the same way, collage can be used in the inquiry process to find the words to express a subjective experience, to initiate a dialogue with participants, or as guided reflection.

Pamela Markus, as mentioned above, is an artist and recent Ph.D. graduate from McGill University. She used collage in her autobiographical thesis entitled *Drawing on experience* (2007) as an elicitation process to articulate her past memories of experiences with art that inform her current art practices as a teacher and an artist. In this example, she was mining her memory for the experiences she had with camp art, both originally as a camper and then for many years as a teacher of camp art at the same summer camp. The process helped her 'find the words for narratives of experience' (p. 98). She describes her process as follows:

The first step was selecting the images. I held the idea of 'camp art' in my mind as I tore images from my magazines. I worked with these images, cutting apart the composite images presented to me in the magazines, and placing them into a personal narrative. In this case I worked on three cards which form a single, unified collage. I attempted to use all of the images that I had torn out, and the cards were complete when the space was filled ...

I translated the images in the collages into words and I listed them: china cups hanging in a row, a concrete disc, framed botanical samples, a glowing candle, leaves under glass, a three-leaf clover, a stone angel, an empty ceramic bowl, a watering can, a bird in motion, and a basket of apples. In this way, the images were then transformed into textual metaphors of experience. The next stage was bringing the words/metaphors to a more conceptual level. ... From the collage and the conceptual interpretation of the images, I began to describe my remembered experience of camp art ... From the narrative fragment, I drew out the words: 'Camp art is accessible; it is nature under glass'. This becomes a rich metaphor for describing the experience of camp art; it is more informative than my attempt to elucidate the experience prior to constructing the collages. ... I opted for images that 'spoke' to me, images that drew me in and fascinated me when I constructed the collages. I relied on this passionate engagement with the image to find the words for the past experiences that inform my present teaching, seeking to unearth emotions and 'see with the heart' as well as with the mind. I create and I learn. (Markus, 2007: 99–103)

FIGURE 7.5   COLLAGE BY PAMELA MARKUS, *NATURE UNDER GLASS*

By using collages to elicit and illuminate the qualities of her experiences with camp art and by juxtaposing these with her formalist experiences in her M.A. in Fine Arts, Pamela realized that

> The art/craft debate had gone on throughout my years in graduate school and I was always torn between the skill and beauty of craft and the challenging nature of fine art; as if it were an either/or situation. When I began to reflect on my own camp art experiences, which were heavily influenced by the 'craft' of arts and crafts, I understood more fully how camp art had enriched and broadened my ideas about art. (p. 60)

Lisa Vaselenak, a recent Ph.D. graduate from the University of Alberta, encouraged the three participants in her study entitled the *The Search for creativity: A visual-narrative inquiry* (2006) to create collages which they then used as part of their ongoing interaction and discussions about life, dreams, memories and creativity in their lives. The collages unlocked distant memories and opened up the depth and peripheries of their discussions. The tangible and often unconscious metaphors depicted in their collages allowed participants to discover important links in their memories and experiences of what it means to be creative, or perceived to be creative, or not. Also, they helped Lisa to find the strands to weave together the threads of these poignant moments into compelling narratives of creativity.

Williams (2000), while working in clinical supervision with nursing students, has used collages a way of eliciting guided reflection. She described how at each session she used collage 'as a starting point for discussion in the supervision setting where reflective questioning by the supervisor is framed around the collage images in order to clarify relationships of the issues presented and the personal meanings and values of these to the supervisee' (p. 273). Not only do the collages initiate discussion and provide focal points for delving more deeply in a relatively unthreatening way, but they also provide tangible 'markers' in the supervision process that can be revisited and reinterpreted over time.

COLLAGE IN CONCEPTUALIZATION

Collage can also be a way of conceptualizing a response to a research question. After a research question has been articulated, a series, or a cluster of collages, are created to respond to the question. The collages are given titles that represent the essence of what is being portrayed. Then, if possible, they are discussed with other researchers working on the same inquiry or with willing colleagues. This helps to bring unarticulated ideas to the surface in much the same way that the reflective approach described above does.

In Chapter 6 on poetic inquiry, it was suggested how clusters of poems can be created around a question or topic to reveal the nuances of a particular experience or phenomenon. The poem clusters act as a way of peeling away and opening up the various facets of the phenomenon in question, allowing a 'walking around' them to get the feelings of the experience. Collage clusters do the opposite. A collage starts from the feeling. Each collage in the cluster reveals a certain intuitive facet of the question/phenomenon that emerges when trying to portray a feeling in response to the research question. Then the collages can be re-examined together. By looking at the colors, shape, content, and composition (Rose, 2001), and finding commonalities across the collages, new conceptualizations can emerge that respond to the question.

For example, during my current, in-progress work with colleagues in a collage inquiry group we have been focusing most recently on 'what it means to be, or feels like to be a woman in academia'. Using 'artcards' or small-scale cardstock the size of sports trading cards, I constructed over several months a series of individual collages that responded to that question. I worked intuitively selecting images and fragments from popular magazines to portray what it feels like to be a woman in academia. When completed, I entitled them *Isolation*, *Invisibility*, and *Inspiration*. The feeling portrayed in each collage came *before* the articulated title. When examined together, the colors varied although all three collages were quite somber, and the content and composition of each were different. What stood out was the centrality of the spherical shape – the floating ball, the lily pads, and the cracked egg – that was in the foreground and dominated each collage. In each it suggested to me that there is a 'breaking away' that occurs for a woman in academia – a breaking away that pushes against invisibility, runs from isolation, and attempts to reach for inspiration.

FIGURE 7.6   COLLAGE BY LYNN BUTLER-KISBER, *ISOLATION*

FIGURE 7.7   COLLAGE BY LYNN BUTLER-KISBER, *INVISIBILITY*

FIGURE 7.8   COLLAGE BY LYNN BUTLER-KISBER, *INSPIRATION*

This is in stark contrast to the prevalent theme that women in academia and in other careers 'push against' the glass ceiling and other patriarchic structures (Buzzanell, 1995). This work has provided me with a new lens for thinking about being a woman in academia that merits further study.

In another phase of the same work, I was trying to portray my evolution over time as a woman in academia. In the cluster of collages below (Figures 7.9, 7.10, 7.11) from left to right I thought I was showing youthfulness dominated by patriarchical structures which are depicted by the prominence of the bottle and cork which is front and at the centre of the collage. The following two collages depict a gradual trend to more freedom shown by the butterfly images and the decreasing size of the bottle. I was trying to show that with age, and the momentum of the women's movement, that my life as an academic became increasingly freer over time. This was my first interpretation of what this cluster represented. It was only after stepping back and sharing with my colleagues that I began to see something else. If I reversed the portrayal and regarded the bottle and cork as representing me and my career, I suddenly saw things differently. Moving from left to right, the first collage shows an imposing embodied self perhaps in pursuit of a more disembodied life in academia represented by the youthful silhouette. Gradually, over time, there is less and less of an embodied self. This suggests that the kind of freedom that academia is encouraged to seek and pursue, is one that mandates a lessening of embodied thinking and feeling.

FIGURE 7.9   COLLAGE BY LYNN BUTLER-KISBER, *ASPIRATION*

FIGURE 7.10   COLLAGE BY LYNN BUTLER-KISBER, *LIMITATION*

FIGURE 7.11   COLLAGE BY LYNN BUTLER-KISBER, *LIBERATION*

Kathleen Vaughn (2005) conceptualized a collage method, a 'fine-arts practice with a postmodern epistemology' by theorizing about collage as a postmodern knowledge system (Brockelman, 2001) and by doing practice-led inquiry through an intuitive, collage-like process that integrated reading, writing, collaging, designing, weaving, and sewing. She has identified through this emergent, embodied process the qualities that are inherent in a collage method. These include creative practice, juxtaposition, interdisciplinarity, a link to daily life, a situated artist/researcher, cultural critique and transformation, open-endedness, multiple, provisional, and interdependent products that reflect and reveal the overall process. Her work underscores the libratory potential of collage inquiry, and provides a very useful way of thinking about art as inquiry, and about inquiry as art from an artist's perspective.

CHALLENGES IN COLLAGE INQUIRY

There are four major challenges that confront researchers conducting collage inquiry. They include: how collage expertise can be developed; when collage should be used in research; how collage inquiry should be evaluated; and how collage work using found images can be carried out ethically.

There is no doubt that collage expertise can be developed by immersing oneself in the medium by reading about, viewing, and practicing the art form. The Internet is replete with sources of collages, and there are copious books on the technical aspects involved in collage (Atkinson, 1996). The opportunities for getting guidance and experience in collage are still quite limited without enrolling in an art program, and some art programs do not even include collage work. For researchers coming to collage rather than the reverse, this limits the number of people who will risk collage, or produces less than desirable work, and as a result, casts aspersions on the gains made to date in arts-informed inquiry. It is a slippery slope. On the one hand, the floodgates can open and 'anything goes', and on the other hand, an elitist form of gate-keeping dominates, repeating the very thinking that postmodernism has tried to overturn. There are collage workshops offered by collagists that can be most helpful, although the participants tend to be other artists rather than researchers exploring art. As well, some of the research conferences, such as the American Educational Research Association, sponsor pre-conference workshops that can be used in this capacity. Some universities are using in-house expertise or hiring outsiders to help researchers expand their artistic repertoires, but for the most part these are scheduled on an ad hoc basis and usually occur at the instigation of a few people and do not become institutionalized practices. Part of this is because these initiatives are added onto already very full schedules and workloads. I believe capacity building would occur in a more systematic, rather than ad hoc manner if ways could be created to integrate the arts into research using existing spaces rather than creating new ones. There is no doubt that collaborative, research partnerships between artists and researchers are a way of building artistic capacity in the 'doing'.

Given the potential of collage to create new understandings and bring unconscious dimensions of experience to the fore, I would advocate that collage inquiry need not be relegated to specific occasions. Rather, the decision is when to use collage as an exploratory/analytical approach, when it should become a public representational form, and when it should be both.

I have discussed elsewhere (Butler-Kisber, 2008) that a concerted effort needs to be directed to integrating how to evaluate visual images, arts-informed work, and more specifically collage in order to judge adequately and justly collage inquiry. Rose (2001) in particular has published an excellent book on visual methodologies which is helpful. Barone and Eisner (1997) provided the first substantial criteria for evaluating arts-informed work (see Chapter 5), and Denzin (2000), Finley (2000), and Richardson (2000) have added to this work. Yet, when it comes to collage, the criteria they have produced tend to be rather generic and not surprisingly, given the historical trajectory of arts-informed research, most often resonate with textual forms of arts-informed inquiry rather than visual ones. Bamford's (2005) criteria for evaluating digital theses provide another helpful addition. She defines value as comprising merit and worth.

> *Merit* is defined as the intrinsic beauty or artistry of the research, while *worth* is defined in a more long-term sense in relation to applicability, usefulness, contribution and desirability of the imaginings formulated as a result of the study … Judgments of merit are bound to characteristics within the research and the research medium itself … worth on the other hand is determined by the context of the research … [and by] … those people with knowledge of the values and context surrounding the study … the notions of 'form' provide a way of determining the value of digitally-based research.

The addition of form(s) to the conversation opens up avenues for possible discussions that relate to non-textual, arts-informed inquiry, particularly when grounded in a postmodern view of form that situates it in the interstices of the boundaries between creator and audience and is 'multilayered, seriated and affective' with 'no set models for effective … forms' (Bamford, 2005).

The conversation around quality and evaluation of collage inquiry needs to continue. The more examples are shared and researchers and artists cross boundaries, the more fruitful the conversation will be.

Finally, the usual ethical issues around voice, reflexivity, and trustworthiness apply to collage inquiry and have been discussed in other chapters. What is unique to the type of collage work described here, one that uses images from popular magazines as a basis for the work, is the issue of copyright. Most information that is available endorses fair use of derivative works, that is, the use of fragments of an original work in a collage. If images are not used commercially for gain or profit, or reproduced in great number, but are used for educational purposes, including work for classes, presentations, and publications in research journals, fair use applies (Rolan, 1996). To date, it appears that no legal cases have occurred around this use of images (Norris, 2008), but perhaps this is because there has been a concentrated focus on derivative work in the music industry, and the resulting copyright issues that have plagued this medium. Increasing interest may be aroused as collage inquiry becomes more prevalent.

There are copyright laws, however, that researchers should know about when doing this kind of inquiry. In the United States, since 1978, a work is automatically copyrighted from the moment it is created, in contrast to pre-1978 when a copyright notice was required initially, and was reviewed periodically to keep the work protected. At the time, it remained copyrighted for 28 years, and could be renewed for another 28. In 1978 the period was extended to 47 years, and in 1998 for another 28 years for a total of 95 years for material created before 1978. Since 1978, however, all work is copyrighted for duration of the creator's life plus 70 years, and since 1989, copyright is automatic and extends for this same period. Works of art in Canada are protected during the life of the artist plus 50 years. Photographs have been covered by these same rules since 1998. Similar laws have been established in other countries.

Some collagists eliminate any copyright issues by using unprotected clip art and/or images from public picture banks which are found readily on the Internet. Others create their own images and/or use found materials. An alternative is to deal with companies that provide licensing for using images. Frequently they charge more modest fees for non-profit work.

This conversation is not over, nor should it be. A useful initiative would be for the large research associations to create guidelines for researchers around these issues. Just as new ethical issues arose in qualitative work when narrative inquiry flourished, in the current infancy, but rapidly increasing collage inquiry, there are sure to be other issues that will arise and need to be addressed.

CONCLUDING REMARKS

In spite of a burgeoning interest in collage inquiry, it still remains fairly isolated and away from the discussions that are taking place around other forms of visual inquiry such as photographic inquiry discussed in the next chapter. The time is ripe for fruitful conversations across fields and perspectives about the array of possibilities for future work and the ways that a helpful and common language for doing these forms of inquiry can be developed.

REFERENCES

Atkinson, J. L. (1996). *A step-by-step guide and showcase.* Gloucester, MA: Rockport.

Bamford, A. (2005). *The art of research: Digital theses in the arts.* Retrieved February 17, 2006, from http://adt.caul.edu.au/etd2005/papers/123Bamford.pdf.

Barone, T., & Eisner, E. W. (1997). Arts-based education research. In R. M. Jaeger (Ed.), *Complementary methods for research in education* (pp. 73–98). Washington, DC: AERA.

Brockelman, T. P. (2001). *The frame and the mirror: On collage and the postmodern.* Evanston, IL: Northwestern University Press.

Burns, D. (2003). Whole systems action research in complex governance settings. Keynote address at the *10th World Congress of Participatory Action Research,* Pretoria, South Africa (September).

Butler-Kisber, L. (2002). Artful portrayals in qualitative inquiry: The road to found poetry and beyond. *The Alberta Journal of Educational Research, XLVIII*(3), 229–239.

Butler-Kisber, L. (2007). Collage as analysis and representation. In J. G. Knowles, T. C. Luciani, A. L. Cole & L. Neilsen (Eds.), *The art of visual inquiry* (pp. 265–281). Halifax, NS: Backalong Books.

Butler-Kisber, L. (2008). Collage as inquiry. In J. G. Knowles & A. L. Cole (Eds.), *Handbook of the arts in qualitative research* (pp. 265–276). Thousand Oaks, CA: Sage.

Butler-Kisber, L., Allnutt, S., Furlini, L., Kronish, N., Markus, P., & Stewart, M. (2005). Collage as inquiry: Sensing doing, and knowing in qualitative research. Paper presented at the *Annual Meeting of the American Educational Research Association*, Montreal, QC (April).

Butler-Kisber, L. & Borgerson, J. (1997). *Alternative representation in qualitative inquiry: A student/instructor retrospective.* Paper presented at the American Educational Research Association Annual Meeting, Chicago. (ERIC Document Retrieval Service No. 420 680).

Buzzanell, P. M. (1995). Reframing the glass ceiling as a socially constructed process: Implications for understanding and change. *Communication Monographs, 62*(4), 327–354.

Davis, D. & Butler-Kisber, L. (1999). Arts-based representation in qualitative research: Collage as a contextualizing strategy. Paper presented at the *Annual Meeting of the American Educational Research Association*, Montreal, QC (April).

Denzin, N. K. (2000). Aesthetics and practices of qualitative inquiry. *Qualitative Inquiry, 6*(2), 256–265.

Denzin, N. K. & Lincoln, Y. S. (2005). Introduction: The discipline and practice of qualitative research. In N. K. Denzin & Y. S. Lincoln (Eds.), *The Sage handbook of qualitative research* (3rd ed.), (pp. 1–32). Thousand Oaks, CA: Sage.

Finley, S. (2000). Arts-based inquiry in QI: Seven years from crisis to guerilla warfare. *Qualitative Inquiry, 6*(2), 281–296.

Hayden, R. (1980). *Mrs. Delany: Her life and flowers.* New York: Amsterdam.

Hellman, L. (1973). *Pentimento: A book of portraits.* London: Little, Brown.

Markus, P. (2007). *Drawing on experience.* Unpublished doctoral dissertation, McGill University, Montreal, QC.

McDermott, M. (2002). Collaging pre-service teacher identity. *Teacher Education Quarterly, 29*(4), 53–67.

McNiff, S. (1998). *Art-based research.* London: Jessica Kingsley.

Mullen, C. A. (1999). Carousel: A metaphor for spinning inquiry in prison and education. In C. T. P. Diamond & C. A. Mullen (Eds.), *The postmodern educator: Arts-based inquiries in teacher development* (pp. 281–309). New York: Peter Lang.

Norris, J. (2008). Collage. In L. M. Given (Ed.), *The Sage encyclopedia of qualitative research methods,* Vol. 1 (pp. 94–97). Thousand Oaks, CA: Sage.

Oshansky, B. (1994). Making writing a work of art: Image-making within the writing process. *Language Arts, 71*(5), 350–356.

Ozawa, S., & Osumi, I. (2002).Trial of collage method to evaluate learning environments including CSCL. *Proceedings of the International Conference on Computers in Education,* Auckland, NZ (December), (pp. 222–226). Washington, DC: IEEE Computer Society.

Parkash, R. (2007). *Collage inquiry exercise.* Unpublished manuscript, McGill University, Montreal, QC.

Pinard, M. (2007). *Collage inquiry exercise.* Unpublished manuscript, McGill University, Montreal, QC.

Pink, S. (2001). *Doing visual ethnography.* London: Sage.

Poggi, C. (1992). *In defiance of painting: Cubism, Futurism and the invention of collage.* New Haven, CT: Yale University Press.

Rainey, L. (1998). Taking dictation: Collage, poetics, pathology, and politics. *Modernism/Modernity,* 5(2), 123–153.

Richardson, L. (2000). Introduction – Assessing alternative modes of qualitative and ethnographic research: How do we judge? Who judges? *Qualitative Inquiry, 6*(2), 251–252.

Robertson, B. (2000). *Why collage?* Retrieved April 5, 2004, from www.collagetown. com/history01.shtml.

Rolan, C. (1996). Fair use: Section 107 of the copyright act. Paper presented at the *National Association of Art Education Conference,* San Francisco, CA (March).

Rose, G. (2001). *Visual methodologies.* London: Sage.

Schwartz, D. (1992). *Wacoma twilight: Generalizations of the farm.* Washington, DC: Smithsonian Institute.

Sturgess, J. (1983). The magazine picture collage: A suitable base for a pre-fieldwork teaching clinic. *Occupational Therapy in Mental Health, 3*(1), 43–53.

Vaselenak, L. (2006). *The search for creativity: A visual-narrative inquiry.* Unpublished doctoral dissertation, University of Alberta, Edmonton, AB.

Vaughn, K. (2005). Pieced together: Collage as an artist's method for interdisciplinary research. *International Journal of Qualitative Methods, 4*(1). Retrieved June 25, 2007, from www.ualberta.ca/-iiqm/backissues/4–1/html/vaughan.htm.

Williams, B. (2000). Collage work as a medium for guided reflection in the clinical supervision relationship. *Nurse Education Today, 20,* 273–278.

8

Photographic Inquiry

Increasingly society has become immersed in a visual world. Photographs have become a prominent way in which life is documented and shared easily and accessibly with user-friendly and diminutive cameras and/or telephones. Life in the 21st century is fast, visual, public, and open to scrutiny in every domain.

> It is misleading to speak of the world as it is, or even of a single world. It makes more sense to think of various versions of the world that individuals may entertain, various characterizations of reality that might be presented in words, pictures, diagrams, logical propositions, or even musical compositions. Each of these symbol systems captures different kinds of information and hence presents different versions of reality. All we have, really, are such versions; only through them do we gain access to what we casually term 'our world'. (Gardner, 1980: 92)

Photographs were used in research by anthropologists before the turn of the 20th century in order to document in detail the ethnographies of the time, for example, in the work of Franz Boas in the Canadian Arctic (Hurworth, 2003). In 1915–1918 and later on, Malinowski and others used photographs to enhance written texts. In the earliest years, still photographs were the prevalent form and then, with the advent of moving pictures, film was used more extensively, ostensibly not only to provide greater detail, but also a 'truer picture' of what transpires in other cultures. Two entire fields of visual anthropology and visual sociology were developed based on the use of images in research. Photographs and film were used as a means for recording and analysis, for elicitation and discovery, for reconstructing dimensions of culture, and for representing ethnographies (El Guindi, 1998: 10). When researchers became more critical of how others are studied, aware of the insidious dimensions of 'photo-colonialism' (Tanjuakio, 2003) in part because of the rapidly expanding field of cultural studies (Harper, 2005), and realized how subjective research really is, there was a growing awareness that visual texts, while powerful and seductive, like all texts, are socially constructed.

> Visual imagery is never innocent; it is always constructed through various practices, technologies and knowledges … a critical approach to visual images is therefore needed: one that thinks about the agency of the image, considers the social practices and effects of its viewing, and reflects on the specificity of that viewing by various audiences. (Rose, 2001: 32)

This chapter examines three specific ways of using photographs and/or film in inquiry: as a means for reflection, elicitation, and representation. It shows, by using an adapted approach for interpreting family photographs created by Richard Chalfen (1998), how a researcher was able to derive a greater understanding of herself as a researcher. It introduces the process of 'photovoice', which uses photographs taken by research participants to record and reflect upon social needs, promote critical dialogue and ultimately reach policy makers (Wang, 1999), and shows how a researcher used an adapted version of this type of participatory action research (Lykes, 2001) to give voice to autistic, adolescent participants in her study. Finally it discusses visual narrative inquiry and how visual narrative episodes (VNE) were created from videotaped data to illustrate the documentation process and resulting teaching/learning events in a teacher–researcher study of an elementary classroom. It suggests ideas for making these visual processes transparent and ways to enhance the work, and deals with ethical issues particular to this type of research.

EVOLUTION OF PHOTOGRAPHIC INQUIRY

From the time of Plato, images were considered just an imitation of reality. The 17th century scientific revolution further denigrated images because it promoted the idea that perceptions realized through the senses were deceptive. With the development of aesthetics that occurred in the mid-18th century, the concept of mediated understanding emerged (Siegesmund, 2008: 940). However, in the early years of visual anthropology and sociology, photographs were used primarily to enhance/illuminate written research texts. Few studies, other than that of Bateson and Mead in their study entitled *Balinese Character* (1942), based on 25,000 pictures taken longitudinally and accompanied with written logs, went beyond superficial interpretations, and thus more closely resembled photographic journalism than research (Becker, 1974). There was a distinct distrust in research circles of how viably photographs and films could be incorporated into research, given the subjective nature of the photographic process. On the other hand, there was a naïve and realist view that photographs and films represented a 'truthful' rendition of what was portrayed. This was countered by the mounting feminist and postmodern critiques of research that emerged in the 1970s, along with the work of phenomenologists such as Heidegger and Merleau-Ponty. These were responsible for the interpretive and narrative turns in inquiry and gave rise to the 'reflective and self-identifying orientations' (Berg, 2008: 935) and the notions of 'mediated understanding and multiple interpretations' (Siegesmund, 2008: 940) in qualitative research. There has been since the late 1980s an increasing interest in the use of visual images in research because of its power to evoke emotional, embodied responses and mediate different understandings depending on its form. The rapid rise of technological refinements and digital possibilities in the last 20 years have made the use of photographs and film swift, easy, and accessible. Photography in particular has become an important dimension of collaborative and participatory action research initiatives because cameras can be used easily and effectively by participants of any age and from any culture, including young children, engaging them directly in the focus and process of the research and thereby making it a much more reciprocal and collaborative endeavor (Prosser & Burke, 2008). The use of visual images in research has taken on an increasingly important role in the creation of field texts, in analytic processes, and in representational forms. Photographs and films/videotapes can be easily transmitted, reproduced, analyzed and distributed electronically, and the costs continue to diminish as the technology flourishes. Photographic inquiry has come of age, and the prospects for the future are boundless.

GENERAL VIEWING OF PHOTOGRAPHIC IMAGES

Part of the reason that the use of photographic inquiry has increased so substantially in recent years is because researchers are committed to reflexivity and want to determine how 'subjective awareness and experience play a role in the production of knowledge' (Berg, 2008: 937). Collier (2001) suggests that when photographs (still or film) are examined as field texts in what he calls a 'direct analysis' (p. 39), the first stage is to examine the corpus of pictures as a whole while making note of initial impressions and feelings. This allows the 'cultural circumstances to speak … in their own terms' (p. 40). Then an inventory of all the images is made using categories that reflect the focus of the study. This is followed by a structured analysis that sifts through the pictures in response to specific questions to help fine-tune initial descriptions and discoveries (p. 43). Finally there is a 'search for meaning' based on the entire visual record so that 'details from the structured analysis can be placed in a context that defines their significance' (p. 39). This process mirrors the thematic forms of inquiry and categorizing approaches (Maxwell & Miller, 2008) discussed earlier in Chapters 3 and 4.

Collier suggests that a more productive form of analysis is what he calls 'indirect analysis', which results from photo elicitation, where participants give their responses to and understandings of the images, discussed in more detail below, and in some instances take the photos themselves. 'The richest returns from photo elicitation often have little connection to the details of the images, which may only serve to release vivid memories, feelings, insight, thoughts and memories' (p. 46). This process gives rise to stories and further dialogue that deepens the understanding of insider or emic perspectives. It emphasizes the contiguous and contextual dimensions of experience and understanding, or a connecting orientation (Maxwell & Miller, 2008) to inquiry.

Collier (2001: 47–52) points out some helpful pragmatic aspects of photographic inquiry. There must be a clear identification of all images, including a dating system, which indicates their relationship to each other and how they are connected to the annotated descriptions. This facilitates comparisons and juxtapositions which are so important in the analysis. Comparative analysis is done more easily with stills because of the controllable viewing pace, the ability to easily rearrange photographs for different purposes, and the more active involvement this engenders. Film, on the other hand, provides contextual information via sound and permits an extensive analysis of nonverbal behaviours depicted in the images. It can be slowed down and frame-frozen to be treated more like still photographs when necessary.

In summary, and importantly, Rose (2001: 32) reminds researchers that:

- visual imagery is never innocent: it is always constructed through various practices, technologies and knowledges.
- a critical approach to visual images is therefore needed: one that thinks about the agency of the image, considers the social practices and effects of its viewing, and reflects on the specificity of that viewing by various audiences.
- the meanings of an image, or set of images, are made at three sites: technological, compositional, and social.
- theoretical debates about how to interpret images can be understood as debates over which of these sites and modalities is most important for understanding an image.
- these debates affect the methodology that is most appropriately brought to bear on particular images.

USING PHOTOGRAPHS FOR REFLECTION

In similar ways as those presented in Chapter 7 on collage inquiry, photographs can be used as an approach for reflection in the research process. Chalfen (1998) has developed a helpful process for a critical examination of snapshots in what he refers to as the 'home mode of visual communication' (p. 215). He suggests that researchers have overlooked the widespread practice of documenting personal images and what can be learned from this form of communication. With the burgeoning and versatile technology available in palm-size digital cameras, cell phones that document visual images, and the more recent and immensely popular use of Facebook, a vast array of images is pushing the boundaries of production, communication and distribution and, hopefully, critical analysis. He suggests that the snapshot is a 'symbolic form embedded in a communication process' which includes the making, interpreting, and the sharing of these images, and that much can be learned about people as social and cultural beings by systematically reflecting on how snapshots are socially constructed.

Chalfen has created a 25-cell grid to be used as a heuristic tool to carefully examine snapshots and elicit patterns of behavior (both typical and atypical) contained therein that are not readily apparent. On one axis of the grid are: participants (all those involved in any aspect of the 'event'), settings (the context of all aspects), topics (the content of the event), message form (the kind of photograph it is), and code (the style and conventions of the photograph). On the other axis are the 'planning events' in preparation for the snapshot, 'on camera shooting' and what takes place, 'behind camera shooting' and what takes place, 'editing events' that transform or rearrange the image, and 'exhibition events' or ways of sharing the photograph (p. 217). With this kind of careful scrutiny, or close reading of the images, the exercise reveals an explanation for how experience is organized in and of itself as well as for 're-play', a way of inquiring about 'our symbolic environment' and the way we make meaning of our lives (p. 230).

Chalfen's approach can be used effectively as a reflective tool if photographing everyday experiences, rather than home or family photography, is part of one's work. For example, one kindergarten teacher who takes photographs as a way of documenting her classroom used an adaptation of Chalfen's grid to look at and reflect on the nature of her photos. She regularly takes portrait-type photographs of her students at the beginning and end of the year and ongoing photographs of the children in their everyday activities, as well as during special events. As a result of the process, she became poignantly aware of things she had not noticed before. Some children were photographed much more frequently that others, in groups and/or individually, particularly one girl. She realized she was favoring some children and excluding others and decided to set up a system to make sure she was more inclusive in both her observations, the prelude to many of her pictures, and the photographs themselves. In photographs of larger groups (more than three in a group), she had many more pictures of the boys than the girls. She began to study whether the size of the groups reflected male and female preferences, or whether something else was at work. These two issues would not have attracted her attention if she had not given this kind of reflective scrutiny to her classroom photographs.

USING PHOTOGRAPHS FOR ELICITATION

The term 'photovoice' emerged in the mid-1990s and has strong links to social action and the field of engaged journalism. As mentioned above, this process uses photographs, often taken by participants, to elicit responses and local understandings of particular phenomena with a view to facilitating social change at both the grassroots and policy-making levels. It should be re-emphasized here that the term 'elicitation' is not being used in the sense of simply drawing out or evoking a response to the image, but rather to engender collaborative reflection to find out how the participants 'use the content of the images as vessels in which to invest meanings and through which to produce and represent their knowledge, self-identities, experiences and emotions' (Rose, 2001: 68).

The earliest instances of photovoice were the posters and documents that criticized child labor of the 1880s (Emme, 2008: 622). Now the success of this approach, coupled with the vast technological advances, has propelled it into many fields of inquiry. It has become a very popular and viable approach to visual inquiry.

There are photovoice organizations in both England and the United States; the former consists of a blend of journalism and ethnographic methods directed to the support of social justice projects, and the latter identified most strongly 'with public health research and community-generated inquiry' (Emme, 2008: 624). The name frequently associated with photovoice is that of Caroline Wang. She has articulated a specific elicitation process for photovoice that is being used or adapted in many places around the world. This includes working alongside participants to create a focus for a series of photographs, sending the participants out into the community to take the photographs, facilitating a group discussion and critical dialogue about the pictures, selecting the photographs for more discussion, facilitating further contextualizing through storytelling, identifying themes, and documenting the stories. This process is embedded in a monitoring structure that makes sure the participants are not deflected from the work due to a lack of support or resources, and often has an overall plan that is worked out with the participants for how to disseminate the findings, reach policy makers and influence policy decisions (Wang, Yi, Tao, & Carovano, 1998: 80–82). These authors contend that the potential advantages to all participants are: 'the contribution to effective … change', and the improvement of status, the 'exchange of new ideas', improvement in the quality of life, and the 'increased credibility by virtue of affiliation and collaboration' (p. 82). They do caution, however, that the research tends to be costly, especially in time. Also, they suggest that the amount of involvement may be unrealistic for certain participants, the participation may be limited for some because of impingements on and/or tensions with other roles in their communities, and that the inquiry may attract criticism for a seeming lack of rigor. Furthermore, the work can have unintended consequences that put participants at risk due to the 'visual evidence' depicted in photographs, and the accessible and powerful messages they portray. Ample advance work on ethics and the power of photographs can help to minimize these drawbacks (pp. 83–84).

Lykes (2001) used photovoice, along with drawing, dramatization, and storytelling for the basis of a study she conducted in Guatemala with a group of women from Chajul following 36 years of living in a war-torn zone and in constant poverty. She describes powerfully how

> photovoice offers an important alternative both at the level of the photograph and, as importantly, at the level of storytelling and analysis. The process of taking pictures within one's local community became an opportunity to develop individual and collective stories that had heretofore been silenced or spoken only privately … The photograph creates its own story and became a site for wider participatory storytelling and analysis … The fixed image serves as a catalyst for an ever-widening discussion of the differing realities [and these] have contributed to our developing a shared understanding of some of the multiple causes of 'the violence' and its local effects while contributing to healing and recovery processes within the group and beyond. (p. 369)

In a pilot study, using an adapted version of photovoice (Todd & Reid, 2004), Terri Todd, a recent Ph.D. graduate from McGill University, was able to give voice to a group of nonverbal, autistic adolescents. They were the participants in her study that focused on the kinds of instructional strategies that promote sustained engagement in physical activities and encourage self-determined behaviors for individuals with severe developmental challenges. The lack of voice among her participants had an emotional component for her given that her grown son was also autistic, but it also limited finding ways of improving programs and schools for them. She decided to take pictures of her participants during the beginning, middle and end of their exercise sessions and then to have them respond to them as 'happy', 'anxious', or 'neutral', using pictograms depicting each of these three emotions. Always sensitive to images that might compromise her participants, she edited out certain pictures. She discovered, to her delight, that her participants could 'tell' her in a concrete way how they felt about each session, and over time she could see that the degree of their engagement was corroborated by their responses. Terri's elicitation approach shows how images can mediate communication with nonverbal participants and draw out emotional and social understandings that otherwise would not be apparent. It suggests a creative way of thinking about photographic inquiry and opens the door to other possibilities.

Several years ago, Michael Whatling, Ph.D. used an adapted version of photovoice for a qualitative inquiry exercise he was doing for a course (Butler-Kisber, 2005). In a school where he was working he gave disposable cameras to three male, grade-four students, Adam, Evan, and Lawrie (pseudonyms), instructing them to walk around the school and take pictures of whatever they thought was important in this context. When the pictures had been developed, he interviewed them asking them to explain why they had chosen to take their particular photographs. The photographs provided a focus for the discussion and helped them to articulate the choices they had made. They also gave Michael directions for probing the discussion. Interestingly, the three boys all chose very different things to photograph. Adam had pictures of the lunchroom, a friend, and the playground. He spoke a lot about the interpersonal and social aspects of school. Evan had pictures of children at play at recess, of several teachers, and of himself thumbing through a book in his classroom. He valued and enjoyed the free play that occurs during recess and spoke about how classroom time often seemed long. However, he knew that both teacher guidance and the work were necessary for preparing himself for the future. Lawrie's photographs focused on some of the traditions and means for self-expression in the school, pictures of the founding 'fathers', the library, and a place in the gymnasium where annually a student performance took place. Michael made a poster of each of the children's photographs and superimposed excerpts from the interviews on them. In his presentation with his peers in the course, he concluded that Adam was most interested in the social and relational dimensions of school. Evan loved the freedom of play, but was willing to endure some of the less engaging dimensions of learning in the interest of preparing himself for the future. Lawrie on the other hand, reveled in school tradition, and the spaces that fostered self-expression.

In a small-group discussion following Michael's presentation the conversation was engaged and lively. It was poignantly clear how the photographs not only opened up avenues for discussion in the interviews that unlikely would have emerged otherwise, but also helped to make the interviews very concrete. Colleagues remarked on how much deeper the interviews seemed to go because of the photographs, and they were awed at the subtleties about schooling that these young boys were able to express. The visuals in the presentation also helped to advance the discussion in ways that would have not occurred if Michael had just reported narratively. In fact, one colleague was able to see something very different when she considered the posters in juxtaposition. She suggested that Lawrie's photographs seemed to focus on the past, Adam's on the present, and Evan's on the future. This opened up new avenues for Michael to pursue, and underscored the revisiting opportunities that photographic/visual materials provide for deepening the analysis.

Futhermore, Prosser and Burke (2008) note several other important advantages of using photographs for elicitation, rather than the more traditional interview format. First, it involves a basic paradigm shift that situates the participants as inquirers in the process as 'researchers with' instead of being simply respondents. The focus on pictures, rather than on each other, creates a 'neutral third party' (p. 410) that negates the need for eye contact and, as a result, makes the atmosphere more relaxed. Finally, in initiatives such as photovoice, where the participants use and direct the cameras and participate collaboratively in the inquiry process, it becomes a creative, engaging and empowering enterprise with much potential for enacting change.

VISUAL NARRATIVES WITH PHOTOGRAPHS AND FILM

Visual narratives are not a new concept. For years photographic journalists have predicated much of their work on producing visual 'stories' accompanied by varying lengths of written text (Becker, 1974) in which the visual images predominate. As mentioned above, visual images have also been used extensively in many fields of research to enhance written narratives. More recently, Bach (2007) has described how she conducted a visual narrative inquiry using the basic tenets of narrative inquiry outlined by Clandinin and Connolly (2000), discussed earlier in Chapter 5. She incorporated visuality, or that 'network of cultural meanings generated from various discourses that shape social practices of vision' (Walker, 2005: 24) to add 'layers of meaning to stories lived and told' (Bach, 2007: 283).

Bach's process included starting with a query or 'puzzlement' (p. 284) and working alongside her participants while they engaged in what she calls four 'camera works' and research conversations, while always attending to the important relational aspects of inquiry. Their collaborative activity began with an autobiographical moment during which time both she and the participants brought together personal photographs and discussed them autobiographically. After spending time discussing technical aspects of photography and ethical implications of visual images, the participants took charge of their cameras and collected photographs that were duplicated so that Bach had a complete compilation of these visual field texts for ongoing reflection. The four camera works consisted of 'creating projective photographs', 'composing self-portraits', 'collecting culture', and 'looking at family albums as pictorial communications' (Bach, 2008: 939).

As part of her search for the recurring rhythms and themes in the field texts, she constructed a set of three columns entitled 'agreed upon image', 'participant story', and 'story of researcher and reader of theories'. This display gave her an overview of her field texts, and allowed her to revisit further with her participants and incorporate their ideas and responses. Extensive conversations and revisiting with her participants allowed her ultimately to weave together, with sensitivity and attention to 'othering' (p. 290), the visual narratives.

Pauline Mesher (2006), a recent Ph.D. graduate from McGill University, used videotaped film from her teacher-researcher study in an early childhood classroom to create VNEs about the children's learning. A former, veteran principal, she decided to return to a classroom of her own for a year so that she could do an inquiry on the important role of documentation for enhancing teacher reflection and the resulting teaching and learning. She decided from the outset to complement her observational and reflective notes with ongoing videotaping to ease the double job of simultaneous teaching and researching, to permit very concrete revisiting of what transpired, and to construct richer field texts. Initially, she had no intention to use the film for other purposes, but the richness of what was portrayed changed her mind. After obtaining additional consent from the parents, and submitting and obtaining approval for an addendum sent to the research ethics board, she conducted a visual narrative (connecting) analysis of the videotapes with a focus on individual student learning. She viewed again all the videotapes in their entirety, and realized how student-teacher conferencing served as 'a pivotal point from which to follow what happened to a particular child in class' (p. 115). She followed 'strands of activity' related to a conference and then 'put them together in a series of clusters that began to suggest how these activities were related' (p. 115). Her use of the computer program Atlas.ti facilitated the work with the videotaped material and the PyroPro video-editing program was used to weave together the VNEs that she ultimately constructed for three particular children. The choice of these children was predicated on the quality and specificity of the videotape segments and the variation in the gender, language proficiency (many children in her class were working in a second or third language), and 'story' of learning that took place that included student reflection on the learning.

She built a storyboard for each of the episodes that consisted of 'communicating a learning dilemma, discussing a learning dilemma, scaffolding a learning dilemma, and subsequent student reflections' (p. 122) and pieced the visual segments together and copied them onto individual DVDs. Pauline explains how she was very attentive to ethical dimensions in using visual images, about remaining as close as possible to the lived experience, and avoiding sensationalizing the VNEs, or compromising the children in any way. She did not adjust the audio even when regular classroom noise muffled some of the conversation. She preferred to allow the viewer to hear her classroom as it was, and inserted a script of the inaudible phrases and sentences onto the film, ones that she could hear when listening intently several times to the videotape but could not be heard on the film. Finally, she constructed short written pieces about each child to contextualize the episode and include her reflective voice.

The resulting VNEs are poignant and compelling. They not only add a vivid dimension to Pauline's thesis, but also they open a window onto the sights and sounds of life in this particular classroom that could not be injected into the written text no matter how prosaic. Because the option of an electronic thesis was not available, a DVD accompanied the work. However, with the advent of digital theses in many universities, and the huge increase in electronic journals, incorporating film into written text is now a reality (Bourassa, 2008; Boyle, 2008), and stretches the imagination for future possibilities.

ETHICAL ISSUES IN VISUAL INQUIRY

The ethical issues that confront researchers working in the area of photographic inquiry include the general ethical issues confronting all researchers discussed in previous chapters. Photographs and films, however, because they are so graphic, and yet have no defined meaning, pose increased vulnerability and intrusion on privacy, can cause embarrassment or cast a participant in a false light, and increase the possibility of appropriation (Gross, Katz, & Ruby, 1988). These dimensions are heightened even further when working with children, or any other vulnerable population. Furthermore, digital technologies increase exponentially the public nature of visual images and their potential exposure to wide and diverse audiences.

The basic tenets of ethical practices in research emanating originally from the Nuremberg Code (see Wikipedia: http://en.wikipedia.org/wiki/Nuremberg_Code) are to respect participants and their autonomy, to do no harm, to maximize the benefits of research, and ensure that there is a fair distribution of the benefits and burdens of research. Nuanced understandings of what these mean in terms of visual inquiry require continuing dialogue and the inclusion and sharing of ethical issues as they are confronted in the work. There are ongoing and important conversations about the ethics involving visual inquiry across disciplinary borders, and technological communication has increased the possibility of convergence and new insights as a result (Papademas, 2004). Still

> [e]thical issues are contextualized, institutionally embedded, organizationally ruled and compounded by postmodern realities that pose paradoxes in the changing visual culture. Negotiating complex social relationships is necessary in order to do ethical visual research that involves the making and using of images, the analysis of their meanings, and the rights and responsibilities associated with the ethics concept. (p. 122)

There is more work to be done.

CONCLUDING REMARKS

Digital technologies have more than advanced the possibilities for using photographs and film in research, they have revolutionized society. Pictures, both still and moving, are taken regularly of the most mundane and spectacular events and shared publicly, immediately, and sometimes repeatedly. The research world has not yet caught up to the world of popular culture, and has lots to learn in terms of inquiry possibilities, but also lots to avoid. The future for photographic inquiry holds promise, but needs caution.

REFERENCES

Bach, H. (2007). Composing a visual narrative. In D. J. Clandinin (Ed.), *Handbook of narrative inquiry* (pp. 280–307). Thousand Oaks, CA: Sage.

Bach, H. (2008). Visual narrative inquiry. In L. M. Givens (Ed.), *The Sage encyclopedia of qualitative research methods*, Vol. 2 (pp. 938–940). Thousand Oaks, CA: Sage.

Bateson, G., & Mead, M. (1942). *Balinese character: A photographic analysis*. New York: New York Academy of Sciences.

Becker, H. S. (1974). Photography and sociology. *Studies in the Anthropology of Visual Communication, 1,* 3–26.

Berg, B. L. (2008). Visual ethnography. In L. M. Given (Ed.), *The Sage encyclopedia of qualitative research methods,* Vol. 2 (pp. 934–938). Thousand Oaks, CA: Sage.

Bourassa, N. (2008). The classroom as studio: The studio as classroom. Education and the arts: blurring boundaries and creating spaces, *LEARNing Landscapes, 1*(3), 115–123.

Boyle, D. (2008). Free yourself from the role. *LEARNing Landscapes, 1*(2), 45–48.

Butler-Kisber, L. (2005). The potential of artful analysis in qualitative inquiry. In F. Bodone (Ed.), *What difference does research make and for whom?* (pp. 203–215). New York: Peter Lang.

Chalfen, R. (1998). Interpreting family photography as pictorial communication. In J. Prosser (Ed.), *Image-based research* (3rd ed.), (pp. 747–762). London: Falmer.

Clandinin, D. J., & Connolly, F. M. (2000). *Narrative inquiry: Experience and story in qualitative research.* San Francisco: Jossey-Bass.

Collier, M. (2001). Approaches to analysis in visual anthropology. In T. van Leeuwen & C. Jewitt (Eds.), *Handbook of visual analysis* (pp. 35–60). London: Sage.

El Guindi, F. (1998). From pictorializing to visual anthropology. In H. R. Bernard (Ed.), *Handbook of methods in cultural anthropology* (pp. 459–511). Walnut Creek, CA: AltaMira Press.

Emme, M. J. (2008). Photonovella and photovoice. In L. M. Givens (Ed.), *The Sage encyclopedia of qualitative research methods*, Vol. 2 (pp. 622–624). Thousand Oaks, CA: Sage.

Gardner, H. (1980). Gifted world makers. *Psychology Today*, September, 92–94.

Gross, L., Katz, J. S., & Ruby, J. (1988). Introduction: A moral pause. In L. Gross, J. S. Katz, & J. Ruby (Eds.), *Image ethics: The moral rights of subjects in photographs, film and television* (pp. 1–34). New York: Oxford University Press.

Harper, D. (2005). What's new visually? In N. K. Denzin & Y. S. Lincoln (Eds.), *The Sage handbook of qualitative research* (3rd ed.), (pp. 747–762). Thousand Oaks, CA: Sage.

Hurworth, R. (2003). Photo-interviewing for research. *Social Research Update, 40.* Retrieved January 14, 2004, from www.soc.surrey.ac.uk/srusru40.pdf.

Lykes, M. (2001). Creative arts and photography in participatory action research in Guatemala. In P. Reason & H. Bradbury (Eds.), *Handbook of action research: Participatory inquiry and practice* (pp. 363–371). Thousand Oaks, CA: Sage.

Maxwell, J., & Miller, B. (2008). Categorizing and connecting strategies in qualitative data analysis. In P. Leavy & S. Hesse-Biber (Eds.), *Handbook of emergent methods* (pp. 461–477). New York: Guilford.

Mesher, P. (2006). *Documentation in an elementary classroom: A teacher-researcher study.* Unpublished doctoral dissertation, McGill University, Montreal, QC.

Papademas, D. (2004). Editor's introduction: Ethics in visual research. *Visual Studies, 19*(2), 122–125.

Prosser, J., & Burke, C. (2008). Image-based research. In J. G. Knowles & A. L. Cole (Eds.), *Handbook of the arts in qualitative research* (pp. 407–419). Thousand Oaks, CA: Sage.

Rose, G. (2001). *Visual methodologies: An introduction to the interpretation of visual materials.* Thousand Oaks, CA: Sage.

Siegesmund, R. (2008). Visual research. In L. M. Given (Ed.), *The Sage encyclopedia of qualitative research methods*, Vol. 2 (pp. 940–943). Thousand Oaks, CA: Sage.

Tanjuakio, J. (2003). Anthropological photography: The West looking at the rest. Retrieved November 25, 2008, from www.tanjuakio.com/joyce/ccit/anthropology_and_photography.htm.

Todd, T., & Reid, G. (2004). Understanding enjoyment and engagement in physical activity for adolescents with ASD. Paper presented at the *Bi-annual Conference of the North American Federation of Adapted Physical Activity*, Thunder Bay, ON (October).

Walker, S. (2005). Artmaking in an age of visual culture: Vision and visuality. *Visual Arts Research*, 59, 23–37.

Wang, C. C. (1999). PhotoVOICE: A participatory action research strategy applied to women's health. *Journal of Women's Health*, *8*(2), 185–192.

Wang, C. C., Yi, W. K., Tao, Z. W., & Carovano, K. (1998). Photovoice as a participatory health promotion strategy. *Health Promotion International*, *13*(1), 75–86.

9

Performative Inquiry

MacLeod (1987), cited in Norris (2000: 40), has suggested that meaning is constructed via word, number, image, gesture and sound and that drama integrates all five. It is perhaps not surprising, therefore, given our multimedia world and search for more holistic modes of research, that there has been an increasing interest in performative inquiry.

> Performative inquiry (Fels & McGiven, 2002) is the exploration of a topic or issue through performance (p. 27). It 'opens spaces of intertextual play within which social responsibility and individual and communal response may be investigated (p. 30), … provides a momentary entrance into 'other' worlds embodied in play and reflection' (p. 32), and 'is a research methodology that recognizes and honours the absences, journey-landscapes, and space–moments of learning realized through performance'. (Fels, 1999: 30)

Current thinking is that performative inquiry counteracts the criticism that representation neglects oppression, injustice, and silenced stories, for it is able to exploit the integrative aspects of meaning, and permit the engagement, accessibility, and participatory dimensions that drama or performance elicits (Denzin, 2005; Jones, 2006). Mienczakowski (1995) has shown the emancipatory potential in performative ethnography in the health sciences, and Saldana's (2005) collection of performance works suggests how ethnodramas can 'enact a politics of resistance and possibility by giving voice to the previously silenced' (Denzin & Lincoln, 2005: x). Performances such as readers theatre (Donmoyer & Yennie-Donmoyer, 1995), and other similar forms which transform data into a script that is then read aloud to an audience often using the participants as 'actors' and/or involving the audience, have become frequent at large research conferences and shown the evocative and pedagogical potential of performative inquiry. What is missing in many of these compelling accounts is a clear and transparent explanation of the process. While all texts might be considered a form of performance, this chapter suggests that script preparation is in itself a form of inquiry and can be used by researchers to interrogate data in different and often revealing ways, or to create a context for focus group interviews, or other forms of 'validatory previews' (Mienczakowski, Smith & Morgan, 2002) and/or as a representational format that engages, enlightens and evokes participation and response. This chapter shares with examples how readers theatre 'playlets' can be created using short narratives or portions of narratives embedded in the data as an analytic process, as an illustrative vignette within a research report, or as a performative series. Finally, there is a discussion about challenges that performative inquirers face and how to help ensure quality products.

HISTORY OF PERFORMATIVE INQUIRY

If we are 'homo performans' and not just homo sapiens as Turner (1982) has suggested, if narrative is the human enterprise (Bruner, 2008), and we make meaning of our lives through the presentation of ourselves in daily activity (Goffman, 1959), then perhaps performance is an embodied, narrative way of understanding in the third dimension. Certainly, performance is usually thought of as some kind of presentation before an audience, but the word 'performative', according to Bhabba (1994) refers to 'action that incessantly insinuates, interrogates, and antagonizes powerful master discourses' (p. 32). It is this call to action that takes performative inquiry beyond the realm of mimesis (imitation of experience), or even poesis (something beyond appearance), to kinesis (reflection and meaning that evokes intervention) (Madison, 2005: 170).

Performative inquiry most aptly describes the current, burgeoning use of performance/dramatization as a mode of inquiry that addresses social issues with goals of change. This is not a new idea. For centuries, drama/theatre has opened up spaces for understanding, critique and social action. For example, the early Greeks used theatre for policy development, Shakespeare's work dealt with social, moral and political issues, and the writers of the French Romantic Period used their work educationally to put lay people in touch with new ideas about democracy (Nisker, 2008: 614). One of the most famous political activists of the 20th century, Augusto Boal, a theatre director, built on the work of Bertolt Brecht and Paulo Freire, and developed 'theatre of the oppressed' (Boal, 1979) to involve impoverished people of Brazil in performances that transformed their oppressive realities into awareness and action. Brecht's contribution to Boal's work was the idea that an audience should be engaged intellectually and not just emotionally, and Freire's was the need for a critical stance to understand and resist oppression. Since the 1960s, Boal's work has had a huge impact on community theatre in Europe and North America.

That drama/theatre intersected with research is attributed to the work of anthropologist Victor Turner (1974, 1982). He recognized performance as a metaphor for an embodied form of research fueled by postmodern notions of multiple realities, a need for interdisciplinary and holistic research processes, and the search for ways of bringing marginalized voices in society to the forefront (Leavy, 2009: 137). Turner worked closely in an interdisciplinary manner with performance theorist Richard Schechner (1985), and they developed the notion of 'liminal space' in performance, 'the space of greatest invention, discovery, creativity, and reflection'

(Madison, 2005: 158). This liberating space 'privileges particular, participatory, dynamic, intimate, precarious, embodied experience grounded in historical process, contingency, and ideology' (Conquergood, 1991: 187 cited in Pelias, 2008: 188). Performative inquiry as embodied narrative, and as both process and product, offered a needed avenue for research that could respond inclusively and ethically to the crisis of representation that occurred in the 1980s.

By the 1990s, many researchers and scholars of theatre were experimenting with approaches to performative inquiry. It was acknowledged as a legitimate form of inquiry at conferences, such as the Annual Meeting of the American Educational Research Association, created performance slots on the program in 1993 (Donmoyer & Yennie-Donmoyer, 2008: 211), and journals began accepting performance-oriented manuscripts. At the moment, 'performative scholars' from around the world are part of a network of interesting exchanges under the auspices of Kip Jones out of Bournemouth University in the UK. The 'call to performance,' to move 'discourse more fully into the spaces of a progressive pragmatism' (Denzin, 2003: 4), has been heard and embraced.

LANDSCAPE OF PERFORMATIVE INQUIRY

Performative inquiry has been taken up by researchers in anthropology, sociology, health sciences and, probably most frequently, in education. It has been referred to as ethnographic performance text, performance ethnography, documentary theatre, docudrama, nonfiction playwriting, theatre of reenactment (Saldana, 2008: 283), reality theatre, performed ethnography, performance science, research-based theatre, applied theatre, data-based readers theatre (Donmoyer & Yennie-Donmoyer, 2008), and popular theatre (Conrod, 2009). While this plethora of terms is confusing, the embodied and emancipatory features discussed earlier are inherent to all. They are informed by a performative epistemology that acknowledges performance as an 'embodied, empathetic way of knowing and deeply sensing the other (Conrod, 2009: 168).

Madison (2005: 161–163) indicates that performative inquiry draws from several different theoretical perspectives. The first is from Austin's (1975) speech-act theory that suggests language has a purpose and function. The second is Searle's (1969) notion that all language is a performance, that is, has intention in the doing. Third is Derrida's (1973) metaphysics of presence, that all we know and say is based on what has transpired before. Fourth comes from Butler's (1998 cited in Madison, 2005: 163) definition that 'performativity … is the stylized repetition of acts …' inscribed on the body from which we create our identities, and that may be largely imbued with hegemonic beliefs and practices (p. 165).

Denzin (2003: 4–5), on the other hand, suggests that the roots of performance come from Mills' (1959) idea of the sociological imagination, Mead's (1938) discursive understanding of the act, Turner's (1986) thoughts on liminality and the construction of performance, and Conquergood's (1998) ideas of performance outlined above. Denzin includes the notion of performance as a sociopolitical act.

The overlapping yet different 'cast of characters' is helpful because it shows how multiple perspectives/disciplines have contributed substantially to the current understanding of performative inquiry, and how the seeds of performance theory have grown and evolved over many decades. Finally, there are strong reverberations across theorists and fields that underscore the interventionist possibilities in performance inquiry.

ETHNODRAMA AND READERS THEATRE

> Performance is innate to humans and ubiquitous in our social interactions. Humans are socialized from childhood … to imitate, to pretend, to role play, to ritualize and to storytell. It is thus a simple transition to act on our performative impulses by developing artistically rendered work that reflects our dramatic nature. (Saldana, 2008: 196)

There are two main umbrella terms, 'ethnodrama' and 'readers theatre', which have been used most frequently to encompass the process of constructing scripts and performing them. Johnny Saldana has been associated prominently with ethnodrama, Jim Mienczakowski and colleagues with ethnodrama in health theatre, and Robert Donmoyer and June Yennie-Donmoyer with readers theatre.

> An ethnodrama is a written, artistically composed arrangement of qualitative data using such dramatic literary conventions as monologue, dialogue, and stage directions. Ethnotheatre is the synchronous, three-dimensional, mounted performance display of the ethnodrama for spectators. (Saldana, 2008: 196)

The goals of ethnodrama are to educate and foster avenues for social change by producing very vivid and credible accounts of lived experience that will generate an aesthetic, intellectual and emotional response from the members of the audience (Saldana, 2008: 283) and move them to deeper appreciations and understandings, and subsequent action or change.

Saldana (1999) suggests that ethnodramas are produced from the constructed field texts that come from documented observations and interviews, or journals, diaries, broadcasts, and articles, etcetera (Saldana, 2005: 1–2). After either carefully grounded thematic (categorizing) and/or narrative (connecting) analyses (Maxwell & Miller, 2008) to produce overall themes or stories, as discussed in chapters three and five, the themes or stories are then transformed into a script that is based on a plot, which forms the structure of the play, the story line that incorporates the sequence of events as they unfold, and the scenes that flesh out the meanings of the events. Attention is given to characterization and how this is portrayed through dialogues and monologues, actions and gestures, and the visual dimensions of costuming, and set design. The researcher can remain very close to actual verbatim text, or less so. This is contingent on the ongoing 'negotiation' between preserving authenticity versus 'rhetorical efficacy, between the desire for honesty and the need to protect' (Pelias, 2008: 190). Consideration is also given to how the researcher decides to situate herself in the script. There are many ways to do this, as a main or lesser character, a narrator, a responder, or as in Boal's 'arena theatre' as the 'joker' who intervenes when necessary to carry the script forward (Lovelace, 1996). It depends on the goals of the performance and the assumptions that underpin the work.

Saldana (1999) highlights how theatre practitioners use many of the very same skills that arts-informed inquirers do that include careful observation and sensory awareness, the ability to analyze texts, nonverbal actions and gestures, and 'read' beneath the surface, the ability to think conceptually and metaphorically, and to use an aesthetic sense for both the visual dimensions and the narrative itself (p. 68). This suggests that a natural bond exists between theatre practitioners and researchers, and that they would make excellent partners while bringing other expertise and experience to the work. In fact, Saldana has worked with a number of researchers to help transform their inquiries into ethnodramas. The most famous of these is 'Finding my place: The Brad Trilogy' (Saldana & Wolcott, 2002), a story of Brad, a high-school dropout with schizophrenia who became a squatter on Harry Wolcott's property, and then, as the participant in a life history inquiry by Wolcott, developed an intimate relationship with Wolcott and eventually attempted to murder him (Wolcott, 2002). This ethnodrama is an excellent example of the features and characteristics of this genre discussed earlier.

Mienczakowski and Morgan (2008) define ethnodrama as:

> a method and methodology synthesizing health and education fields where we combine qualitative research processes with action research, grounded theory and narrative. … Essentially ethnodrama relies upon the voices, lived experiences, and beliefs of its subjects to inform its content, shape and intent. (p. 451)

Their processes are built on participatory assumptions that guide action research. They use the usual means for constructing field texts through interviews and observations but integrate a series of 'validation processes' and other participant involvement throughout this work (Mienczakowski & Morgan, 2001). They return their field texts several times to the participants to triangulate ideas and get feedback, encouraging the participants to indicate what they think the audience of medical health workers, caregivers and young people should or want to know. The participants help prioritize what is relevant. The researchers incorporate as much verbatim text and as many voices as possible, aspiring for a 'polyphonic script' that resonates with participant experiences. They do not fictionalize characters unless endorsed by the participants, and do not let aesthetic possibilities override authentic portrayals. They pay attention to what are often deficit notions about disease, and are careful not to depict 'pathologized' characters. Program booklets are created to help explicate the context and try to end on a note of hope before engaging with the audience in a post-presentation discussion (pp. 219–221). Experts are always on hand to debrief if necessary. Their goals are to achieve empathetic understanding and learning, expand perspectives, and to reach a wide range of audiences. This kind of participatory and 'confrontational' performative inquiry is not without issues and drawbacks that will be discussed below.

Readers theatre (RT) is a joint dramatic reading from a text, usually with no memorization, no movement and a minimum of props, if any at all. Participants read aloud assigned parts from prepared scripts often derived from literature. Unlike traditional theatre, the emphasis is on oral expression of the text, rather than on acting and costumes. The 'actors' do not exit the 'stage' but rather turn their backs to the audience when not speaking. RT has been used extensively in schools for several decades to increase oral reading fluency while engaging students in literature and performance.

As mentioned earlier, Donmoyer and Yennie-Donmoyer (1995) were the first to adapt RT as a 'mode of data display' and to formally present their work at the Annual Meeting of the American Educational Research Association in 1994. Entitled, 'In Their Own Words: Middle School Students Write About Writing', Donmoyer and Yennie-Donmoyer analyzed student essays about what helped or hindered them in school as writers, and constructed a montage-like script to 'display a plethora of perspectives rather than merely juxtapose antithetical points of view … and avoid … binary thinking that scholars from Dewey to postmodernists suggest is both problematic and a characteristic of expository discourse' (Donmoyer & Yennie-Donmoyer, 2008: 213). They found, perhaps unsurprisingly, that the script construction mirrored in many ways the thematic (categorizing) analysis of qualitative inquiry; they even suggest that the aesthetic considerations for performance were not very different from the rhetorical ones used in research reports, and that 'stage directions functioned like punctuation' (p. 214).

The advantages of RT are that the researcher is able to stay close to the inquiry process, the voices of the participants are embodied and clearly present, the participants can very easily be part of the performance, and the performance not only engages the audience emotionally and intellectually, but also provides a generative moment for discussion (pp. 216–217). RT perhaps provides the 'water wings' for performative inquiry, allowing researchers to get more than their feet wet before diving into ethnodrama.

Example

A very useful exercise in performative inquiry is to construct a 'playlet' or mini RT from an interview field text (the oral dimension of an interview lends itself much more readily to performance than observational field texts). Tips for constructing and performing the script include:

- It is not necessary to use an entire transcript. Excerpts can be used very effectively.
- Delineate the plot, storyline, and scenes within the transcript with a view to initiating a discussion that will follow the performance.
- Determine what portions of the text to leave in to be true to the storyline, characters, or topic, and which portions can be deleted.
- Delete the less critical passages: descriptions, transitions, etcetera.
- Rewrite or modify those passages that need to be included but require adaptation.

- Keep passages short.
- Divide the parts up for the characters/readers.
- Insert a narrator with lines to read if needed, to explain or move the performance forward.
- Make sure each reader is positioned within view of all members of the audience. It is important that the audience can hear lines and see the facial expressions and any gestures.
- Stay away from props and movement unless it is very minimal as this detracts from intellectual response. The oral aspect and presence of the readers provide the embodied dimension.
- If the readers are to be placed in front of the audience all at once, it is helpful to have them stand in a semicircle so that each reader can be seen by all the other readers and the audience.
- Don't allow one reader to block the audience's view of another reader.
- Readers should not look at, talk to, or react to the other readers/characters unless predetermined to achieve a specific effect. The narrator may face and speak to the audience.
- As an alternative to having all the readers stand facing the audience in the performance area, readers can turn to face the audience when reading and then turn their backs to the audience between passages. Turning can be distracting, however, if not done gracefully.

Melanie Beaulac, a Ph.D. graduate in criminology from the Université de Montréal, using themes from her interview field texts for her thesis on restorative justice, constructed the following RT playlet, entitled 'From confrontation to comprehension', for a class exercise (June 2007).

Prologue: (The prologue was written as a context for the assignment and not shared with the 'audience' until after the performance. It could be adapted very easily to a booklet form for the audience during the discussion following the performance.)

Restorative justice is not a new concept. It is an old form of justice that native people, in particular, have used for centuries to resolve the problem of crime or deviance in their societies. Restorative justice could be defined as a negotiation and problem-solving process between a victim, a mediator, a perpetrator, and some members of the community after a crime. It is a form of justice where the victim and/or 'indirect victims' (close relatives or friends) are at the centre of the justice process, which means they are invited to share their thoughts about the consequences of the criminal act, and about the reparation/punishment they judge fitting for the perpetrator of the crime. In this way, the victim has a voice which is completely the opposite of the penal justice system, where the state is the one in charge, where the victim is the passive 'actor' and where, therefore, the offender never faces the real consequences of his actions.

What follows is a representation of a relatively new kind of restorative justice process where the victim and the offender do not know each other, but have

(Continued)

(Continued)

experienced the same type of crime from different perspectives. This initiative is meant to help the victim and the offender to experience personal growth. Participation is voluntary in this program, which consists of eight meetings of three hours each that includes three or four offenders, three or four victims, two members from the community, and one mediator. I have been responsible for an ongoing evaluation of the program since 2005. This short readers theatre presentation is my understanding of the restorative justice process commonly experienced by a victim and an offender.

Readers theatre playlet

Scene:

Narrator: Erica (pseudonym) is a 45-year-old woman who has been subjected to two burglaries in her home in one month. The first time she was absent, but the second, she was at home. She has been severely traumatized (depressed) since then and she is very angry. Steve (pseudonym) is a 29-year-old man who has been found guilty for the second time of burglaries and hold-ups in the area. He portrays a 'tough guy' but in actuality he is a calm person who is fed up with living a criminal life. In one of the penitentiary's classrooms, the entire group of four victims, four offenders, two members of the community and one mediator sit in a circle for a discussion. What follows is the conversation that takes place between Erica and Steve at one point.

Script:

Erica: What is your problem!?! You think that it's a game!?! You think it's funny to make people afraid and steal from them!?!

Steve: I don't understand you victims. How can you be so sensitive? I mean, we don't hurt you, we take some stuff and then we go ... and we just take a few minutes to do our thing ... so what's the big deal, honestly?

Erica: Ha, ha, maybe it's clear for you, but for us it's another matter! We don't know your intentions when you commit your crime ...

Steve: Well, you have a point. I know it may seem odd, but I never realized that before.

Erica: And another point, you think that when you steal it's just material stuff that you're taking, that it doesn't hurt anyone ... that the insurance company will reimburse us anyway ... Well you're wrong! Some of the things stolen from my house had particular meanings for me.

Steve: Like ... ?

Erica: An old glass. It was my mom's, a plastic glass because she was always dropping everything... To me it was precious.

Steve: I'm sorry. I don't ..., don't know what to say.

Erica: They also took away my security, and my children's security. At one point our thoughts were always, 'They will come back, they will come back.' It was awful … that feeling … I can't describe it … You see, that's what you have done.

Steve: You're right, I accept the blame.

Erica: But why, why did you choose to live that way? I mean, weren't you ever tempted to get a normal job?

Steve: I don't think it's something you choose. In fact, I've had many jobs but each time it never lasted for long … When you party every night, you know, it's hard to wake up the next morning! (*laughs*). In fact, I've always hated to work for a boss that thinks he's god. I've always preferred to run my own 'business'.

Erica: But why did you have to party every night and run an illegal business?

Steve: I don't know, I guess I never knew better. That's how my parents lived, probably still live … I don't know, I'm not in contact with them anymore, and anyway, I don't give a f–k!

Erica: … But why?

Steve: There are things I'd rather keep in the past … far away from me.

Erica: (*silence*)

Steve: I … I don't want to play the victim, but my family was not … is not … what you'd call the perfect little family … My father's alcoholic and was very violent when I was younger. Let me tell you, he's f–king crazy. The times he hit me, my mother or my sister … I can't count. And what he's done to my sister, that … I will never forgive him … I know I did many bad things in my life, but that … f–k … oh, no … oh, no, that's disgusting.

Erica: And your mother?

Steve: As crazy as her husband! I think, she never really … (*silence*). Sometimes I wonder if she thinks about me or my sister … I mean, would she still prefer her drugs over her children now, at her age … (*silence*)? Probably… I don't know …

Erica: (*silence*) Your story is so sad, Steve … I'm lucky to have my husband and children around me … to support me.

Steve: You are lucky. I hope … I hope one day I will be able to make a family like yours.

Epilogue: (In this epilogue, Melanie shares her goals for the performance and her process of script production.)

In this exercise, I wanted to treat the two principal themes in the story of my characters: their mutual confrontation and their mutual comprehension. These are the general themes that were very recurrent in my data and summarized well, in my opinion, the restorative justice process lived by most victims and offenders. From my data (verbatim transcripts about property crimes from the perspectives of both victims and offenders), I chose passages that showed as specifically as possible these two, general themes. Most of the lines in fact were parts of anecdotes that the participants had shared during our interviews. After that, I deleted the passages

(Continued)

(Continued)

that were redundant or not particularly pertinent. Then, I assembled the lines that I had extracted and constructed a story. At that point it was not really fluid. I tried to imagine the kind of atmosphere, interventions, and pauses that would have produced the lines of the participants. I rewrote some of the sentences, changed some words, switched sentences into questions, injected some silences and pauses, and conveyed emotions using punctuation. I decided that the script worked best with two characters. Throughout the process, I tried to remain close to the meaning in the participants' original words, but of course my interpretation had an impact on the construction of the script. However, I did try to base my interpretation on the emotions and impressions that I experienced during the actual interviews. Naturally I would validate my interpretations with the participants. (Beaulac, 2007)

This playlet initiated an excellent discussion about the potential in performative inquiry for understanding different perspectives, seeing things in new ways, evoking an embodied response, and opening up avenues for action and change. It also initiated a helpful exchange about the process of analysis and script production and is an example of how a performative text, or series of texts, might be used as an analytic tool, or to illustrate a specific aspect of a study.

VALIDATORY PREVIEWS

As mentioned earlier, Mienczakowski et al. (2002) suggest using a series of validatory previews with participants before the final script is completed. This is the same idea as checking back with participants about the content and tone of a research report, or any other form of representation. Matthew Meyer did just that for his dissertation entitled 'Transitional wars: A study of power, control and conflict in executive succession: Theatre as representation' (1998).

With a background in theatre, and many years in teaching theatre and doing productions in high schools, Meyer decided to use performance as a part of his inquiry process. He has suggested, as Norris (2000) has, that playwriting mirrors much of the inquiry process. From interview field texts about the succession process of leadership in a school district in the Greater Montreal area, he first created a novella for 'his eyes only' so that he could 'play with ideas, stretch characters, create situations and develop dialogue' (Meyer, 1998: 112). Then he wrote the script and presented a 'staged reading' with 'minimal staging and without full theatrical effects' (p. 148), and a cast of seven readers, all educators, to a small, invited audience that included the members of his dissertation committee and other educators. The performance took place in a theatre in a local high school.

Upon entry, audience members received a 'biographical information sheet' (p. 149) in which they gave some personal background information and their immediate response to the play following the performance. Then they moved into six breakout groups for focus group discussions for approximately 30 minutes. These were audiotaped for subsequent analysis. This validatory process was an excellent means for helping him shape the final performance script which is part of the thesis, and which he has used in subsequent, professional development work with educational leaders. It also opened up avenues for further exploration in his inquiry process. He was able to show that

> *Transitional Wars*, as a research study employing the medium of theatre *as representation,* did successfully portray the executive succession issue and the 'real life' administration and social issues of the play's script and characters. It was also successful in provoking discussion in many areas of educational administration. Clearly, *theatre as representation* could be successfully used as a potential learning tool for administrators' professional development. (Meyer, 1998: 160)

CHALLENGES IN PERFORMATIVE INQUIRY

There are several challenges that performative inquirers face. As in other arts-informed inquiry, there are those who will continue to question the legitimacy of performance as research. While this perspective has diminished in the last decade, the best way to counter the criticism is to produce quality work, make the inquiry process transparent, include validatory previews and analyses throughout the process with participants, adhere to a reflexive stance and ethical practices, build a dialogic framework into the performance, and avoid sensationalizing (Mienczakowski et al., 2002). Like all arts-informed work, ensuring quality requires study of the art form itself to build expertise by immersing oneself in it, and working with artists. Collaboration between researchers and theatre experts as in the work of Wolcott and Saldana outlined above offers excellent possibilities.

The biggest challenge with grave ethical implications is the negative impact a performance can have, particularly on a vulnerable audience (Mienczakowski & Moore, 2008). Performances are powerful because of their embodied form, but in performing there is always 'slippage between what the body knows, what it can say, and what the audience can interpret' (Pelias, 2008: 192). Pelias goes on to suggest that this can serve to reify a phenomenon rather than to question it or further marginalize, rather than legitimize and emancipate a particular group (Mienczakowski & Moore, 2008). Attention to rigorous inquiry and ethical practices outlined above, and the creation of authentic, not just aesthetic, and dialogic performances can counter these challenges.

The third challenge is that reviews of performative inquiry are frequently made by those who have no background for evaluating the work. Uninformed judgments have severe consequences for both publication and funding possibilities, and for building the field (Saldana, 2008). Alexander (2005: 428) uses Richardson's (2000) criteria for arts-informed work suggesting that evaluation of performative inquiry should focus on content, form and impact. An evaluation of content is based on a clear understanding of intent – purpose and goals, a built-in reflexivity and critical reflection throughout the process, and a credible portrayal. An evaluation of form is based on the degree of craft displayed in 'the sensuousness of articulate embodied thought, with the clarity and efficacy of good research grounded in ethical care and thick description' (pp. 429–430). And finally, impact is based on the effect the performance has on the performers and the audience and what new avenues of thinking and possible action are opened up as a result (p. 430).

Kerry-Moran (2008) concurs with the need to attend to content, form and impact in evaluating performative inquiry, but interestingly suggests that attention should also be directed to the evaluators and the qualities they bring to the evaluation or review. She holds up the role of the dramaturge as a model, one who is knowledgeable about the art form of performance, works in collaborative, theatre teams to improve and strengthen production in a formative and ongoing process, and one who is always 'actively researching and developing skills appropriate to each project …' (p. 497). These are lofty, but not impossible goals for evaluators. They merit further consideration and discussion. Certainly the quality of inquiry is incumbent upon both researchers and evaluators.

CONCLUDING REMARKS

Performative inquiry encompasses all the senses. Performance offers a metaphor for all that is done in qualitative inquiry, both in the doing of the research and in the representation, whether the product is a written text, story or poem, or a collage, photograph or film, or any other form. It offers an important lens for thinking about inquiry that is embodied, relational, participatory, and geared to action and social change. Promise lies in the continued exploration of this form of inquiry.

REFERENCES

Alexander, B. K. (2005). Performance ethnography: The reenacting and inciting of culture. In N. K. Denzin & Y. S. Lincoln (Eds.), *The Sage handbook of qualitative research*, (3rd ed.), (pp. 411–441). Thousand Oaks, CA: Sage.

Austin, J. L. (1975). *How to do things with words*. Cambridge, MA: Harvard University Press.

Beaulac, M. (2007). *Readers' script exercise*. Unpublished manuscript, McGill University, Montreal, QC.

Bhabba, H. K. (1994). *The location of culture*. New York: Routledge.

Boal, A. (1979). *Theatre of the oppressed*. New York: Theatre Communication Group.

Bruner, J. (2008). *Making stories: Law, literature, life*. Cambridge, MA: Harvard University Press.

Butler, J. (1998). Performative acts and gender constitution: An essay in phenomenology and feminist theory. *Theatre Journal, 40*, 519–531.

Conquergood, D. (1991). Rethinking ethnography: Cultural politics and rhetorical strategies. *Communication Monographs, 58*, 179–194.

Conquergood, D. (1998). Beyond the text: Toward a performative cultural politics. In S. J. Dailey (Ed.), *The future of performance studies: Visions and revisions* (pp. 25–36). Washington, DC: National Communication Association.

Conrod, D. (2009). Exploring risky youth experiences: Popular theatre as a participatory performative research method. In P. Levy (Ed.), *Method meets art: Arts-based research practice* (pp. 162–178). New York: Guilford.

Denzin, N. K. (2003). *Performance ethnography: Critical pedagogy and the politics of culture*. Thousand Oaks, CA: Sage.

Denzin, N. K. (2005). Emancipatory discourses. N. K. Denzin & Y. S. Lincoln (Eds.), *The Sage handbook of qualitative research* (3rd ed.), (pp. 933–958). Thousand Oaks, CA: Sage.

Denzin, N. K., & Lincoln, Y. S. (2005). Foreword. In J. Saldana (Ed.), *Ethnodrama: An anthology of reality theatre* (pp. ix–xi). Walnut Creek, CA: AltaMira.

Derrida, J. (1973). *Speech and phenomena.* Evanston, IL: Northwestern University Press.

Donmoyer, R., & Yennie-Donmoyer, J. (1994). *In their own words: Middle school students write about writing.* Performance presented at the Annual Meeting of the American Eductional Research Association. New Orleans, LA.

Donmoyer, R., & Yennie-Donmoyer, J. (1995). Data as drama: Reflections on the use of readers' theater as a mode of qualitative data display. *Qualitative Inquiry, 1*(4), 402–428.

Donmoyer, R., & Yennie-Donmoyer, J. (2008). Readers' theater as a data display strategy. In J. G. Coles & A. L. Knowles (Eds.), *Handbook of the arts in qualitative research* (pp. 209–224). Thousand Oaks, CA: Sage.

Fels, L. (1999). *In the wind clothes dance on a clothesline: Performative inquiry – a (re)search methodology.* Unpublished doctoral dissertation, University of British Columbia, Vancouver, BC.

Fels, L., & McGiven, L. (2002). Intercultural recognitions through performative inquiry. In G. B. Brauer (Ed.), *Body and language: Intercultural learning through drama* (pp. 19–35). Westport, CT: Ablex.

Goffman, E. (1959). *The presentation of self in everyday life.* Garden City, NJ: Doubleday.

Jones, K. (2006). A biographic researcher in pursuit of an aesthetic: The use of arts-based (re)presentations in 'performative' dissemination of life stories. *Sociology Review,* II(1), 66–76.

Kerry-Moran, K. J. (2008). Between scholarship and art: Dramaturgy and quality in arts-related research. In J. G. Coles & A. L. Knowles (Eds.), *Handbook of the arts in qualitative research* (pp. 493–50). Thousand Oaks, CA: Sage.

Leavy, P. (2009). *Method meets art: Arts-based research practice.* New York: Guilford.

Lovelace, A. (1996). A brief history of theatre forms. *Motion Magazine.* Retrieved August 14, 2008, from www.motionmagazine.com/theater.html.

MacLeod, J. (1987). *The arts and education.* Paper presented at the keynote address at the Fine Arts Council of the Alberta Teachers' Association and the Faculty of Education. University of Alberta Invitational Seminar. Edmonton, AB.

Madison, D. S. (2005). *Critical ethnography: Method, ethics, and performance.* Thousand Oaks, CA: Sage.

Maxwell, J., & Miller, B. (2008). Categorizing and connecting strategies in qualitative data analysis. In P. Leavy & S. Hesse-Biber (Eds.), *Handbook of emergent methods* (pp. 461–477). New York: Guilford.

Mead, J. H. (1938). *The philosophy of the act.* Chicago: University of Chicago Press.

Meyer, J. M. (1998). *Transitional wars: A study of power, control and conflict in executive succession: Theatre as representation.* Unpublished doctoral dissertation, McGill University, Montreal, QC.

Mienczakowski, J. (1995). The theater of ethnography: The reconstruction of ethnography into theater with emancipatory potential. *Qualitative Inquiry, 1*(3), 360–375.

Mienczakowski, J., & Morgan, S. (2001). Ethnodrama: Constructing participatory, experiential, and complleling action research through performance. In H. Bradbury (Ed.), *The handbook of action research* (pp. 219-227). London: Sage.

Mienczakowski, J., & Moore, T. (2008). Performing data with notions of responsibility. In J. G. Coles & A. L. Knowles (Eds.), *Handbook of the arts in qualitative research* (pp. 451–458). Thousand Oaks, CA: Sage.

Mienczakowski, J., Smith, L., & Morgan, S. (2002). Seeing words – hearing feelings: Ethnodrama and the performance of data. In C. Bagley & M. B. Cancienne (Eds.), (pp. 34–52). New York: Peter Lang.

Mills, C. W. (1959). *The sociological imagination.* New York: Oxford University Press.

Nisker, J. (2008). Health-policy research and the possibilities of theater. In J. G. Coles & A. L. Knowles (Eds.), *Handbook of the arts in qualitative research* (pp. 613–623). Thousand Oaks, CA: Sage.

Norris, J. (2000). Drama as research: Realizing the potential of drama in education as a research methodology. *Youth Theatre International, 14,* 40–51.

Pelias, R. (2008). Performative inquiry: Embodiment and its challenges. In J. G. Coles & A. L. Knowles (Eds.), *Handbook of the arts in qualitative research* (pp. 185–207). Thousand Oaks, CA: Sage.

Richardson, L. (2000). Evaluating ethnography. *Qualitative Inquiry, 6*(2), 253–255.

Saldana, J. (1999). Playwriting with data: Ethnographic performance texts. *Youth Theatre Journal, 13,* 60–71.

Saldana, J. (Ed.), (2005). *Ethnodrama: An anthology of reality theatre.* Walnut Creek, CA: AltaMira.

Saldana, J. (2008). Ethnodrama and ethnotheatre. In J. G. Coles & A. L. Knowles (Eds.), *Handbook of the arts in qualitative research* (pp. 195–207). Thousand Oaks, CA: Sage.

Saldana, J., & Wolcott, H. (2002). Finding my place: The Brad trilogy. In H. Wolcott (Ed.), *Sneaky kid and its aftermath* (pp. 167–210). Walnut Creek, CA: AltaMira.

Schechner, R. (1985). *Between theater and anthropology.* Philadelphia: University of Philadelphia Press.

Searle, J. R. (1969). *Speech acts: An essay in the philosophy of language.* Cambridge, UK: Cambridge University Press.

Turner, V. (1974). *Drama, fields, and metaphors: Symbolic action in human society.* Ithaca, NY: Routledge.

Turner, V. (1982). Performing ethnography. *The Drama Review, 26,* 33–35.

Turner, V. (1986). *The anthropology of performance.* New York: Performing Arts Journal Publications.

Wolcott, H. (2002). *Sneaky kid and its aftermath.* Walnut Creek, CA: AltaMira.

10

Future Directions

Qualitative inquiry whether thematic, narrative, or arts-informed has evolved into what is now a particularly interesting place. It has become a legitimate form of research embraced by inquirers world-wide, and has produced a sense of excitement because of the relative speed with which it has diversified and grown in the last decade. Digital technology has made the possibilities for creating new research avenues, expediting the communication of work, and shrinking the distances among scholars. There are some worries about a backlash against qualitative inquiry that has emerged in the accountability and evidence-based research movement (Ellis et al., 2007). To counter this, and to meet the needs of a new generation of qualitative inquirers, several key directions need attention and work.

This book is predicated on the need for researchers to have access to transparent accounts of inquiry processes, on one hand, to show rather than just tell and as a result to produce more trustworthy and credible accounts of thematic, narrative, and arts-informed processes. On the other hand, and perhaps even more importantly, there is a reason for elaborating on inquiry processes. These transparent accounts provide ways for other researchers to use and adapt the work, thus adding to the evolving nature of qualitative inquiry. It is hoped that this work will encourage others to do the same.

The theme of evaluation cuts across every chapter in this book – in thematic, narrative, and most importantly in arts-informed inquiry. There have been worthy, but only partial attempts to deal with evaluation. Most of the emphasis has been on how to produce exemplary literary/narrative products and not on the other genres of arts-informed work, for example, poetic, collage, photographic, and performative inquiry. The subtle differences among these forms of inquiry require specific attention and elaboration. More space, time, and emphasis need to be devoted to evaluation at conferences, in journals and other forms of scholarly communication. Evaluation must become an integral part of ongoing inquiry conversations, not tacked on as an afterthought or relegated to separate discussions.

The 'craft of representation' is a needed area of work. Seasoned researchers are exploring avenues of inquiry that require technical skills to make the work worthy and legitimate. Novice researchers are eager for help to acquire the knowledge and skills that will give them sufficient expertise to get their work accepted and published. What is needed is more cross-boundary sharing and collaborating. Artists and researchers should be talking and working together more often, as should researchers from varying disciplines and who conduct different types of inquiry. From these conversations, networks of support can develop and flourish (Ellis et al., 2007). Methodology courses need to be structured along these lines inviting graduate students to cross boundaries to learn from different examples and perspectives. Included in methodological preparation is the need for providing expertise and time for developing the artistic and technological skills that will improve the quality and expand the growing possibilities in the various types of inquiry.

To counter any backlash that is occurring against qualitative inquiry, and to retain and develop more fully an ethical stance in all aspects of research, there needs to be an upfront and continuous questioning of the 'so what' or utility of our work. Does our work make a difference, and if so for whom, and how and why? These kinds of discussions cannot remain relegated to scholarly circles in academe. They must reach the public domain in ways that are accessible, informative, and engaging.

REFERENCES

Ellis, C., Bochner, A. P., Denzin, N. K., Goodall, H. L., Morse, J. M., Pelias, R. J., & Richardson, L. (2007). Coda: Talking and thinking about qualitative research. In N. K. Denzin & M. D. Giardina (Eds.), *Ethical futures in qualitative research: Decolonizing the politics of knowledge* (pp. 229–267). Walnut Creek, CA: Left Coast Press.

Index

Supporting researchers for more than forty years

Research methods have always been at the core of SAGE's publishing. Sara Miller McCune founded SAGE in 1965 and soon after she published SAGE's first methods book, *Public Policy Evaluation*. A few years later, she launched the Quantitative Applications in the Social Sciences series – affectionately known as the 'little green books'.

Always at the forefront of developing and supporting new approaches in methods, SAGE published early groundbreaking texts and journals in the fields of qualitative methods and evaluation.

Today, more than forty years and two million little green books later, SAGE continues to push the boundaries with a growing list of more than 1,200 research methods books, journals, and reference works across the social, behavioural, and health sciences.

From qualitative, quantitative and mixed methods to evaluation, SAGE is the essential resource for academics and practitioners looking for the latest in methods by leading scholars.

www.sagepublications.com